# The Price of Poverty

# The Price of Poverty

*Money, Work, and Culture*
*in the Mexican American Barrio*

Daniel Dohan

UNIVERSITY OF CALIFORNIA PRESS
*Berkeley · Los Angeles · London*

University of California Press
Berkeley and Los Angeles, California

University of California Press, Ltd.
London, England

© 2003 by the Regents of the University of California

Library of Congress Cataloging-in-Publication Data

Dohan, Daniel, 1965–.
   The price of poverty : money, work, and culture in
the Mexican American barrio / Daniel Dohan.
      p.    cm.
   Includes bibliographical references and index.
   ISBN 0-520-22756-5 (cloth : alk. paper)—
ISBN 0-520-23889-3 (pbk. : alk. paper)
   1. Mexican Americans—California—San Jose—
Economic conditions.   2. Mexican Americans—
California—East Los Angeles—Economic conditions.
3. Urban poor—California—San Jose.   4. Urban
poor—California—East Los Angeles.   5. San Jose
(Calif.)—Economic conditions.   6. East Los Angeles
(Calif.)—Economic conditions.   7. San Jose (Calif.)—
Ethnic relations.   8. East Los Angeles (Calif.)—Ethnic
relations.   9. Hispanic American neighborhoods—
California—Case studies.   I. Title.
F869.S394 D64   2003
330.9794'74'00896872—dc21            2003002460

Manufactured in the United States of America
12  11  10  09  08  07  06  05  04  03
10  9  8  7  6  5  4  3  2  1

The paper used in this publication is both acid-free and
totally chlorine-free (TCF). It meets the minimum
requirements of ANSI/NISO Z39.48–1992 (R 1997)
*(Permanence of Paper)*. ⊗

# Contents

# Figures and Tables

FIGURES

TABLES

# Preface

In the heart of "Eastern City" there is a slum district known
as Cornerville, which is inhabited almost exclusively by Italian
immigrants and their children. To the rest of the city it is a
mysterious, dangerous, and depressing area. . . . Cornerville
people appear as social work clients, as defendants in criminal
cases, or as undifferentiated members of "the masses." There
is one thing wrong with such a picture: no human beings are
in it. Those who are concerned with Cornerville seek through
a general survey to answer questions that require the most
intimate knowledge of local life. The only way to gain such
knowledge is to live in Cornerville and participate in the
activities of its people.

> William Foote Whyte, *Street Corner Society:*
> *The Social Structure of an Italian Slum*

Many studies of urban poverty begin on the inner-city street corner. This
study begins on two—corners separated by more than three hundred
miles of distance and a year of time.

Julián, my guide, drove me to the first corner in October 1993. It was
the beginning of ten months of fieldwork in San Jose, California, and
Julián had generously agreed to show me around the low-income neighborhoods of the city. He had grown up not far from the corner, and after
I met him at his parents' home, we went there immediately. The corner
was part of a strip-mall shopping center—a corner the *Mexicanos* of San
Jose referred to as *Miami,* after a salsa club that had closed its doors not
long before I arrived in the city. *Miami* stood over a congested intersec-
tion where four-lane roads met at a long-cycle stoplight, and it stood
nearly in the shadow of a spaghetti bowl of concrete exit ramps where
two freeways twisted together. It marked the geographic heart of
Mexican American San Jose, with the city's established Chicano barrios

spread out to the north and east—it is a short walk from *Miami* to the bungalow in the Sal Si Puedes barrio where César Chávez grew up—and the newer barrios of immigrant *Mexicanos* stretching south and west. In 1993, *Miami* was a *Mexicano* place. Boutiques stocked *piñatas* for birthdays and frilly dresses for *quinceañeras,* the discount store sold sturdy work clothes, the supermarket had aisles marked "Bread/Pan" and "Frozen/Helados," and the *panaderías* (bakeries) offering *novias, pan dulce,* and other Mexican *postres* drew the city's Mexican Americans to the strip mall. The wide sidewalks and expansive parking lot had also been turned over to commerce. In the evenings and on weekends, one lane of Strong Road and the parking areas to the side of the laundromat were converted into a used car lot. Julián had not brought me to *Miami* for any of these things, however; we had come for the day laborers, the *jornaleros.* On most days, they gathered at the mall entrances and sidewalk on Broad Street before dawn. These were men—fifteen to fifty— who had grown up in Jalisco, Michoacán, and other states in Mexico. Some had arrived only a few days or weeks ago, while others had lived for years in overcrowded apartments and subdivided ranch-style houses nearby. All of the *jornaleros* came to *Miami* early in the morning to wait for a pickup truck to pull up and take them off for a day moving rubble at a construction site or trimming shrubs at one of Silicon Valley's high-tech corporate campuses.

My friend Andrés drove me by the second corner in January 1995, the first month of a year of fieldwork in Los Angeles. Andrés had grown up in East LA, the expansive Mexican American settlement that sprawls inland from downtown into the San Gabriel Valley, and we began our tour of the barrios at his father's home furnishings store. I had just spent ten months living and conducting research in the barrios of San Jose, so much of the East LA that Andrés and I toured that day felt comfortable and familiar. The barrios had the same wide avenues and the same fence-enclosed one-story bungalows and ranch houses as the Silicon Valley. Many of the residents, like the people with whom I lived and spent time in San Jose, were recent *Mexicano* immigrants. The second corner was different; on a large laminated map hanging on the wall of his store, Andrés's father pointed it out. It was the heart of a very poor neighborhood, he said, an area with many second- and third-generation Mexican Americans, not recent immigrants. It stood at the edge of one of the large public housing projects that together create a half-circle separating East LA proper from the railyards and warehouses near the Los Angeles

river. In 1995, locals referred to the corner as the "hot spot." Not far
from it, a sound-wall separated the near-identical low-rise buildings of
the projects from a massive freeway, and I soon came to associate the
muffled roar of traffic with project living. Longtime residents showed me
pictures of their community over the years. The earliest photos were part
of promotional brochures distributed by the LA Housing Authority.
They showed mostly Anglo residents posing next to new cars in front of
new buildings. The freeway did not exist in those pictures. It first
appeared in the background of pictures taken in the 1950s. The residents
in the foreground of those pictures were increasingly Mexican American
and black. In 1970s photos the sound-wall covered the freeway, and all
the residents seemed to be people of color. By 1995, after bursts of inter-
racial violence in the late 1960s and 1980s, the projects became—with
the exception of one elderly African American who had stayed on—
*puro Chicano.* Like the corners of *Miami,* the roads and sidewalks near
the hot spot were a place for socializing and for commerce. In the late
afternoon, residents stopped to chat at the hot spot on their way to the
*tienda* (corner store) or exchanged greetings through car windows on
their way to and from work. Commerce at the hot spot also picked up in
the late afternoon and continued until late at night. It was dominated by
the corner regulars, a group of young men who had grown up in the
cramped project apartments and were members of the local street gang.
Each afternoon, they gathered to socialize, to drink beer, and to sell
cocaine and PCP to passing pedestrians and motorists.

I begin this book with a comparison of everyday life at *Miami* and the
hot spot—a rough comparison that lacks depth and focus. What we
appear to see at *Miami* are Mexican immigrants lining up to do hard
labor at low wages—jobs that U.S.-born residents will not take. At the
hot spot we seem to see U.S.-born minorities working in the drug economy, maybe because they cannot find other work or maybe because the
money on the streets is better than anything they can earn legally. This
rough comparison seems to conform to widely held images of poverty
among U.S. immigrants and U.S. minorities. In the pages of this book, I
examine those widely held images by focusing on everyday life at *Miami*
and the hot spot and in the two Mexican American barrios that surround
them and of which they are a part.

I call these barrios Guadalupe and Chávez. Like nearly all of the
proper names in this book, these are not the real names of these barrios.
But these names do communicate something about these neighborhoods.

I call the San Jose barrio Guadalupe after Mexico's patron saint as a reminder that this barrio is populated largely by Mexican immigrants. Similarly I selected the name Chávez, recalling the prominent Mexican American labor leader César Chávez, to refer to the Los Angeles community because this barrio is largely dominated by U.S.-born Mexican Americans.

I spent nearly two years living and observing everyday life in these barrios during 1993–95. *Miami* and the hot spot are just two of the places where I spent time during fieldwork, and the people I hung out with there and the events I observed there contributed just a small portion of the data for this project. But everyday life at *Miami* and the hot spot does provide a convenient window into the experience of poverty in Guadalupe and Chávez barrios. In important ways, everyday events at *Miami* capture the experience of poverty in Guadalupe and other immigrant areas, and in certain important respects the goings-on at the hot spot capture the experience of poverty in Chávez and in other neighborhoods of persistent poverty. In short, these street corners bring to life the puzzle I grapple with in the pages of this book.

My aim here is to provide a rich understanding of the similarities and differences in the experiences of immigrant poverty in Guadalupe and persistent poverty in Chávez. I ground this understanding in an examination of everyday economic life in the barrios. Poverty is, by definition, a lack of income, so it makes sense to start a comparison of poor communities with the one thing definitely held in common: a shortfall of income generation. And it makes sense to start with an examination of work—the most important source of income in just about every community.

Work became a focus of this study early on—after I had lived in Guadalupe barrio for only a few weeks. In the barrios of San Jose, as on the street corner of *Miami,* most residents were working, but few were happy about their employment situation. It was easy to understand why. Like many workers in the San Jose barrios, the day laborers at *Miami* were paid miserable wages, and they were never certain whether they would find any work at all. The jobs they did find were difficult, often involving early starts and long commutes, backbreaking labor or dangerous working conditions, demanding bosses and little autonomy. In Guadalupe, I pursued questions about working poverty. What is its daily routine? How do these routines reflect residents' thoughts and feelings toward work and nonwork life? What are its social consequences?

These questions about work deepened and shifted after I moved to

Los Angeles. It is important to recognize that most of the residents of the East LA housing projects did not work at the hot spot. In fact, it would be a horrible misrepresentation to imagine for a moment that many Chávez residents at all were directly employed in the drug economy. But economic life at the hot spot does convey certain features of economic life in the projects. Like the drug sellers at the hot spot, a significant number of project residents went through periods of unemployment or underemployment, and many residents "hustled" to make ends meet. There were many different ways of hustling, but most hustles meant hard work rather than easy money, and hustling usually meant putting at risk one's body, freedom, and reputation. As I came to appreciate the role of hustling in Chávez, I began to ask a different set of questions about work. Are project dwellers hustling because they can't find jobs? How do they think and feel about hustling? Hustling often involves participating in stigmatized activities such as the illicit economy or public assistance programs. How does this affect social life more broadly in the community?

INVESTIGATING EVERYDAY POVERTY

As Americans, we have addressed these questions time and again. Often we have done so by analyzing what William Foote Whyte calls, in the epigraph above, "a general survey." At other times, we have followed Whyte's footsteps by describing everyday life in a single "Cornerville" community. Both of these approaches have their advantages. The survey, by analyzing how different people respond to identical questions, helps us explain the causes and consequences of poverty. The community study uses rich description to help us understand the nature of poverty in its lived complexity. The explanation of the general survey and the understanding of the community study both play an important role in studies of poverty.

In this study I attempt to combine aspects of the general survey and the community study in hopes of gaining some of the advantages of both. Borrowing from the survey, I analyze comparative data that address a similar set of questions. This provides the grounds for an explanation of the causes and consequences of poverty in Guadalupe and Chávez. Borrowing from the community study, I examine everyday community life in depth. This allows me to provide a rich description of the nature of poverty in the lives of barrio residents. My explanation of the causes and consequences of barrio poverty reflects my attempt to take into consid-

eration the rich complexity of ordinary lives. My description of the
nature of barrio poverty hangs upon an explanatory frame that gives it
structure and organization. Both explanation and description reflect my
experiences of comparative participant-observation in Guadalupe and
Chávez barrios.

I lived in Guadalupe barrio from October 1993 through August 1994.
Five months after leaving Guadalupe barrio, I moved to Los Angeles in
January 1995 and lived near Chávez barrio until December 1995. Altogether, I spent nearly two years deeply immersed in the daily life of the
neighborhoods and their residents. I ate and drank with residents, played
with them, worked with them, celebrated *quinceañeras* and birthdays
with them, and mourned with them when tragedy struck, as it did too frequently. I spent occasional nights on their floors and politely put off several invitations to go on extended trips to Mexico. In short, for nearly two
years I lived as a member of these low-income communities, playing a role
within the community even as I always remained an outsider.

Many times during the fieldwork, and especially at moments of
extreme discomfort or joy, I found myself reflecting with incredulity at
the situation in which I found myself. Late one night in Los Angeles, I
found myself immersed in these reflections after I had thrown myself to
the ground to avoid becoming an unwitting victim of a drive-by shooting. A few weeks earlier I had had similar reflections while sitting on the
back patio of a project unit in the midst of a joyful birthday party. In San
Jose, I had these feelings of incredulity while drinking beers and socializing after weekend pickup soccer games. And these feelings came to me
after a long conversation with my landlady during which I told her I had
no further ideas about how to extricate her son from the legal troubles
that could lead to his deportation. I imagine that most ethnographers
have these feelings at one time or another during their fieldwork. For me,
they were intense because prior to undertaking the fieldwork for this
book, my life experiences had never taken me to places like Guadalupe
and Chávez.

I grew up in a prosperous Boston suburb. My interest in urban
poverty grew from reading works of social criticism such as *Native Son,
Manchild in the Promised Land,* and *The Autobiography of Malcolm X.*
My desire to study urban poverty firsthand developed as I immersed
myself in the scholarly literature on urban poverty and the so-called
urban "underclass" as a graduate student in the early 1990s. While I
admired scholarly attempts to identify the roots of "underclass" poverty,

I was frustrated at the mismatch between how they studied and wrote about urban poverty and how Richard Wright, Claude Brown, and Malcolm X described their experiences growing up and making do in the urban ghetto. The social critics described a rich, three-dimensional ghetto social world that appeared to have escaped the attention of the policy makers and social scientists. Along with many other scholars, I hungered for an analysis of poverty that acknowledged and explained the rich social world of the low-income community. This book is part of a growing library of urban ethnography that seeks to provide such a rich and textured understanding of the everyday world of the urban poor in contemporary America.[1]

# Notes and Acknowledgments

There is a voluminous research literature on poverty, immigration, and Mexican Americans, and for the most part I have tried to restrict my references to this literature to endnotes. While some notes merely reference a particular citation, others contain short discussions of theoretical issues or point out further empirical examples of the material I discuss in the text. Occasionally I use notes to convey parenthetical information that seems important for the flow of the main text.

I have tried to adopt a consistent set of rules for the terms of identity I use in this book. In San Jose, residents generally referred to their identity as *Mexican* or *Mexicano/a* or according to their state or city of origin in Mexico. In Los Angeles, residents generally identified with the terms *Mexican, Mexicano/a, Mexican American,* or *Chicano/a.* To avoid confusion, unless I have otherwise noted, I use the terms *Mexican* and *Mexicano/a* to refer to individuals who were born in Mexico but live in the United States; the term *Chicano/a,* unless otherwise noted, refers to individuals who were born in the United States and trace their ancestry to Mexico. The term *Mexican American,* unless otherwise noted, refers to individuals of either Mexican or U.S. birth who trace their ancestry to Mexico.

No ethnography, particularly that brand oxymoronically labeled "solo ethnography," comes to fruition without assistance from many institutions and individuals. It is a pleasure to acknowledge efforts to facilitate and improve this work while reserving for myself responsibility for shortcomings that remain.

This project began as a doctoral dissertation with support from a Dissertation Grant from the Program on the Urban Underclass of the Social Science Research Council, which funded fieldwork in San Jose, and a Doctoral Dissertation Improvement Grant from the National Science Foundation (Award No. 9501509), which funded fieldwork in Los Angeles. At the University of California (UC) at Berkeley, I received support from the Vice Chancellor for Research Fund and the Department of Sociology as well as from an award from the Carol Hatch Ethnography Fund. After I finished the dissertation, the Robert Wood Johnson Foundation's Scholar in Health Policy Research Program and a Post-Doctoral Fellowship in Alcohol Studies at the Alcohol Research Group/Prevention Research Center sponsored by the National Institute of Alcohol Abuse and Alcoholism provided a home at the UC Berkeley School of Public Health while I wrote this book.

During fieldwork, I received guidance and aid from Jesús Mártinez, Richard Wood, and Christian Zlolniski in the Bay Area and Abel Valenzuela, Father Greg Boyle, Heather Trim, Larry Jacobson, Patti and Merrill Bauman, Jackie Levitt, and María Cabildo in Los Angeles. Christian and Abel deserve special mention, as they have ministered to this project in different ways for many years. My dissertation committee at UC Berkeley, Martín Sánchez-Jankowski, Ann Swidler, Mike Hout, and the late Mike Rogin, guided the design and conduct of the research and provided valuable feedback on the dissertation that represented a first attempt to analyze everyday economic life in Guadalupe and Chávez. The involvement of Ann and Martín continued as I wrote this manuscript. Ann's understanding of how culture works inspired much of the analyses I present here. Martín inspired, facilitated, encouraged, and cajoled in ways too numerous to mention. My debt to him runs deep and not just because he made this project possible.

Many people provided comments and feedback at various stages of the writing. Elizabeth Armstrong, Dalton Conley, Eric Klinenberg, Hal Luft, Ruth Malone, Anne Piehl, Jennifer Reich, Laura Schmidt, Loïc Wacquant, Jim Wiley, and members of the Writing Seminar at the Institute for Health Policy Studies at UC San Francisco provided valuable comments on individual chapters. Dalton and Eric both read and commented not only on several chapters but on full drafts of the complete manuscript. Laura midwifed this manuscript. She read most chapters several times and read the full manuscript at least twice. But even this tremendous effort pales in comparison to the assistance she provided by creating an intellectual and institutional home for this project and its off-spring at the Alcohol Research Group. I am grateful to the extraordinary support provided by Naomi Schneider at UC Press during the preparation of the manuscript.

Family of all types have provided patient and enthusiastic support. East Coast siblings, aunts, uncles, and cousins provided emotional support and intellectual engagement. Marc Dohan and Marion Magill shared their knowledge of and contacts in Los Angeles. Chris Gaut, Tiffany Camarillo, and their families and Peggy Woodring, Joanne Fabian, and their families assisted in small ways that made a large difference. During difficult and joyous moments over the many years of this project, Phaedra Bell has sustained me with a love and support that is impossible to adequately acknowledge here. The birth of our daughter Raisa during the final stages of writing has put everything in perspective.

Finally, I thank the residents of the low-income barrios of San Jose and East Los Angeles who allowed me to share pieces of their neighborhoods and lives. Some of the important things I learned from them are reported here—hopefully in a form they would consider accurate. I am grateful in particular to the members of two families who were my landlords in San Jose and in East Los Angeles.

With gratitude, I dedicate this book to my parents.

# PART I

# Introduction

# CHAPTER I

# Institutions of Poverty

Increasingly, the Mexican American experience of poverty matters not only in the barrios but also for our nation as a whole and its future possibilities. Mexican Americans have long made up the largest share of Latinos in the United States, and they are projected to become the largest non-Anglo group in the near future as their population surpasses that of African Americans. Mexican Americans have traditionally been considered a rural population, but low-income Mexican immigrants have been settling in large cities for decades. In recent years, long-established low-income barrios have grown and *Mexicanized* while new barrios have sprung up in cities across the country from New York to Kansas to Seattle.[1] In cities with long-established Mexican-origin populations such as Los Angeles, San Antonio, and Chicago, persistent poverty is a problem for many U.S.-born Mexican Americans. Thus, urban poverty among Mexican Americans is heterogeneous. Immigrant poverty afflicts many newcomers to the United States, and persistent poverty burdens U.S.-born Chicanos as it does other American ethnoracial minorities. This book seeks to further our understanding of these experiences of urban poverty among Mexican Americans by comparing immigrant poverty among newcomer *Mexicanos* with persistent poverty among U.S.-born Chicanos.

Mexican American poverty provides a crucial and underutilized perspective on poverty in general. The low-income barrios occupy a position betwixt and between two commonplace understandings of American poverty. On the one hand, they resemble the European immigrant slums of William Foote Whyte's "Eastern City": places where residents speak a foreign language, follow foreign customs, and exit as they settle into U.S. society. On the other hand, the barrios have features in common with the impoverished African American ghettos of our contemporary cities: places where U.S. citizens assigned the status of an ethnoracial minority are segregated and relegated and where problems such as gangs, drugs, crime and family breakup are all too common.

Despite the resemblances, I believe it is a mistake to cast the low-income barrio as a "special case" of the slum or ghetto. To the contrary, I argue that examining Mexican American barrio poverty on its own terms yields new insights into urban poverty in general. Some scholars and policy makers maintain that urban poverty arises from structural problems in the inner city, such as poor-quality schools or lack of jobs; others argue that it reflects individual dysfunction among the poor themselves, such as a devaluing of work or a lack of commitment to two-parent families. I began this project hoping to contribute to this "structure versus individual" debate, but my research in the low-income barrios has led me away from it. During fieldwork in the barrios, I saw how social institutions shaped the nature and consequences of poverty in the Mexican American barrios. My argument here is that analysis of these institutions of poverty—which spring from and sustain the social, political, and cultural environment of the low-income urban neighborhood—provides a useful yet neglected vantage point from which to explain and understand urban poverty not just in the barrios but also in slums, ghettos, and other low-income communities. A central goal of this book is to supplement extant structural and individual perspectives by focusing on the role of social institutions in the creation and re-creation of urban poverty in contemporary America.

EVERYDAY POVERTY IN GUADALUPE AND CHÁVEZ

My introduction to everyday poverty in the barrios began when I moved into a room in a Guadalupe home a few days after Julián showed me San Jose's low-income landmarks. My landlady Gloria and her family had just moved in themselves. They had come to California from El Salvador in 1989 and lived in the Latino Mission District in San Francisco for a few years before moving south to settle in San Jose. The family first moved to an apartment a few miles from Guadalupe, and in October 1993, Gloria was happy to find a vacant rental house in Guadalupe barrio. I was fortunate to find Gloria. I was talking to a local community organizer when Gloria came by and casually mentioned that she was looking to rent out one of her bedrooms to a boarder if the organizer happened to know of anyone. "How about this *muchacho?*" he suggested, and Gloria was my landlady before either of us really knew what had happened.

While neither Gloria nor I knew much about each other when we met, I did know something about the Guadalupe barrio. I knew already that many of my neighbors in Guadalupe were recent immigrants, that mostly these immigrants came from the western Mexican states of Michoacán and Jalisco, and that for many years Guadalupe and the *ranchos* and *colonias* of these states had been joined by migrants' circular travels.[2] I knew that Guadalupe barrio was poor. The 1990 U.S. census showed that Guadalupe barrio was among the more impoverished areas in San Jose; approximately one in five residents in the Guadalupe census tract had an income below the poverty line. While I leave a full discussion of census figures to the book's appendix—which includes a detailed discussion of how Guadalupe compares to the other barrios of San Jose and to the city as a whole—it is worth noting here that I suspect this 20 percent figure understates the extent of poverty in Guadalupe itself. The census tract that included Guadalupe also included some higher-income areas adjacent to the barrio, and as a receiving area for recent immigrants, it is possible that during the years since the census data were collected, additional poor people moved into the barrio.

Whatever the precise rate of poverty in Guadalupe, conditions in many barrio households were difficult. Overcrowding was the rule, and Gloria's home exemplified this. To pay the rent on her three-bedroom house, Gloria turned over one bedroom of the house to me and a second bedroom to another boarder. She slept in the third bedroom along with her daughter and a third boarder. Her two teenaged sons stayed in the living room. Nearly all the houses and apartments of Guadalupe were similarly overcrowded with large families, multiple boarders, or multiple families doubling or tripling up in all available rooms.

The streets of Guadalupe also communicated the feel of a low-income community. The primary grocery outlets of the neighborhood were mom-and-pop *tiendas.* Several blocks of the neighborhood had been turned over to used car dealerships and auto parts stores. Among the *panaderías, taquerías,* and beauty shops of the remaining blocks stood a food pantry that distributed free bags of groceries, two charitable thrifts where locals sifted through stacks of donated clothes, and a soup kitchen that twice weekly provided hot meals to dozens of destitute individuals and families.

As someone steeped in the scholarly literature on poverty, I also noticed signs of poverty that were absent in Guadalupe. In my first weeks in the barrio, I was struck by the social problems I *did not* find—problems such as joblessness, street crime, and welfare dependence that we often associate with urban poverty in America. Instead of joblessness, each morning I saw the old cars and pickup trucks that jammed Guadalupe's streets, driveways, and front lawns move off in every direction, taking residents to their low-tech jobs—such as janitor, landscaper, home health aide—in the high-tech Silicon Valley. Rather than street crime, Guadalupe evenings saw residents gathered over open car hoods or supervising children's play within fenced-in yards while Mexican *rancheras* blared from car stereos and open windows. The streets seemed peaceful even though there were two homicides in Guadalupe during the first three months I lived there. As for welfare dependence, I met few residents who received public assistance, and Gloria's was the exceptional household in the neighborhood that was headed by a mother raising children on her own. On both sides of us, across the street, across the back alley, and around the block, the families of Guadalupe were headed by two parents.

Though poor, Guadalupe barrio avoided the social problems of an impoverished "urban underclass," and some residents and knowledgeable outsiders took pains to point this out. One researcher who had studied San Jose's poor barrios for several years told me soon after I arrived, "Look around you here. Is this the 'underclass'? The poverty in San Jose is different. Unemployment is not the problem here; underemployment is the problem. . . . Everyone is off at work. Poverty here is not being out of a job. Poverty here is that the jobs are so bad that you cannot get ahead."

During my months of residence in San Jose, I saw how poverty in Guadalupe emerged out of low wages and underemployment. I listened to residents talk about the challenges they faced as Silicon Valley businesses used subcontracting strategies to reduce their hourly wage. I watched as families, in order to put in long hours at low-wage jobs, arranged their lives around impossibly hectic schedules that left little time to socialize or even to get a good night's sleep.[3] I saw residents come and go along the links of international migration chains, and I listened to parents and children talk about the opportunities and difficulties that came with their move from Mexico to the relative prosperity of the United States.[4] After nearly a year of fieldwork in San Jose, I saw how the everyday experience of poverty in Guadalupe barrio revolved around the lousy jobs that residents found in Silicon Valley *el norte.*

I left Guadalupe barrio keenly aware of how "underemployment, not unemployment," undergirded poverty in immigrant barrios such as Guadalupe, but my expectation was that the situation would be different in other Mexican American barrios. To check these expectations against reality, I moved to East Los Angeles—a move Gloria considered ill-advised because, she warned me, "the people down there are crazy. . . . There is a lot of shooting, a lot of gangs." The year of LA fieldwork to come would deepen and shift the understanding of barrio poverty I had begun to develop in Guadalupe.

After Andrés first guided me to the hot spot, several weeks passed before I succeeded in gaining a toehold in the Chávez community. During these weeks of meetings, introductions, and negotiations, I found an apartment near Chávez in East LA, and I familiarized myself with the social geography and street life of this Mexican American city within the southern California megalopolis.

East LA is a low-income area, and large parts of it reminded me of Guadalupe barrio. Overcrowded houses and barracklike apartment buildings covered dozens of square miles stretching east from downtown into the suburbs of the San Gabriel Valley and south toward LA's satellite cities of Long Beach and Santa Ana. After my time in Guadalupe, I felt at home in the residential blocks of East Los Angeles, where fenced-in yards surrounded overcrowded homes, sidewalks and driveways were jammed with workers' old cars, and quiet daytime streets erupted with traffic and socializing when residents came home from work in the evening.

Public housing in East LA was a different story. There was more street life, more graffiti, and a more tangible feeling of trespassing in a defended neighborhood.[5] Over time, I became comfortable in these neighborhoods and learned how to "read" their public signs of difference. I saw that some street life revolved around the drug economy, that some reflected the efforts of local members to "represent" their organized street gang, and that most was the socializing and errand running of people who lived in a community of cramped apartments and substantial unemployment. I learned to distinguish street gang *placas* that promoted the organization's claim to territory from the tags of teenagers who simply wanted to advertise their name. I learned that people in the streets had a sense of who was coming and going in their neighborhood, and I learned whom they were looking out for.

Chávez and other public housing in East LA differed from Guadalupe and other barrios of private housing in ways that went beyond the street. According to the 1990 census, more than half of the residents in the Chávez census tract had income below the poverty line. No part of East Los Angeles was more impoverished. As I document in the book's appendix, census figures on employment, family structure, and use of public assistance also show that Chávez barrio is more socially and economically distressed than the East LA barrios in general and more distressed than Guadalupe. According to standard measures, which typically use 40 percent as a poverty rate benchmark, and according to a quick visual inspection or "windshield survey," Chávez barrio *is* different. In contrast to East LA barrios of private housing and in contrast to Guadalupe, these measures identify Chávez as an "underclass" community.[6]

It was impossible to ignore the ways in which Chávez differed from Guadalupe and similar barrios in East LA. But as I spent more time in Chávez I increasingly looked past the differences to see that the projects had much in common with barrios of private housing. Behind the graffiti-covered walls of Chávez apartment buildings, households in Chávez looked much like those in Guadalupe and the other low-income Mexican American barrios where I spent time in East Los Angeles. Most were overcrowded because many children, extended kin, or multiple nuclear families squeezed into two- or three-bedroom units.

Household routines in Chávez were also familiar from my time in Guadalupe. Most Chávez residents struggled to make ends meet in low-wage jobs. Every morning the parking lots emptied and the streets filled with old cars carrying residents to often-distant job sites, and every evening the streets, parking lots, and front lawns filled as Chávez residents returned home. Many Chávez residents suffered from the same job-induced maladies that afflicted residents of Guadalupe, such as continual sleep deprivation, no time to relax with family, long commutes, and employment insecurity. As it did in Guadalupe, the everyday experience of poverty in Chávez revolved around lousy jobs and residents' limited opportunities for advancement.

Like my Guadalupe landlady Gloria, Chávez residents recognized problems such as "crazy people," shootings, and gangs in their community. But many echoed the feelings of Ana-Berta, a forty-five-year-old mother of four who was one of the first residents I met in the barrio. Ana-Berta's experiences and understandings of the social problems in Chávez were complex, and I address them in some detail in Chapter 7. Here, however, it is important to note Ana-Berta's first thoughts on the subject, which she shared with me soon after we first met. "We have our problems here," she said. "But you're not going to write just about the drugs and the gang, right? We have a lot of good people here, too."

## STRUCTURES OF POVERTY, EXPERIENCES OF POVERTY

Ana-Berta was right, of course. In the months following our conversation, I met many good people in Chávez, just as in the months preceding our conversation I had met many good people in Guadalupe. Meeting good people makes ethnography enjoyable and is one of its central occupational hazards. Enjoyment and hazard reflect the mandate of ethnography itself—to foster an understanding of peoples' lives and provide insights into their worlds.[7] In no small measure, the ethnographer's task is to delve into people's lived experiences to bolster our understanding of how structural circumstances and individual behaviors combine in everyday life.

Immigrant poverty provides a clarion example of how the structural and individual blend in a complex social reality. Scholars have emphasized that low-wage jobs, such as those in Guadalupe barrio, reflect newly emerging structural circumstances at a global scale. Globalization theory points out how political, economic, and historical ties between the world's regions and nations influence the creation of jobs and the flow of workers. From this perspective, the fact that Silicon Valley's low-wage workforce hails from Mexico reflects the will of financiers in New York, London, and Tokyo as much as it does the decisions of laborers in Guadalajara and Mexico City.[8] Globalization complements long-standing theories that emphasize how individual decisions, such as the decision to migrate, shape the economic fortunes of newly established ethnic communities. Privileging the individual behaviors of the people who move from one country to another, the theory of selective migration argues that migrants often have different motivations and aspirations—an unusually strong work ethic or a more powerful drive to succeed—than their compatriots who stay put. These individual characteristics affect how immigrants work in the United States. Even when confined to less desirable sectors of the labor market—whether due to lack of education, language barriers, or even anti-immigrant discrimination—selective migration explains the origins of an immigrant workforce who are willing to work harder than many U.S.-born natives and who are willing to take jobs that many natives do not want.[9]

A parallel set of structural and individual factors shape the world of the persistently poor. The same global economic changes that have brought immigrants to U.S. cities seeking work have motivated employers to move better-quality jobs out of the cities in search of cheaper labor. This deindustrialization has had profound consequences for impoverished African American ghettos and Puerto Rican barrios, whose residents have found that long-standing jobs have disappeared.[10] Scholars note that communities overwhelmed by the structural-economic dislocations of deindustrialization may develop distinct cultural worlds.[11] Extreme economic distress may lead to a paucity of shared resources in a community or a breakdown of trust among friends and neighbors. This can hamper residents' ability to combat crime or to take advantage of the opportunities for upward mobility that do exist.[12] But some scholars, questioning the structural perspective, maintain that persistent poverty reflects individuals' rejection of mainstream norms and values. According to this view, American society has tolerated and even encouraged individual behaviors that have had negative consequences for poor people and impoverished urban communities. The theory of perverse incentives notes that in post-1960s America the significance of material wealth has been celebrated while the importance of steady work has been dismissed. In the same period, federal welfare programs that provide cash assistance to unemployed single mothers have given low-income Americans a reason not to work and not to marry.[13]

Structural theories of globalization and deindustrialization as well as individual theories of selective migration and perverse incentives provide guideposts for understanding the experience of contemporary barrio poverty. Globalization permits the widespread employment of impoverished Mexican immigrants in Silicon Valley homes and businesses, and deindustrialization means that the factories that supported earlier generations of East LA Chicanos no longer provide jobs to their children. Selective migration means that the *Mexicanos* who leave for and settle in Guadalupe are more likely to be willing to work eighty-hour weeks at minimum-wage jobs in fast-food restaurants, and the perverse incentives offered by public aid programs help explain why similar work-related sacrifices make less sense to residents in Chávez.

Yet even as these theories help us explain the situation of the low-income barrio, they provide only an incomplete picture of its social dynamics. In the low-income barrio we see daily interactions and hear personal narratives but can only infer and interpret how these are connected to underlying structural forces or personal motives.[14] For example, ethnographers in immigrant communities cannot see globalization create low-wage jobs; nor can they see the process of self-selection by which migrants decide to move in their pursuit. Recent ethnographies have, however, shown how gender, jealousy, and loyalty inform and transform migration among recent immigrants.[15] By the same token, ethnographers who examine persistent poverty cannot see deindustrialization make work disappear, and they can do little more than speculate about whether perverse incentives keep the persistently poor out of the labor market.[16] But they can show how street life, crime, and public housing shape present behavior and future possibilities among the persistently poor.[17] Ethnographers do not *see* globalization, deindustrialization, selective migration, or perverse incentives. They use these structural and individual theories as guideposts for making sense of the interactions and narratives that constitute the substance of everyday life in low-income communities.

What ethnographers do see are small-scale patterns of everyday life in poor communities and the local context within which those patterns unfold and make sense. International migration presents itself as a chain of social connections among individuals, families, and communities rather than as a demographic flow. In the ethnographer's view, street gangs operate as an organization within the fabric of the low-income community; they do not simply arise in response to blocked economic opportunity. Ethnographic interviews with low-income women show us that public aid is neither the last resort of the desperate nor the first choice of the manipulator but rather one part of the process of household budgeting. In short, ethnography reveals how large-scale forces and individual motivations work themselves out in patterns of everyday life within the local context of the low-income community.

## SOCIAL INSTITUTIONS AND THE BARRIO ECONOMY

During fieldwork, I saw the residents of Guadalupe and Chávez generate income in a multitude of ways. This diversity of income-generating behaviors testified to the difficulties of material survival and advancement in the unpromising and uncompromising economic environment of the barrios. Low-quality jobs dominated employment opportunities in both barrios; residents mostly worked in nonunionized positions that paid near-minimum wage and provided little employment security. Few residents had the educational credentials to open doors into better jobs, and few even had access to the kinds of schools that might provide such credentials. Almost none had wealthy or powerful friends or relatives who could provide direct material support. And, like all U.S. residents, barrio residents had access only to meager benefits from state-sponsored aid or other charities. In these circumstances, material advancement was far from certain, and material survival could at times be challenging.

Residents in both barrios engaged this harsh economic environment along three fronts. They made do as best they could working at low-wage jobs, they took advantage of available opportunities to generate illegal income, and they participated in a variety of public assistance programs. The dizzying variety of income-generating activities in the barrios thus boiled down to various combinations of these three things: taking a job, pursuing opportunities in the underground economy, and participating in public aid. Moreover, in Guadalupe and Chávez the quality of economic, political, and social life reflected not only pervasive material insecurity but also the local institutions that mediated residents' engagement with that insecurity. In short, life in the barrios reflected not only *that* barrio residents lived in a harsh economic environment but *how* barrio residents grappled with the challenges of economic advancement and survival.

What I refer to here as "institutions of poverty" shaped how residents of Guadalupe and Chávez struggled to advance by shaping how residents engaged in and combined jobs, underground economy, and public aid.[18] Residents decided which low-wage jobs were worth pursuing and which to avoid within the context of social institutions. Social institutions helped them assess the risks and rewards of the illegal economy. And social institutions helped them make sense of and manage the inevitable stigma that attended public aid receipt. In my analyses of everyday income generation in Guadalupe and Chávez, I point out how three institutions in particular—social networks, illegal organizations, and welfare subcultures—shaped residents' struggles for advancement and survival.

First and foremost, *informal social networks* in Guadalupe and Chávez played an important role in shaping how residents participated in low-wage jobs.[19] Social networks shaped the meaning that residents of the two communities assigned to low-wage jobs.[20] In both communities, local social networks mostly included family and low-income Mexican Americans known through the neighborhood, school, or work. In Guadalupe, these local social networks were supplemented by transnational ties to communities in Mexico. Social networks—local and transnational—are usually conceived of as an element of social structure. In terms of their effects on everyday economic life in Guadalupe and Chávez, however, social networks had important consequences for cultural orientations. Transnational social networks led Guadalupe residents to assign a different meaning to low-wage work than purely local networks did in Chávez.[21] Embedded in ongoing interactions with friends and relatives in Mexico through reminiscences, visits, phone calls, and letters, Guadalupe residents saw low wages as relatively valuable, believed they would work in low-wage jobs for only a limited period of time before returning to Mexico, and took their tenure in low-jobs as indicative of upward economic mobility. Given their U.S.-only orientation, it is not surprising that Chávez residents more commonly saw low-wage jobs as economic and social dead ends. Differences in low-wage laboring in Guadalupe and Chávez show how structural circumstances have cultural consequences that affect everyday economic life.

Second in economic significance were the *indigenous organizations* that had an impact on illegal activities.[22] These organizations shaped how residents integrated law-breaking into everyday life in Guadalupe and Chávez.[23] Residents of both communities participated in illegal activities. In Guadalupe, many residents who had migrated from Mexico without proper documents worked in the informal economy—otherwise legal economic activities that took place outside the purview of government regulation. In Chávez, residents more commonly worked in the illicit economy, which produced and distributed goods and services that were themselves illegal. Individuals involved in both kinds of illegal activities faced obstacles to participation—the difficulty of finding employers who hired undocumented workers in Guadalupe and the difficulty of avoiding police interdiction in Chávez. Local organizations such as street corner day labor markets in Guadalupe and street gangs in Chávez provided a collective solution to the individual difficulties of illegal work. These local organizations integrated illegal activities into everyday community life. In Guadalupe, local organizations erased the distinction between legal and informal economic activities in everyday life, thus "legalizing" illegal activities. Suppression, incarceration, and violence make it impossible to "legalize" illicit activities. In Chávez, local organizations "normalized" illicit activities by providing an institutional means for managing the material and symbolic costs of participation in the illicit economy. The differential organization of illegal activities shows how structural arrangements and cultural orientations jointly affect everyday economic life.

The final way that barrio residents grappled with the daily economic conundrum of barrio life was by participating in public aid programs, and *subcultures* affected how this participation unfolded in everyday life.[24] Differences in barrio subcultures created distinct experiences of public assistance receipt in Guadalupe and Chávez.[25] In keeping with dominant attitudes and values in the United States, residents of both Guadalupe and Chávez believed that receiving public assistance was not a legitimate means of earning income and that welfare recipients should be stigmatized. Nonetheless, economic necessity forced some residents in both communities to rely on public aid to make ends meet. Public assistance in both communities was thus marked by an inconsistency between what residents said and what they did. Subcultural practices in both communities allowed residents to make sense of and manage this inconsistency in everyday life by simultaneously recognizing the legitimacy of welfare stigma and the necessity of welfare receipt. Because economic need was more acute and aid receipt more common in Chávez than in Guadalupe, however, the subcultures surrounding public assistance in the two communities were not identical. In Guadalupe, residents steadfastly maintained that any receipt of aid was illegitimate, but time-limited use of aid to relieve economic hardship could be justified on a case-by-case basis. In Chávez, relatively widespread reliance on aid for longer periods of time meant that residents tended to invoke the stigma of welfare receipt more selectively—often in the instrumental or even strategic pursuit of personal, social, or political advantage within the community. Neither case-by-case justification of aid receipt nor instrumental invocation of stigma was a self-sustaining cultural practice; each simply made sense of welfare reliance created by structural circumstances. Thus, the everyday dynamics of welfare participation show how structural circumstances affect symbolic expression.

From William Foote Whyte's analysis of street gangs and rackets in Boston's prewar North End to Joan Moore's examination of changing commercial, family, and educational institutions in the face of resumed Mexican migration in 1990s East LA, urban ethnographers have focused on how social institutions shape everyday life in low-income urban communities.[26] This study adds to that tradition by examining income-generating institutions in the barrios. A central tenet of this analysis is that income generation in the barrios occurs along the contours of local social institutions. Understanding the experience of poverty thus requires examining those institutions and the local cultural orders that they sustain. I argue here that neither the structural forces that underlie economic opportunity nor the individual actions that produce income sufficiently describe why income generation occurs the way it does in the low-income community. The effects of structural change must be traced downward to their concrete manifestations in particular communities at the same time that individual motives must be traced upward and placed in the local context within which they make sense. Here, I show how the structural and individual intersect to create everyday poverty in the California barrios.

## AN OVERVIEW OF THE BOOK

This book is organized around the income-generating activities of the barrios. I discuss, in turn, residents' work lives, the way they earned money illegally, and how they participated in public assistance programs. Of course, in real life all of these activities were intertwined in complex and multifaceted ways. The case studies of Chapter 2 and the book's conclusion describe and discuss this complexity. For several reasons, however, I mostly discuss work, crime, and welfare separately. Focusing on one kind of income generation at a time allows me to highlight how social institutions shape income generation in the barrios. This is particularly true because my analysis of work, crime, and welfare suggests that each of these different income-generating activities was dominated by a different kind of social institution. Thus, discussing each activity in turn allows me to show different institutions of poverty in action and to focus the reader's attention on one institution at a time. Another reason to discuss work, crime, and welfare separately is that the three activities did not play equally important roles in everyday economic life. I start with work because it was the most important source of income and the most important determinant of everyday economic life in Guadalupe and Chávez. Illegal activities were second in importance and thus come second in exposition, and public assistance was third.

In the next chapter, I finish laying the groundwork for the argument by analyzing aggregate data that point out the differences between Guadalupe and Chávez. This concludes the introductory section of the book. Part II of the book analyzes wage laboring in Guadalupe and Chávez. The chapters of this section highlight the social institution of informal social networks. Part III turns to illegal activities. Its chapters focus on the indigenous organizations that shaped economic crime in the barrios. Part IV addresses participation in public assistance, and I highlight there how community subcultures constituted a social institution that shaped how residents participated in public assistance programs.

In Part V of the book, I provide an overview of the economic organization of everyday barrio life, and I discuss what the analysis of barrio poverty tells us about poverty in other communities and more generally.

In this holistic discussion of urban poverty in the barrios and in the nation, I note the influence of social structure and community culture on the everyday lives of the poor. My argument here is not that these factors are unimportant. It is, rather, that they do not tell us all we need to know about life in low-income communities. Social institutions organize the experience of poverty. They sometimes do this in accordance with structural and cultural circumstances. They sometimes do so despite them.

# CHAPTER 2

# Income Generation
# in the Barrios

The Guadalupe barrio lies only a few miles from the corporate campuses of some of the country's best-known Silicon Valley companies, but visitors might not realize they are so close to the high-tech center of the United States. In some ways, Guadalupe more resembles the turn of the twentieth-century immigrant slums famously documented by Jacob Riis in *How the Other Half Lives* than the capital of the information economy at the turn of the twenty-first.[1] The residents of Guadalupe were mostly born and raised abroad in the western Mexican states of Michoacán and Jalisco. Most residents left school years before they learned hardware design or software languages. The language of Guadalupe is Mexican Spanish, which dominates the streets and the stores and is the language of celebration in all but one of the half-dozen masses each weekend at the local Catholic parish. In other ways, however, the barrio and the campuses are closely intertwined. Guadalupe residents clean the high-tech offices, prepare the food and wash the dishes in the trendy restaurants that celebrate Valley prosperity, and care for the elderly parents and pre–school-age children of the high-tech workforce.[2]

If Guadalupe represents the face of new immigrant poverty in America, Chávez barrio represents a different but still new American poverty. Located several miles from downtown in East Los Angeles, Chávez is one small part of the largest contiguous settlement of Mexican-origin people outside Mexico itself. Many neighborhoods in East LA have the same *Mexicano* atmosphere as Guadalupe barrio, where a recent migrant population relies on Spanish as the language of everyday life. But even though nearby industrial areas in Commerce, Vernon, and LA itself have experienced an economic transformation in recent decades, East LA is no Silicon Valley. Many of the manufacturing plants that provided steady employment at midcentury have downsized or shut their doors. The contrast between Guadalupe and Chávez is even more striking than that between San Jose and LA. While Guadalupe-like immigrant slums surround Chávez, the barrio itself is in many ways more like the housing projects of Rust Belt cities thousands of miles distant than the slums around the block. Chávez residents, like the subjects of *There Are No Children Here,* Alex Kotlowitz's child's-eye view of public housing in inner-city Chicago, daily encounter a public and vibrant drug economy on their street corners and a welfare economy that raises the prospect of long-term dependence on public assistance. These social dislocations—along with poverty rates exceeding 40 percent, public housing that cries out for renovation, and unmistakable "quality-of-life" crimes such as graffiti and public drinking—signify persistent poverty in urban America. Chávez residents know their neighborhood's reputation. Motorists drive in from nearby neighborhoods or take advantage of convenient freeway exits to buy illicit drugs from street dealers. The local gang and the regular eruptions of violence bring community activists, news reporters, movie and sports stars, and police cars and helicopters.

Seeing Guadalupe and Chávez side by side sparks questions. How are differences in the economic organization of Guadalupe and Chávez expressed in the daily lives of residents? Does the economy of the Silicon Valley protect Guadalupe from persistent poverty? How do the residents of Chávez manage the economic dislocations that have changed the face of employment in Los Angeles?

The goal of this chapter is to address these questions in a way that recognizes the similarities in the everyday lives of residents in Guadalupe and Chávez at the same time that it acknowledges differences between San Jose and Los Angeles. I start with case studies of two residents to give a sense of the similarities in income-generating routines in Guadalupe and Chávez. Most of the rest of this chapter then uses quantitative summaries of field note data to frame these case studies and introduce questions about how social institutions shape everyday life in the barrios—questions that I then address in the chapters in Parts II through IV.

## EVERYDAY INCOME GENERATION
## IN GUADALUPE AND CHÁVEZ

The experiences of José Mendoza and Ted Galindo, an eighteen-year-old resident of Guadalupe and a 23-year-old resident of Chávez respectively, provide one view of everyday economic life in the barrios. I describe their income-generating activities in extended vignettes. I refer to specific passages in these long vignettes as exemplars of more general patterns of income generation that I document with a quantitative analysis of my field note data.

### Guadalupe: José's Story

In early 1993, José Mendoza walked across the border from Tijuana with his stepfather Jesús and the clothes that fit into an old suitcase that is now under the bed in their Guadalupe apartment. Jesús had lived and worked in San Jose during previous trips to the United States, and José's mother, María, was waiting for them when they completed the trip north.

The food-processing plant where María worked hired José for $5.00 an hour into a part-time job, but "part-time" was a misnomer. To get to work, José either had to drive with María—which meant spending her full workday at the plant—or endure a time-consuming and unpredictable commute on public transportation. In early summer, 1994, José adopted the same solution as most Silicon Valley workers to the frustrations of the commute; he bought a car. The dangerously dilapidated 1978 Ford nearly killed José and Jesús when one of its tires exploded on the freeway, and José went back to the bus for two weeks while he saved up to have it towed and repaired. Though hazardous, the car allowed José to come and go to the plant according to his own work schedule rather than at the whim of his mother or of the Santa Clara County public transportation.

Coming and going as he pleased was crucial because José's work hours varied widely. And his wages, of course, varied with his hours. Some weeks, he brought home a couple hundred dollars, while other weeks he netted only $50 or $60. Contributing to household expenses consumed some of what he brought home. But with five earners and only three dependents in a small two-bedroom apartment, day-to-day expenses were not overwhelming. Aside from a few months when his international long-distance bill skyrocketed, José generally had money to spend on himself and to save. Until the spring of 1994, when he began saving for the Ford, he spent most of his money on keeping in touch with friends in Mexico (the long-distance calls were mostly to a young woman he was courting) and for clothes and electronics he would show off on visits home.

As the Silicon Valley went on summer vacation in 1994, the plant slowed down, and José's work hours dipped. Few hours brought financial pressure, and José first turned to welfare and then to crime to make ends meet.

A local food and clothing bank provided the welfare. The church-based charity worked with local supermarkets to issue food vouchers to those in need, and José obtained vouchers several times. This short-term use of welfare provided crucial support when work at the plant first began to unexpectedly slow down. After several months, however, José's hours at the plant did not pick up, and he turned to crime for a more permanent solution to his financial woes.

José had two kinds of criminal opportunities. One of his uncles was involved in the drug trade. José said that his uncle earned a good income—enough to rent a two-bedroom apartment for just himself, his wife, and two children and to fill the apartment with a cable-equipped large-screen television set—by "sitting around at home all day waiting for his beeper to go off." In terms of his uncle's profession and his own access to the drug trade, José was exceptional in Guadalupe. There were no public drug markets in the barrio, and residents often commented derisively on the few local "cowboys" who—it was rumored—bought their gaudy clothes and customized "ground effects" trucks with the profits from drug selling. Like his neighbors, José did not find the drug trade an attractive opportunity; not only did he make fun of the cowboys' consumption habits, but also he knew of the practical difficulties—such as the time his uncle's business partner left his family and possessions behind in a desperate flight to Mexico.

The crime José turned to was more subtle and so commonplace in Guadalupe barrio that it rarely was commented upon in everyday life. His boss at the food-processing plant told José that a social security card would earn him a lateral move to a job which had more dependable hours. Of course, José had no way to obtain a social security card legally. His border crossing a year previous was ostensibly for a short visit to Los Angeles relatives, not resettlement in Silicon Valley. José's other uncle, however, knew how to overcome this problem. It was to buy a false card, a *chueco,* from the young men in a particular San Jose parking lot, and the uncle instructed José on whom to contact, what to expect, and how much to pay. A few weeks later, José presented his *chueco* and resolved the financial crisis by working long hours as a truck driver's assistant.

### Chávez: Ted's Story

Ted Galindo had grown up in Chávez barrio and lived there all his life, but in 1995 he was not officially a resident of the housing development. Early in the year, he, his mother, and his two sisters agreed to remove Ted from the apartment lease in order to lower the rent on their unit. With fewer official lessees, however, the housing authority soon moved Ted's mother and sisters into a smaller, two-bedroom unit. Ted lost his private bedroom, and he spent his nights on a couch in the living room—an arrangement that meant he had little privacy and little ability to pursue his relationships with women.

Beyond the practical difficulties it introduced, staying in the living room was annoying on a more philosophical level. Although his mother insisted that he contribute more to household expenses than his sister, she and her child were given exclusive use of one of the apartment bedrooms. Ted's mother insisted this was necessary because the sister was officially on lease and her staying in the living room would not only be inconvenient for everyone in the apartment—due to the baby—but would also raise the possibility that their manipulation of the lease would be detected. Ted was furious about how living expenses and living space were divided between him and his sister. He said that his sister was lazy and that she should get out of the house and go to work, like him.

While Ted benefited from public aid through housing, most of his income came from low-wage work. During 1995, he worked as a clerk at a sandwich shop, as a busboy and dishwasher at a restaurant, and at a small downtown firm that provided security for sporting and entertainment events all over the LA Basin. Ted dressed in the required uniform of black pants, black shoes, and white shirt; he often left for his security jobs in the late afternoon and did not return home until early the next morning. He also was often looking for a ride to work because events were frequently inaccessible via public transportation. Despite having held a variety of full- and part-time jobs since finishing high school, Ted could not afford a car. Several times, when his arranged ride fell through at the last moment, Ted walked around Chávez in his black pants and white shirt looking for someone to drive him to Shriner's Convention Center in South Central LA or to a club in the San Fernando Valley. A few times, I drove Ted to his security jobs. These drives through East LA were like a tour of his employment history. In every block, it seemed, Ted could point to a restaurant or a convenience store where he had worked for a few months at some point in his life.

Ted pined for a car and apartment of his own. He complained about the terrible bus system that meant he had to spend extra hours every day getting to and from work, about the frustration of never being able to leave Chávez to go to the beach or visit friends, and about his lack of privacy at home. He was particularly vocal on the streets with friends and especially after he had a few beers. One night, too much beer and frustration at not being able to bring his girlfriend home exploded in a fight with his girlfriend's brother. I talked to Ted, fuming and whirling around with a knife in his hand, on the streets of Chávez after midnight. "I just want a car so I can get the fuck out of here," he cried.

One way to make enough money at least for a car and perhaps for the security deposit on a private apartment would be through illicit activities. But Ted had trouble getting access to better opportunities in the illicit economy such as in the drug trade. The incident with his girlfriend's brother was seen as typical; as her brother saw it, Ted had a tendency to "snap" that made him hard to trust in a difficult situation. In addition, Ted had a reputation for unduly avoiding violence. No one was surprised, for example, when Ted was a no-show at a weekend football game between Elm Street and a nearby street gang. Everyone expected the game to be violent, and several Elm Street members sustained fairly serious injuries in an intragang scrimmage when the opposing street gang failed to turn up.

Financially, Ted spent most of 1995 between a rock and hard place. At home, his mother and sister made so little money from public assistance that his wage earnings were a crucial part of the household's economic strategy.

Month to month, Ted was not able to save much money at all. The improvements he wanted to make in his life—buying a car and moving out of the projects—seemed maddeningly out of reach.


PATTERNS OF INCOME GENERATION

Income generation played a large role in everyday barrio life, dominating the daily routines of José and Ted. José spent many hours each week working and in a frustrating commute, and his migration to Guadalupe barrio was related to income generation. For Ted, as well, income generation shaped where and how he lived. Although Ted spent less time working than José, commuting and the uncertainties of work hours in the jobs he held meant that much of his life was, nevertheless, devoted to the logistics of earning a living. Tabulations from field notes I recorded in Guadalupe and Chávez suggest that income generation played an important role in the lives of other barrios residents as well. Figure 1 provides a graphical summary of the data I collected on income generation. It shows that the overwhelming majority of the residents with whom I spent time in both communities—87 percent in Chávez and 91 percent in Guadalupe—generated income in some way during the time I knew them.

During fieldwork, I attempted to collect data on the income-earning activities of all residents with whom I came in contact. I did this by spending time with people and actually watching what they did to earn income; by speaking with them informally about where they were working or how they were paying the rent; by noting what other people in the barrios said about the income sources of family, friends, and neighbors; and by simply asking residents how they were making do. Most of the time, I felt I was able to collect reliable information about residents' income-earning activities. I asked working residents what kind of job they held and how much they earned at it. I accompanied hustling residents to flea markets or watched them sell food, clothing, or illicit drugs in the neighborhood. Residents talked about how much their friends and neighbors earned, and I used this information as long as I heard it from several different seemingly neutral sources and as long as it accorded with what I directly observed about the person's situation. Sometimes, residents showed me pay stubs or tax returns.

Still, in some cases, I never satisfied myself that I knew how someone actually earned his or her income. For example, during the winter and spring of 1994 I saw a young Guadalupe resident named Tomás fairly

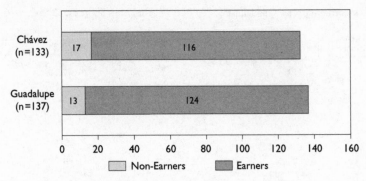

Figure 1. Earners and Nonearners: Guadalupe and Chávez

regularly, but I never was sure how he supported himself financially. I saw him at the day labor markets, but I also saw him on the streets during business hours, which suggested to me that he was not working full time at day labor. In addition, he had his own room in a well-maintained apartment building, which suggested that his income was both steady and reasonable. In conversations, I probed several times about how he paid the rent on his apartment, and he always said through day labor. I developed some theories: that family in Mexico or Texas were sending him money, that he was working a night job, or that he earned money through illicit activities he did not want to talk about. Sometimes, I had confirmed or rejected theories such as these through conversation with friends or relatives, but Tomás had no family in San Jose, and I always spent time with him alone, so I did not know his friends or even if he had any. In short, even though I spent time with Tomás over the course of several months and even though I felt I knew a lot about some aspects of his life, I never satisfied myself that I knew how he actually earned his income.

By the time I left the field, I had collected what I considered reliable information on the income-generating activities of 137 Guadalupe residents and 133 Chávez residents. I did not carefully select this group of people to represent all residents in Guadalupe and Chávez, and I do not claim that these data represent the income-generating activities of the barrios. But these data do provide a way of summarizing what I saw and experienced in these barrios during the course of fieldwork. To ease exposition, I refer to these data as a sample and use the data to speak of income generation in Guadalupe and Chávez generally without always including all the appropriate caveats about the limitations and specificity

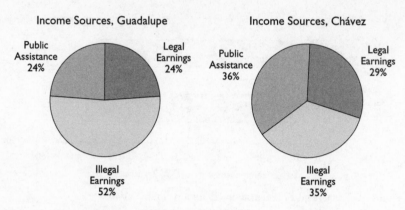

Figure 2.  Income Sources: Guadalupe and Chávez

of my data. I am comfortable with these shortcuts because I did make a concerted effort to circulate throughout the barrio and gather data that were as representative as possible. I will also try to provide reminders that these data represent and summarize what I saw during fieldwork but not necessarily barrio life as a whole.

The experiences of José and Ted are also notable for the variety of ways in which the young men earned their income. In addition to working, both considered involvement in economic crime, and both received income from public assistance. In this respect, José and Ted were typical of the residents I spent time with in the barrios. Figure 2 shows how the residents I knew in Guadalupe and Chávez earned their income on a day-to-day basis. They had income from three sources—legal earnings, illegal earnings, and public assistance. Many barrio residents (including José and Ted) had income from more than one kind of source, so in constructing Figure 2 I counted each distinct kind of income-generating activity by each barrio resident separately. For example, the wages José Mendoza earned at the food-processing plant and the food vouchers he obtained from the church count as two distinct kinds of income-generating activity. For this reason, José Mendoza is represented twice in Figure 2.[3]

Figure 2 shows that legal, illegal, and public assistance earnings were common in both barrios. About one in four of the residents I knew, 24 percent in Guadalupe and 29 percent in Chávez, had some income from legal sources such as wage labor. The barrios differed in illegal earnings and public aid. More than half of my Guadalupe group (52 percent) had illegal income, while in Chávez the figure was 35 percent, just over a third. Chávez residents had more experience with public aid, however, with more than one out of every three residents I knew receiving aid there (36 percent) while fewer than one in four (24 percent) had aid in Guadalupe.

The stories of José and Ted and Figures 1 and 2 highlight two important similarities in income generation in Guadalupe and Chávez: nearly all the adults I knew earned income in some way, and residents of the barrios earned income from a variety of different sources. These figures also suggest that there were some differences in income generation in the two barrios. Differences in the experience of work, crime, and welfare in Guadalupe and Chávez require more attention, and I turn to those now.

*Work*

José and Ted both had complex and variable work experiences. They both sought and found work, but the jobs they held paid low wages, provided unreliable working hours, or proved unstable over time. There were also differences in how steadily and how legally the two young men worked—differences typical of what I saw in Guadalupe and Chávez more generally.

The Guadalupe residents I knew were underemployed at times, but they were rarely jobless, even though for many residents working constituted a violation of law. José's own experiences—often underemployed but never jobless during the months I knew him—illustrate this. That said, although his everyday experience of work was unremarkable, technically José never worked legally. As the figures in the first column of Table 1 show, this pattern was common in Guadalupe barrio. In Guadalupe nearly everyone (93 percent) who earned income held a job. But fewer than half (44 percent) of those who held a job had legal permission to work in the United States. In conversations about job histories, moreover, I found that only half of Guadalupe residents, 62 of the 124 earners I knew in the barrio, had ever held a legal job in the United States.

The residents I spent time with in Chávez were often not only underemployed but unemployed, as Ted's experiences illustrate. Ted was often underemployed in the jobs that he held, and in addition he had experienced multiple spells of joblessness as he moved from one position to another, often seeking a better position or in frustration after a bad experience at a workplace. The second column of Table 1 shows how this kind of job-holding pattern manifested itself in the barrio in general. In contrast to the situation in Guadalupe, less than two-thirds (59 percent)

TABLE I. JOBHOLDING IN
GUADALUPE AND CHÁVEZ

| Measure | Guadalupe | Chávez |
|---|---|---|
| Jobholder, 1993–1996 | 93% | 59% |
| Legal job, 1993–1996 | 44% | 51% |
| Ever held a legal job | 50% | 93% |
| $n$ (earners 16+) | 124 | 116 |

SOURCE: Field notes recorded October 1993 through August 1994 in
Guadalupe and January through December 1995 in Chávez.

of Chávez residents with earnings had a job at some point during my
fieldwork. A slight majority of those jobs were legal (51 percent)—not
much different than in Guadalupe—but there was an enormous difference when it came to reports of lifetime experience in legal work. In
Chávez, among the residents I knew, nearly all (93 percent) who had
earnings said they had at some point worked in a legal job.

The experiences of José and Ted and the tabulations from field notes
suggest that neither Guadalupe nor Chávez was experiencing a devastating collapse of the job market. These figures do show, however, that residents in the two communities had different experiences in local labor
markets. Guadalupe residents were more often holding down jobs, even
if many residents were working in the informal economy. Chávez residents often had experience working, but many remained out of the labor
force.

What these case studies and aggregated field notes cannot tell us, however, is how these different relationships to the job market work themselves out in everyday life. What local differences within the barrios led
to higher rates of employment in Guadalupe than in Chávez? How are
differences in job holding in the barrios related to different orientations
toward work in the barrios? Where do these different work orientations
come from?

I address these questions in Chapters 3 through 5, where I analyze the
ethnographic data more closely. Detailed field notes show that some of
the difference in job holding in Guadalupe and Chávez reflected differences in the economic climates of San Jose and Los Angeles (the appendix also addresses this issue). Jobs seemed harder to come by in LA,
more LA residents unsuccessfully sought work, and San Jose residents
seemed to have an easier time locating and securing jobs. The field notes
also show the limitations of these between-city explanations of differ-

ence, however. Everyday life in Guadalupe and Chávez was distinguished not only by structural differences in opportunity but also by differences within the two barrios. Residents of Guadalupe and Chávez had different understandings of the meaning of the jobs they did find. Guadalupe's immigrants commonly devoted themselves to low-wage jobs in a manner that the natives of Chávez explicitly ridiculed and rejected. I show in Chapter 5 how this difference in the meaning of work affected attachment to the labor market. I also show how these differences in meaning arose from the different informal social networks that dominated everyday life among Guadalupe's immigrants and Chávez's natives. These social networks—elements of social structure that also shape local cultures—are a social institution that mediates labor market attachment in low-income areas.

## Crime

To document patterns of employment in Guadalupe and Chávez, I focused on residents who worked for wages, whether or not those wages came from legal jobs. Now I focus on activities of residents—of those I knew, more than half in Guadalupe and over one-third in Chávez—who earned income through some kind of illegal activity. I define *illegal* strictly. Illegal income-generating activities include income gained through illicit activities such as drug selling, car theft, and other economic crime. Illegal income-generating activities also include wage labor in the informal economy in which illegality is confined to violations of employment laws concerning tax payment, workplace safety, minimum-wage provisions, or immigrant documentation. The distinction between illicit and informal is subtle but important. *Illicit* activities are devoted to the production and distribution of goods and services which are themselves illegal; *informal* activities produce and distribute legal goods and services, but the means of production and distribution violate the law.

Both José Mendoza and Ted Galindo participated or tried to participate in illegal activities. José had little choice in the matter. Because he had come to the United States without work documents, José broke the law simply by holding a job, and his work thus fell into the informal economy, activities that produce legal goods and services while violating laws governing *how* those goods and services are produced. José also considered participation in the drug economy that attracted Ted. The drug economy is part of the illicit economy, which produces and distributes illegal goods and services. The experiences of José and Ted show that different kinds of illegal activities played different roles in the barrio economy.

Illegal activities were common in both Guadalupe and Chávez, but residents of the two barrios participated in different kinds of illegal activities. To document patterns of illegal activities I present further analysis of the field note sample of 124 Guadalupe residents and 116 Chávez residents aged sixteen and older who had earnings during the period of fieldwork. The analysis is summarized in Figure 3, which shows the proportion of residents with different kinds of illegal earnings.

More than half of the residents I knew in Guadalupe barrio had income from illegal activities, as Figure 1 showed. Figure 3 shows that in Guadalupe barrio, illegal work among these residents was confined to the informal realm. Three of five residents had illegal income because, like José Mendoza, they worked in the informal economy. The other 40 percent of Guadalupe residents with illegal earnings also participated in the informal economy, but they combined informal earnings with income from legal earnings, public aid, or both.

The pattern of illegal activities among residents I spent time with in Chávez provides a sharp contrast in two respects. First, in addition to illegal earnings from informal activities, in Chávez the illicit economy was important. Altogether, 58 percent of Chávez residents with illegal earnings participated in the illicit economy—nearly the exact same proportion (59 percent) who had illegal earnings from informal activities. Second, only a small proportion of residents with illegal earnings relied entirely on either the informal (4 percent) or the illicit (6 percent) sector. As Figure 3 clearly shows, nearly all of the Chávez residents I knew participated in illegal activities by combining income from informal or illicit sources with income from legal work and from public assistance. Contrary to popular images of easy money in the drug economy, residents in Chávez did not support themselves, to say nothing of getting rich, by devoting themselves to illicit activities. The aggregate data show that while illegal income earning was widespread in both communities, residents of Guadalupe and Chávez participated in different illegal activities, and they participated in different *ways*. Most residents in Guadalupe, like José Mendoza, participated in informal work as a substitute for legal jobs. The residents of Chávez used illegal activities to supplement and complement earnings from other sources, as Ted Galindo sought to do.

In Chapters 6 and 7, I document how these different patterns of involvement with the illegal economy worked themselves out in everyday life. Detailed field notes show how illegal workers in the two barrios

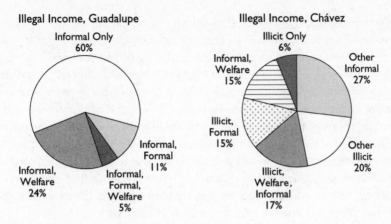

Figure 3. Illegal Income: Guadalupe and Chávez

relied on different kinds of illegal organizations in managing their day-to-day affairs. In Guadalupe, informal workers and employers met at local day labor markets and hiring halls. These organizations provided an institutional framework for informal activities to operate "below the radar" of local law enforcement and allowed Guadalupe residents to substitute informal for legal work. In Chávez, the gang and the hot spot facilitated illicit work. In contrast to the informal organizations of Guadalupe, however, the gang and other illicit institutions in Chávez attracted suppression efforts by local law enforcement. Illicit work could not substitute for a legal job, but illicit organizations were prevalent enough in Chávez that residents came to accept the risks and rewards they offered as one way among several to earn income. The difference in illegality in Guadalupe and Chávez was not, therefore, only a technical difference in whether legal goods or services were produced but also a practical difference in how communities organized illegal activities among their residents.

## Welfare

While work and crime were the two most important sources of income in Guadalupe and Chávez, a substantial number of barrio residents supplemented these earnings with income from public aid. The experiences of José Mendoza and Ted Galindo reveal several qualities of aid receipt in the barrios. First, as José's experiences show, barrio residents often found themselves turning to aid following an interruption in earnings from other sources. Ted's experiences reveal two other truisms of welfare in the barrios: that it was difficult to survive on welfare alone and that barrio residents often felt free to criticize aid recipients, as Ted felt free to criticize his sister and mother. The experiences of José and Ted also suggest subtle differences in public aid in Guadalupe and Chávez. For example, José and his family turned to local charities for assistance when work at the food plant slowed down, while Ted and his family relied on public aid from the state, in the form of Aid to Families with Dependent Children (AFDC) and public housing, to make ends meet. Figure 1 showed that, in my fieldwork experiences, fewer residents participated in aid in Guadalupe (24 percent) than in Chávez (36 percent), but the experiences of José and Ted suggest that the differences in the experience of aid in the two barrios may go beyond these basic figures.

Public assistance in the United States is not a monolithic entity but rather an uncoordinated network of programs that provide cash and in-kind support according to means-tested and other criteria under the auspices of a wide variety of governmental agencies.[4] In the barrios, public aid revolved around five such programs: AFDC, unemployment insurance, General Assistance (GA), food stamps, and Supplemental Security Income (SSI). Residents of the barrios, as the experiences of José Mendoza show, also took advantage of private charity, which was provided by local churches or other nonprofits.

Figure 4 shows what kind of aid was received by residents I knew who participated in public aid programs in Guadalupe and Chávez. In Guadalupe, nearly half of residents who received public aid received unemployment insurance. A third received food stamps, and a nearly a sixth had AFDC. Very few residents had income from SSI, and no one received GA. The situation in Chávez was quite different. In Chávez, AFDC and food stamps each accounted for nearly a third of public aid receipt in the barrio, with GA accounting for nearly another fifth and SSI 7 percent. Unemployment insurance, which was received by nearly half of the public aid recipients in Guadalupe, accounted for aid among only one of seven recipients in Chávez. In Guadalupe and Chávez, public aid played an important role in everyday economic life, but the residents I met during fieldwork tended to participate in different kinds of aid programs, with unemployment dominating in Guadalupe but not in Chávez.

I examine how barrio residents used aid as well as the consequences of aid use for everyday community life in Chapters 8 and 9. There, I use detailed field notes to show that residents of both barrios tended to turn to aid when income from other sources ran short rather than as a preferred alternative to working. The differences between aid use in Guada-

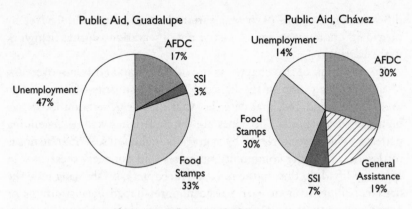

Figure 4. Public Assistance: Guadalupe and Chávez

lupe and Chávez arose because the financial misfortunes that necessitated aid use were more common in the latter barrio than in the former. Detailed field notes also show that public assistance played an important cultural role in everyday barrio life. The meaning of public aid and the stigma associated with its receipt differed slightly in the two barrios. Residents who used aid in Guadalupe, including José Mendoza, were harshly criticized no matter what particular circumstances surrounded their aid use. In Chávez, the reaction to aid recipients varied according to type of program and relationship to recipient. Criticism often expressed revulsion not only toward public assistance in general but also toward the behavior of certain recipients in particular. Thus, Ted Galindo's comments expressed not only—or perhaps not mostly—his objections to the AFDC program in principle but also his specific belief that his family's participation in AFDC had resulted in hardships for him personally. More aid did not mean that Chávez residents were less willing to work or more willing to accept the dole than Guadalupe residents. But more aid did matter for the culture of everyday life.

The rhythms of daily economic life in Guadalupe and Chávez were quite similar. As in the lives of José Mendoza, Ted Galindo, and their families, daily routines revolved around generating income. For the most part, income generation in the barrios took place on the job. But in both barrios, crime and public assistance also played an important role. I have sought to provide a feel for everyday economic life in the barrios by describing the experiences of José and Ted, as I knew them, in the mid-1990s. I have also sought to provide an overview of the similarities and differences in patterns of income earning in Guadalupe and Chávez by providing quantitative summaries of my observations during fieldwork in the barrios.

We can think of this chapter as providing a skin-and-bones overview of income generation in the barrios. The skin consists of stories, like those of José and Ted, that describe what income generation looks like on a day-to-day basis. The bones are the underlying income-generating patterns, which are conveyed by aggregated field notes. What remains is to describe how the community animates and connects these two in everyday life. I do this, in the next seven chapters, by showing how the daily economic lives of barrio residents are shaped by institutions of poverty and how these institutions create the distinct patterns of income generation of Guadalupe and Chávez.

# PART II

# Work

AMERICANS SEE JOBS AS THE best path for economic advancement and the most constructive foundation for social life. We associate joblessness with personal destitution, intergenerational poverty, and community problems such as crime and violence. Our awareness of the hardships of joblessness need not, however, blind us to the difficulties of working. Among the people whom I knew and spent time with in Guadalupe and Chávez, jobs were the most important source of income and the most important element of everyday economic life. Residents of these barrios, like most Americans, wanted to work. Most believed that, ideally, working would provide the economic foundation for personal advancement and community stability. But at the same time most barrio residents knew that available jobs usually fell short of this ideal. The low-wage jobs most residents found paid too poorly to support personal advancement and provided work too unpredictably to provide much community stability. In Guadalupe and Chávez, jobs were an important source of income and stability, and they were also a source of great challenges and frustration.

I stated in Chapter 1 that income generation in the barrios centered on the problem of surviving and advancing in an unpromising and uncompromising economic environment. The chapters of this section describe and analyze wage labor, the most important element of that economic environment. I describe daily routines among barrio residents who held jobs, how residents made sense of the opportunities they encountered on the labor market, and how they managed the frustrations they inevitably encountered. I also analyze how and why wage labor differed in Guadalupe and Chávez barrios. As I described in Chapter 2, there were substantial differences in the way that residents of the two communities engaged in wage labor; working was a bigger part of everyday life in Guadalupe than in Chávez. In this section, I explain these differences in working by focusing on the role of informal social networks in the two communities. I argue that these social networks are an important social institution in the barrios. Researchers have long argued that social networks help residents of low-income communities find jobs and keep working. I point out that in Guadalupe and Chávez, these same informal social networks also shaped subjective orientations toward the jobs that

were available in local labor markets. In particular, residents' embeddedness in transnational social networks, which existed in Guadalupe but
not in Chávez, shaped the meaning of low-wage jobs. As a social institution, informal networks supported differences in wage laboring in the
two barrios.

The chapters of this section develop this explanation in three steps.
Chapter 3 focuses on the experience of unemployment and shows how
residents of the barrios found low-wage jobs. In Chapter 4, I discuss the
work ethic and describe the social, cultural, and emotional experience of
staying in low-wage jobs. Together, Chapters 3 and 4 document similarities in the structural circumstances and the values and norms surrounding work in Guadalupe and Chávez. In Chapter 5, I show how different
institutional contexts caused these similar structural and cultural factors
to work themselves out in different ways. As mentioned above, transnational social networks were crucial. In Guadalupe, embeddedness in
these networks led residents to embrace "overwork" in low-wage jobs; in
Chávez, purely local embeddedness led residents to "hustling"—income
generation that combined low-wage work with other kinds of income
generation.

CHAPTER 3

# The Job Market

Often, the jobs in Guadalupe and Chávez resembled the "prizes" awarded to "lucky" contest winners in the classic joke: first prize was one job; second prize was two jobs. In the barrios, working was better than idleness. Jobs *were* prized. But given the monetary rewards and conditions on the job, the prize was one that few residents embraced without ambivalence.

Nearly everyone I knew in Guadalupe and Chávez worked in jobs that paid low wages, provided unsteady working hours, and provided few possibilities for upward mobility. Even though these jobs fell within a small slice at the bottom of the labor market, they were the most important source of income for residents in both Guadalupe and Chávez barrios.[1] Guadalupe residents worked as janitors, home health care workers, gardeners, construction laborers, table bussers, dishwashers, store clerks, and fast-food cooks. Some Guadalupe residents worked in the light industry of the Silicon Valley, including assembly of computer chips, food packaging, and warehousing. In Chávez, residents worked in the same jobs as in Guadalupe: fast-food cook, janitor, construction laborer, table busser, dishwasher, and warehouse laborer. Workers in Chávez also found positions in small manufacturing shops working as chromers, sheet metal workers, or painters; a few worked in larger unionized establishments, but most did not. Some Chávez residents had jobs in government or human services, such as community outreach worker, youth counselor, secretary, or intake nurse. No matter what the specific title, tasks, or employer, for most residents I knew in the barrios, jobs had

37

unpleasant drawbacks: low wages, unreliable hours, negligible security, or some combination of all of these problems.

The job market thus represented a conundrum for residents in both barrios. Good jobs—jobs that might turn into a career and lift a family out of poverty—were hard to come by. The wages from more readily available work often failed to gain residents and their families much economic security. This chapter explores this conundrum through an analysis of residents' experiences and understandings of local work opportunities. I show how a variety of challenges made job markets in Guadalupe and Chávez more a source of ongoing difficulty than a source of manifest opportunity. These challenges included employers who appeared to have little interest or incentive to invest in their workforce or to provide a safe and pleasant work environment; residents' relatively low levels of human capital—English-language skills and educational attainment in particular—that closed off better-quality jobs; and the difficulty of addressing these problems through organized and individual appeals for change. The challenges of the job market provide the context for understanding the experience of unemployment, and I conclude this chapter by describing the experience of unemployment for several barrio residents.

WORKERS AND EMPLOYERS

Most residents I knew in Guadalupe and Chávez worked in jobs that paid poorly, provided part-time or irregular hours, and provided unsteady tenure over the long term. Many residents in the barrios saw these qualities of jobs as a reflection of employers' power and desires. In the view of residents, employers were solely interested in making money and cared little whether a job was competently completed, under what conditions, or with what implications for their employees' quality of life.

The on-the-job experiences of a group of men in Guadalupe exemplified these views. The men were all janitors in large office buildings in and around San Jose, and they regularly had lunch together at Rita's restaurant in the late afternoon before starting their swing shifts. I joined them occasionally and over the course of several months developed a sense of their frustration with their work.

During my first lunches with the group, I discovered that much of the men's frustration stemmed from their feeling that they were not able to do their work properly. The men all had a substantial knowledge about cleaning techniques. One afternoon before lunch, for example, I watched as Victor, who was running his own janitorial business at the time, instructed a young man about how to properly clean the linoleum floor in his office. He outlined the steps to be followed and explained why certain cleaners had to be used in a particular order. Victor warned the young man against taking shortcuts such as one-coat solutions that, he warned, clean the floor fine but over time corrode the linoleum. He pointed out bare spots on the floor that reflected this kind of shoddy technique.

At Rita's, many complaints concerned how employers did not let the men do their jobs properly. All of the men worked for *contratistas,* contractors who supplied the large firms of the Silicon Valley with an outsourced labor force. These firms had made it possible to replace the higher-paid in-house janitors that the firms used to hire directly. As the *contratista* system became established in the South Bay, the various contractors bid against each other for cleaning jobs. Wages declined and workload increased as the costs of the competition were passed on to the workers. Scholars have documented these changes in the Silicon Valley and in other cities in California.[2] The janitors knew about it from personal experience. At Rita's the men talked about how the *contratistas* were paying less or hiring poorly trained workers. Frequently, according to the men, the *contratistas* hired the most recently arrived immigrants who were least able to defend themselves. One day Luis complained about how his boss had suddenly expanded the number of offices in his assignment; now there were only four workers per floor in his bank building downtown.

In the midst of these changes in contracting, Victor started his own cleaning service with a few contracts at local churches. His business was meant as an alternative to the *contratistas,* he told me. He emphasized that his workers were properly trained, even if he himself had to retrain them in unlearning improper techniques they had picked up in other jobs. His service cost a bit more than others, he knew, but he also believed that by properly cleaning his workers saved money on wear and tear. In addition, Victor's service offered social benefits. It was a Catholic business that sought to promote social justice. He paid his workers a living wage, and he hoped to eventually turn the business over to his workers and move on to new entrepreneurial pursuits himself. But the business ran out of steam after only a few months and long before Victor had achieved his social justice goals. Like the other businesses in San Jose, Victor concluded, the churches ultimately just wanted the lower price. He had to let his workers go, and like them he returned to the employ of *contratistas.*

The treatment that workers received at the hands of the janitorial *contratistas* exemplified more general patterns. The employers of Guadalupe and Chávez residents did not invest in their employees. Intense competition among employers and the availability of workers led to the degradation of conditions at work, the deterioration of hourly wages, and an increase in work duties. Rather than moving up into positions of greater pay, autonomy, or power over time, workers in Guadalupe and Chávez often found that low-wage jobs in San Jose and Los Angeles seemed to become progressively less rewarding.

A small number of residents in each barrio proved the exception to this rule, however. They worked in positions where tenure was rewarded. Oscar, a Guadalupe resident, ran the presses at a local printing company, and after several years he was promoted to the job of plant supervisor. His on-the-job familiarity with the machinery was the key element that gained him a promotion. In his new job, he earned overtime pay, supervised the younger press operators, and had substantial autonomy given that his boss, the plant manager, relied on him to communicate with the Spanish-speaking workforce. In Chávez, Cynthia recalled how her mechanic's skills had allowed her to rise to a position of autonomy and responsibility in a small transportation company. She had been hired as a van driver, but her supervisor noticed that she was able to repair her own van whenever it broke down. This led to a promotion where she operated almost as a freelance driver/mechanic within the company. She managed her own schedule, repaired her van and those of other drivers as needed, and recalled it as the best job she had ever held.

Occasionally, as Oscar and Cynthia could attest, barrio residents worked in jobs that provided positive experiences of engagement, autonomy, and advancement, but experiences such as those of Luis, Victor, and the other janitors in Guadalupe were more often the rule. Residents' experiences told them that most barrio employers preferred paying a low wage to supporting conscientious workers.

## THE ROLE OF HUMAN CAPITAL

Residents in Guadalupe and Chávez found working in low-wage jobs unrewarding in many ways, so it was not surprising that many sought to move into better positions. Moving out of low-wage jobs could be difficult, however, because the residents I knew often found that the better jobs toward which they aspired appeared to require credentials, skills, or experience—in short, human capital—that they did not possess. In Guadalupe, residents frequently felt they did not speak English well enough to get better jobs, and residents in both barrios often felt that better jobs demanded better credentials and substantive skills than they had been able to acquire in local schools.

In Guadalupe generally, residents took it as an article of faith that speaking English was necessary to get a better job. This faith was born of repeated experiences such as occurred one day in a local hiring hall where many Guadalupe residents sought work. Mary was a bilingual volunteer who worked in the center, screening incoming calls from potential employers and attempting to match job seekers to jobs. I saw the following events in July 1994:

> Mary has several jobs she is trying to fill and stands in front of the room of fifteen men and women who are seeking positions. Most of the jobs she has are for two- or three-day stints as gardeners or domestics, but one is for a full-time position behind the counter at a soon-to-open deli. Many are interested in the position, but Mary quickly eliminates them all from consideration. "You need to speak *English* to do this job," she tells the group. "I speak English," replies René, who has his hand up. Mary says to him, in a pretty good imitation of a fast-paced New Yorker, "I'll take a turkey on rye with pickle and mustard, hold the lettuce and mayo." And then slower and with more careful diction, "What did I ask for?" René confesses that he did not understand. "A-ha!" she exclaims, and she snaps her fingers a few times. "You need to be quick *quick* to do this job." René ends up settling for a short-term gardening job that does not require English. Over the next hour, several others who express keen interest in the deli job also fail the language test, and later Mary turns over the job to an Anglo-American woman.

The events at the hiring hall that summer afternoon provided an unusually stark illustration of how language barriers restricted residents' attempts to get better-paying and more stable jobs. In other cases, residents found that knowing English was not necessary to get a job but was crucial for mobility within the work site. The experiences of Oscar illustrated this dynamic. His English-language skill, rudimentary to be sure, coupled with his long tenure was enough to move him into a supervisor's position at the print shop. The many workers at the site who spoke no English whatsoever never got the chance to impress the owner with their own qualifications to move up in the organization.

In Chávez, where facility with English was rarely an obstacle, many residents found that their educational attainment and credentials frustrated their attempts to attain better-paying and more stable jobs. The experiences of Lisa, a twenty-four-year-old Chávez resident who was a clerk at a health care clinic, provide an example. A mother of two, Lisa had left high school when her first child was born and had not received her diploma. I recorded the following field note at work soon after Lisa and her friend and co-worker Rosa had been briefed about the future of the clinic by a senior administrator. The administrator headed the East Los Angeles health care consortium that operated the small Chávez clinic with funds from a special grant, and the grant had not been renewed. Rosa was directly employed by the consortium; the end of the special grant did not threaten her position. Lisa's salary came from the grant, however, so her position was vulnerable.

Lisa and Rosa begin to talk about going back to school. Lisa wants to return for her Graduate Equivalency Degree (GED), and Rosa says that the clinic would support her if she wanted to go back. Rosa says that she herself went back for her GED but it took her about five tries before she finally got it. She kept signing up and going and then quitting and then going back and so on. Lisa says that she went back to school, too, but after a while in the continuation school [where students work toward the GED] they switched her into a job-training program. That program was good because she learned all these skills and got the job at the clinic, but they said she would also finish her GED and she never did. She was going to one of the local high schools, but it got to be too much. She was going to work and then to school. She'd leave the house before her kids were up and get home after they'd go to bed so she would never see them. It was too hard never seeing her kids, she says, so she dropped out. Now she wants to return to the continuation school in order to get her high school diploma. The class meets nine to eleven in the morning and she thinks that maybe the clinic will let her get away from work for that time in order to attend. If she gets that diploma, she thinks she'll be able to keep her job with the clinic, because with the GED the clinic will be able to hire her to its full-time staff.

For several years, before returning to school and joining the clinic, Lisa had relied on public assistance. Her enrollment in the job-training program, where she learned medical-clerical skills, helped her overcome the barriers to employment that she had faced as a single mother without educational credentials or employment experience. My impression was that Lisa was a well-prepared and competent worker. Being from Chávez and bilingual allowed her to adeptly handle the clinic's patient population, all of whom were residents of Chávez and other nearby low-income neighborhoods. Staff and clients sang her praises. Nevertheless, with only a few months at her first full-time position, Lisa still felt tenuously attached to the job market. She believed that the lack of a GED made her more likely to be laid off than clerks who had the credential. It seemed that neither practical skills as a clerk nor practical knowledge as a long-time resident of the low-income barrios offered the same employment security as a GED.

As it turned out, when the special grant that paid Lisa expired, the clinic kept her on staff by moving her into a new position. The administrator spent a few hours training her to handle the financial screening and paperwork that would be crucial for the small clinic's continued existence. In her new position, Lisa's rapport with community members was particularly valuable. She knew whether incoming clients were Chávez residents or not, and in many cases she knew what kind of access they had to health insurance. Lisa used the threat of charging for services to turn away some clients from the clinic, and for some whom she believed really needed care she forged paperwork to get them through the initial screening process.[3]

The experiences of René and Lisa highlight how human capital shaped residents' experiences on the job market. On the one hand, lack of human capital—René's lack of English and Lisa's lack of credentials—could hamper workers. Once they were working, as the experiences of Oscar and Lisa illustrate, workers in both communities often turned out to be competent and valued workers. Even for the most competent workers, however, lack of credentials remained a source of insecurity and vulnerability.

## ADDRESSING LABOR MARKET PROBLEMS

Residents of Guadalupe and Chávez were aware of the problems posed by low-quality jobs and their own limited human capital, and they attempted to address them directly. Some workers tried to organize. In Guadalupe, attempts by resident and nonresident activists to organize janitors were hotly contested by employers, who assumed they would have more difficulty keeping wage rates low if workers of Guadalupe and other barrios were represented by a union. In a general sense, Guadalupe residents knew about and supported the union's efforts and goals, but when it came down to particulars many residents wanted concrete evidence that the fledgling union was turning money and support into better working conditions and higher wages for workers. The following field notes, which capture a conversation among three middle-aged Mexican immigrants, convey how union promises to improve wages and work conditions played out in Guadalupe.

Martín and Macario are discussing the corruption of unions when Héctor joins the conversation. Héctor was an official in one of the big unions in Mexico City before coming to San Jose, and he begins to defend the union. He says that it is the only way janitors will get ahead with the *contratistas*, if they all organize together and get better working conditions. But Martín is skeptical. "No, I'm not going to pay them [the unions] any more money," he says. "I already paid them so much money, but they don't do anything with it. They just take it. They opened the new union headquarters—that nice new building—but at the opening celebration, how many people there were workers in the union? Only ten people of that big crowd." Héctor pleads with Martín that the union needs to stay strong because contract negotiations are coming up soon, but Martín is not moved by this argument. They have just nearly doubled his workload at his job at one of the large Silicon Valley computer companies. "How am I going to do the job right now?" he asked. "Now I have 250 offices, five conference rooms, and five large bathrooms to clean between 6:00 p.m. and 2:00 a.m. The union just makes noise, but they should stop that [the increasing workload]. There's no way to clean that much in one shift. So now I'm going to have to rush through and not clean things right, and the job will not be done right."

Unions represented a compelling argument about how to address the problems of low wages and poor working conditions. By negotiating collectively with employers, unions could improve the conditions at work by pressuring employers into raising wages and establishing and enforcing work rules. Residents in Guadalupe supported these ideas, but their everyday experiences told them that support of these ideas did not quickly translate into practice. Most of the Guadalupe residents I knew did not attend organizing meetings, and union activists and community leaders—not rank-and-file workers—dominated the meetings I observed. The union's presence in the city and signs of its increasing power in local affairs, signs including the opening of the new union headquarters, failed to inspire much interest or commitment in Guadalupe residents.

Residents in the low-income barrios also addressed problems of low-wage labor markets through direct appeal to local help-providing organizations. Government and nonprofit agencies often provided assistance to residents of both barrios as a matter of course, but they rarely addressed employment problems directly. Nevertheless, residents believed that these agencies had tremendous resources at their disposal, and they appealed to them for help on the labor market, as Chávez residents Paul and Elena did in the spring of 1995. The two went to see a housing authority official to appeal the case of a tenant who faced a heavy fine and possible eviction for failing to pay rent. The tenant had fallen behind in her rent payments when her husband became unemployed following an accident on the job.

Paul and Elena went down to the central office for public housing for the city for a meeting with one of the midlevel managers there. This official was a Chicano who had grown up in one of the working-class suburbs of the San

Gabriel Valley, and on previous occasions Paul had had cordial and friendly relations with him. Elena said that today the official had been rigid and unhelpful when it came to dealing with the problem of the tenant, and Paul lost his temper. Paul blamed the problem on the housing authority official. "They forget where they came from," he said. "Just sit on their ass, pushing paper around and collecting thirty or forty thousand dollars a year. Their job is to help people out in the projects, but they don't care about them at all."

When it came to the daily problems that inevitably though unpredictably arose for residents dependent on low-wage labor markets, residents of both barrios regularly turned for assistance to public and nonprofit agencies—the housing authority, job-training centers, nonprofits dedicated to helping immigrants adjust their legal status. Like Paul and Elena, however, residents often came away from these experiences frustrated. Government and nonprofits addressed the difficulties of low-wage work through official programs: job training, summer employment, legal outreach, parenting classes, and the like. But agency staff often appeared unresponsive and occasionally appeared hostile to direct appeals by residents for concrete assistance or even simple understanding. Many residents saw this unresponsiveness as a function of staff persons' distance and insulation from residents' everyday concerns and dilemmas. Thus, Paul blamed the housing authority official's unresponsiveness on the fact that he held a secure, well-paid job. The distance between those who helped from those they helped made it difficult for residents to bring leverage to bear on staffers during times of need. In everyday life, though regularly appealed to, the helping agencies of local government and nonprofits failed to provide reliable and timely assistance for low-wage workers.

Residents of both barrios also made direct appeals to another powerful local influence, the employers themselves. In Chávez, many residents believed they had some leverage over local employers. In the past, direct pressure on local merchants had led to the hiring of public housing residents. When a shuttered store in Chávez prepared to reopen under a new owner, Ron, a former gang member and active member of the Chávez community, explained, "They're opening up that store again. . . . They closed it down last year, and then these Chinos [Asians] are opening it up again. But we have to make sure that they do something for the community. They would just hire their own people to work that store, but we're going to make sure they hire some homeboys. I already talked to people about it. If they don't hire homeboys to work there—and not just one but a bunch of guys—then we're going to boycott." The owners of the new store seemed likely to respond to pressure from the community because they needed to capture the business of Chávez residents if they were to succeed. In addition, Ron hinted that their property was at risk if they did not maintain good relations with the community. He was not surprised that the new owners made a point of hiring some Chávez residents when the store opened some weeks later.

Employers also occasionally responded to more personal appeals. When Guadalupe resident Oscar and his wife Natalia had their first child in San Jose, they were shocked by the expense. But Oscar had already established a good working relationship with the head of the printing company, and he was able to secure a loan to cover the hospital bills. Paying the loan back through paycheck deductions pushed Oscar, Natalia, and their children into reliance on public assistance for a period of time, but without the cash from Oscar's boss, the family had no idea how they were going to pay the thousands of dollars of medical expenses incurred during the routine delivery.

## UNEMPLOYMENT

Guadalupe and Chávez residents saw the job market as a place of opportunity for highly skilled and credentialed workers or for workers with union protection, government employment, or a decent boss. But most of the people I knew in the barrios did not work in this job market. They lacked skills or credentials required for more desirable positions, their employers seemed interested only in maximizing profits, and they worked without union or government protections. These qualities of local job markets provide the context for understanding unemployment among barrio residents.

Unemployment has distressing or even devastating consequences for low-income workers and their communities, and the unemployment rate is an widely understood and easily grasped indicator of the quality of life in a low-income community. Scholars and policy makers measure unemployment by using a survey to determine how many workers in a community or the nation are actively looking for work. A 5 percent unemployment rate, for example, indicates that for every hundred workers interviewed, five said that they were out of a job and looking for work. The 5 percent figure counts only "workers," so it specifically excludes children (people younger than eighteen), retired people (those older than sixty-four), and anyone of "working age" (eighteen to sixty-four) who is not actively looking for work, such as homemakers. The picture of unemployment conveyed by this survey measure is that unemployed people are a group of people who spend their days searching in vain for an employer willing to take them on.

I did not use a survey to measure unemployment in Guadalupe and Chávez, but I tried to directly assess which workers in these communities were actively looking for work. This turned out to be a difficult task. For every resident who was clearly spending his or her days in a frustrated search for employment, there were many more who were having trouble finding a job they wanted to take. I met men and women struggling with unemployment in both barrios, but, for reasons I discuss in detail in Chapter 5, these problems were especially pressing for young men in Chávez barrio.[4] The experiences of Benji, a Chávez resident in his early twenties, were fairly typical of residents who spent considerable time in a frustrated search for work, while for Christian, another Chávez resident, unemployment played a complex role in a complex work history.

After Benji had graduated from high school in the early 1990s, he had looked for work near Chávez but had been unable to find anything satisfying. Believing that some more years of education and some concrete job skills would ease his way into steady work, Benji enrolled in a course to learn cable television maintenance and repair. He held some temporary positions while training, and the school had implied that they would find him a job once he graduated. As graduation neared in the early summer of 1995, he optimistically predicted he would find a job, earn more money, and establish an independent household. However, several months after the completion of the training course, Benji had still not found secure employment, and he continued to live in his mother's apartment in the projects. Still, he remained optimistic. He took it as a positive sign that he had found temporary jobs. Given the popularity of cable television, Benji was sure it was just a matter of time until he found a steady job that would allow him to get together the money for the security deposit on his own apartment.

Unemployment seemed to sneak up on Christian. He was a twenty-four-year-old lifetime resident of Chávez, and he had not graduated from high school. He began grappling with unemployment after completing jail time for his role in an attempted armed robbery of a local *tienda*. For four months after getting out of jail and re-entering his mother's home in Chávez, Christian stayed away from criminal enterprises, dividing his time between caring for his baby daughter, working occasionally at construction or car repair, and performing as part of a local rap group. He was essentially idle during these months. Initially, Christian believed that the period of idleness was a time during which he and the band members were working on new material and preparing to go into the studio to record their first full-length CD. If he had been responding to a survey, I am not sure whether he would have said he was idle and looking for work during these months. But after performing at several events, the lead singer of the band split off from the group to pursue a solo career. "When we did that gig over in Las Vegas, this agent saw Pedro and really liked him. But this guy said that he wanted Pedro but not the rest of the band, and Pedro left us. That was fucked up," explained Christian.

Christian had not seemed troubled that he was unemployed while the band was working gigs and preparing for studio sessions. Now, with the band ruined by the leader's defection, Christian became more discouraged about the long period of time he had gone without a regular job. He began to spend more time hanging out on the streets, and he complained that he was depressed and bored. He knew that his background made him an unattractive prospect for most employers, and he figured his best chance of finding employment was in construction, where he had some experience and contacts and where he could take advantage of special programs to employ public housing residents, high school dropouts, and ex-felons. A steady construction job did not come quickly or easily, but after an additional two months Christian found a position at a nearby site and entered a one-month period of reduced hours and wages while he underwent training. Finally, after seven months of more or less complete idleness—some partially self-imposed and some at the mercy of the labor market—Christian began working full time. He was guaranteed only a few months of work. When the specific project he was working on ended, the firm probably would let him go and he would again be on the job market.

Christian believed that lacking a high school diploma and carrying a criminal record extended his period of unemployment. At the same time, much of his unemployment reflected his own hopes for success with the band. For Christian, the meaning and role of unemployment changed over time, with a period of voluntary loose connection with the labor market gradually becoming a time of frustrated exclusion from work. Significantly, Christian's experience on the job market was similar to that of Chávez residents who, on the face of it, seemed more employable and more focused on finding regular employment.

The experiences of Benji and Christian illustrate the role of unemployment in the lives of many barrio residents. Most people could find some kind of work, as Benji did after graduating from high school, but often these easily found jobs offered few financial rewards or career possibilities. Searching for a better position could consume many months, and, as Christian found, the reward at the end of this long search often would be a position that promised only a few months of pay before the job search would have to be resumed. Better qualifications, such as Benji's technical training, might increase the wages earned in a particular job, but this training by no means guaranteed residents an easier job search or shorter periods of unemployment while job searching.

When we measure the unemployment rate with a survey, we attach a clear meaning to the notion of "high unemployment"—frustrated workers, economic struggle, and negative consequences for the community. Sometimes barrio unemployment carried these connotations. But unemployment had a variety of other meanings as well. Benji's original experience with unemployment came when he left the labor market to go to cable school, while Christian stayed off the job market to pursue band life and take care of his daughter. Technically, while Benji was in school or Christian was in the band, neither was unemployed. In the barrios, choices such as these were often understood as choices or opportunities. At the same time, one wonders: If Benji had landed a good job straight out of high school, would he have gone to cable school? And would Christian have stayed in the band so long or been as willing to be a fulltime parent if he had been able to find a job coming out of jail?

The unemployment rate is a measure of frustration—of the number of people who want to work but cannot find a job—that is easily and reliably measured with just a few survey questions. In everyday barrio life, however, unemployment includes a variety of complex relationships between residents and jobs. What kinds of jobs do residents believe are available to them? What constitutes the volition to work? Would a resident take any job? Or did it make more sense to be picky and search for an attractive opportunity? Residents frequently transitioned into and out of jobs. Understanding these dynamics requires an appreciation for what residents expected to gain from working, what workers had to offer employers, and how workers sought to improve their collective position on the labor market.

Contrary to my expectations, during fieldwork I saw residents in both Guadalupe and Chávez confronting a similar catalog of job market difficulties: employer exploitation, difficulty competing for better-quality jobs, limited power to effect positive change, and regular unemployment. I was not surprised that barrio residents found the labor market frustrating, but I did not expect to find residents in *both* barrios frustrated by the same sorts of problems. I had expected residents in Chávez, with its higher unemployment rate, to be manifestly less connected to local jobs than the people I knew in Guadalupe. I had expected that the residents of persistently poor Chávez would have much more difficulty finding *any* sort of job than the people I knew in Guadalupe. To be sure, unemployment was more frequently a problem for people I knew in Chávez than it was in Guadalupe, but both communities had strong connections to the labor market. Neither barrio appeared to be experiencing a job market collapse.

This is good news for the barrios, but it is also puzzling news for researchers. Often researchers interpret high unemployment rates as a reflection of job market collapse. With a poverty rate above 50 percent and unemployment at 20 percent, the statistics paint Chávez as a community where work has disappeared. The theme of this chapter, however, is that residents in both Chávez and Guadalupe found opportunities for income earning on the job market even though pursuing these opportunities meant confronting substantial challenges and frustrations. Thus, I see the job market in the barrios as a source of prickly prizes that residents pursued despite practical challenges and personal ambivalence. In the next chapter, I delve further into the nature of barrio jobs by examining how residents held on to the prizes they garnered in local job markets.

# CHAPTER 4

# The Experience
# of Low-Wage Work

Barrio residents often found that low-wage jobs made greater demands on them off the job than at the work site. Many residents I knew in Guadalupe and Chávez held jobs that appeared to require few job skills other than on-time arrival. But finding a job, getting to work on time, and mustering the emotional fortitude to manage the challenges of an unforgiving work environment all made substantial demands on residents' lives outside the workplace.

This pattern of barrio work reflects the fact that low-wage jobs generally require little formal education and few hard-to-obtain job skills and that most low-wage workers bring limited credentials and few valued skills to them.[1] Because jobs require few work-specific skills, workers have a hard time differentiating one job from another. Because workers have relatively few job-specific skills, employers often look for workers of a particular temperament rather than a specific set of skill characteristics.[2] Workers who hope to hold on to a low-wage job for long must supplement their meager wages with resources culled from family and community to make ends meet.[3] Work routines in low-wage jobs thus reflect qualities of everyday life far from the work site. Even low-wage jobs that demand relatively little from workers while they are at the job site can make heavy demands on workers' everyday lives at home.

With few work-specific qualities leading specific residents to specific jobs, more personal characteristics of workers shaped the experience of low-wage work among residents I knew in Guadalupe and Chávez. One important personal quality was knowing how to find a job. In the barrio labor market, where it seemed many residents could do most jobs, finding a job depended as much on knowing which jobs were open and how to apply as on finding a match for one's particular skills or experiences. For residents who held low-wage jobs, the experience of work unfolded in the context of friends and family who helped pay the rent, helped take care of children, and provided transportation to and from the job site. Employers demanded few skills, but they did not tolerate worker absence; barrio residents' employment depended on their personal support system. The first sections of this chapter analyze how the Guadalupe and Chávez residents I knew found jobs and kept jobs. Knowing how to find a job and keep a job shaped residents' feelings and attitudes toward work. I turn in the final section of this chapter to an analysis of the work ethic in the barrios and a discussion of the complex relationship between everyday labor market experiences and residents' orientations toward work in general and toward low-wage jobs in particular.

## FINDING A JOB

In both Guadalupe and Chávez, residents seeking jobs turned to their personal networks of family, friends, and neighbors as well as to local organizations that specialized in job placement.[4] Seekers often started with information from family, friends, and neighbors. In many of the barrio households I knew, members worked in the same work site, in the same kind of job, or in the same kind of business. But residents did not circulate all job-related information through their personal networks in the same way. Information about low-quality jobs circulated widely in both barrios, but residents often shared information about harder-to-find and better-quality positions sparingly and strategically.

In both Guadalupe and Chávez, some information about job openings circulated widely. Generally, however, I noticed an inverse relationship between how quickly information about a job opening spread and the quality of the job; news about low-quality jobs spread quickly, while information about good jobs circulated less widely. For example, local fast-food establishments near both barrios frequently sought workers, but these jobs seemed unattractive to many residents. They paid poorly and, more significantly, could promise only few and unsteady work hours. In Chávez, a local McDonald's restaurant posted a "Help Wanted" sign in late spring, 1995. Ben was a recent high school graduate who lived with his mother and sisters in public housing near Chávez and frequently came to visit his aunt and friends who lived in the Chávez projects. His girlfriend was six months pregnant, and they planned to marry in a few weeks' time. Ben was unemployed when he heard through a friend of the sign at the McDonald's. During a trip through the McDonald's drive-through lane a few weeks earlier, Ben had made small talk with the young woman working at the window. Hoping to get some free food, he complimented her hair and smile, asked where she attended high school, and asked whether she liked working at the restaurant. None of the sweet talk worked, and we paid in full for our meals. Ben said at that time that if he had to work in McDonald's he would at least find a way to get his friends some free food. When he heard that the McDonald's was now looking for workers, he repeated the sentiments he had expressed that day. "I would never work in a place like that," he said. He pointed out that they paid minimum wage or maybe $4.50 an hour and that they gave only a couple hours of work a week. Maybe for someone in school who just needed a little extra money that job would be okay, he thought, but Ben needed to support his wife, and soon he would also have a child to raise. He didn't see how a job at McDonald's would help. The job referral was, in Ben's opinion, completely worthless.

In contrast to the ready circulation of information about lousy jobs, residents who knew about attractive opportunities often used the information strategically. They told family members or other significant individuals in their life about the job but did not share the information with casual friends or acquaintances. Manuel was the eldest brother in a family of twelve children in Chávez barrio. He had risen to the position of foreman in a local manufacturing plant, and as such he had inside information about the availability of stable jobs. (Manuel no longer lived in Chávez but in a small house nearby.) Manuel had used his influence at the plant to get two of his brothers, Smiley and Juan, jobs there. Both hirings were significant. Manuel helped secure Smiley's release from prison by providing him with a steady job upon re-entering the community. Juan, the second oldest son in the family, had long struggled with alcohol problems, so getting him a position at the plant despite the heavy drinking constituted a real coup. Juan's job was in a relatively undemanding part of the plant. As Smiley related it, Manuel got him a job that Juan could do completely drunk. One evening over a poker game in his sister's apartment in Chávez, Smiley and Manuel regaled the players with stories of Juan's antics on the job, which included passing out in the back of the company's warehouse after consuming a bottle of wine.

Whatever its effects on the productivity of the plant where he worked,

Manuel's generosity toward his brothers put him in good stead with the family. I was first introduced to Manuel at a large family gathering. One of Manuel's younger brothers was pointing out his brothers and sisters one by one and providing a capsule summary of their place in the family and his opinion of their place in the world. Of Manuel he said, "That's Manuel over there with the mustache and the Dodger's cap. He's my oldest brother. He's a foreman over at a factory where they make plastic containers and stuff like that. He's basically the only one in my family who's not a fuck-up." Manuel's strategic use of information about job openings at the plant where he worked raised his standing in the eyes of other family members. His brothers and their families were grateful to have steady jobs. Manuel's parents and other family members were glad that Manuel was able to facilitate Smiley's release from prison.[5]

The efforts of family members to aid one another were limited by the nature of most individuals' attachment to the labor market. The way in which Manuel aided his family members and enjoyed the reciprocity due him was typical of helping behavior in both Chávez and Guadalupe barrios. However, barrio residents only rarely had the opportunity to support each other in this way. Residents looking for steady work in good jobs were more often disappointed with the assistance of family and friends. Most residents had difficulty helping family members and friends find good jobs because they were not employed in good jobs themselves. Those working for better employers often had little power to influence the hiring process. At times, residents' position in better-quality workplaces placed them among the last to know that their organization was looking for more workers. For example, Tina, a resident of Chávez who worked part time as the receptionist at the local office of the housing agency, found herself on several occasions in the unenviable position of parrying accusations by friends and family that she had withheld information about desirable government job openings. The housing agency hired gardeners and construction workers to work on projects in the neighborhood, and residents coveted these jobs. But these hiring decisions took place at the housing authority's central office, not in the local branch that serviced Chávez. Nevertheless, residents reproached Tina— both in person and behind her back—for not sharing information about hiring opportunities and decisions, even though, in fact, Tina had no way of obtaining this information. Barrio residents often found jobs with the assistance of family and friends, but social networks rarely steered residents into good jobs.

For good jobs, residents often had better luck through formal job-getting organizations than through social networks of friends and family. The quality and effectiveness of these formal job-getting organizations depended primarily on the stability of the resources they were able to draw on. Smaller institutions depended for their funding on charitable contributions from private groups (often religious) and on small grants from local government. They took advantage of volunteer contributions of time and effort (again, churches of various denominations played a significant role here), and they depended on neighborhood employers' sense of enlightened self-interest to find job openings for their clientele. Larger institutions depended on funding from federal, state, and local government. They hired professionals who consulted and advised clients on how to obtain jobs, and they hired other professionals who actively pursued and developed job prospects in businesses throughout the metropolis. Residents in both barrios took advantage of both types of job-placing organizations, although in general these services helped more people I knew in Guadalupe than in Chávez. The smaller job placement services in both barrios opened their doors to all comers, while the larger operations usually required an application. For those who were accepted into their programs, larger job-placing organizations provided intensive classroom preparation, substantial assistance on the job market, an attendance stipend for most residents, and a reputation for successful placement. Most of the residents I knew at the larger job-training institutions participated through unemployment or public assistance programs sponsored by federal and state governments. Thus, one of the ironies of the job-finding process in the barrios was that the misfortune of unemployment was one of the most common routes into better-quality jobs for barrio residents.

The experiences of Nora, a forty-two-year-old single mother from Guadalupe, and her twenty-one-year-old son Robert illustrated how unemployment could provide a path toward future employment. While Nora participated in a training program at a large job placement service in Guadalupe, Robert enrolled in a smaller jobs program elsewhere in the barrio. Their experiences highlight interesting differences in the formal organizations that helped barrio residents find jobs. Nora and Robert's experiences are also interesting because they were third- and fourth-generation Mexican Americans living in Guadalupe barrio. As it turned out, Nora's job-training experience paralleled that of many of the first-generation immigrants I knew in Guadalupe, while Robert's experience was more commonly echoed among the residents I knew in Chávez.

In the fall of 1993 and winter of 1994, Nora attended the Jobs for

People in the Community (JPC) program in Guadalupe. This was her second time at JPC; her first enrollment came soon after Robert was born,
when she had been laid off from a cannery that relocated outside the
Silicon Valley. In the early 1990s, Nora credited her enrollment to a provision of the Immigration Reform and Control Act (IRCA) of 1986
known to barrio residents as "Farmworkers." The joint federal and state
program provided assistance to low-income people who themselves had
been farmworkers or who had grown up in a household headed by a
farmworker. A cherished provision of Farmworkers provided funds to
enroll in JPC following a job loss as well as a stipend during the course of
the training program. Nora's mother had worked in the fields, so Nora
enrolled in JPC under the benefit.

I haven't seen Nora inside JPC for a couple of weeks, since she finished
her course work, but she returns today to print out her resume. As she tries
to coax the old printer in the back of the classroom to life, she tells me about
her work history. After her first time at JPC, she had gotten a job as a janitor,
but then she moved into a different job in the same company—assembling
computers. But the company was bought out in 1985, and they laid off nearly
the whole workforce and moved the plant out of state. So Nora worked in a
cannery for two seasons and then at a meatpacking plant. But the meat plant
lost a lot of orders and put her on a shortened workweek, and she couldn't
make enough to get by. Then she found out about Farmworkers and was able
to enroll in job training again. She almost didn't get the Farmworkers because
her mom had worked in the fields so long ago. I recall when Nora received the
lump sum payment that marked successful completion of her course work, a
reward all Farmworker enrollees could receive. She kissed the check and called
out, "Thank you, mom, for working in the field and in the cannery."

About three months after finishing the course work for her second
stint at JPC, Nora found a position in a high-tech firm in Silicon Valley.
Before she found that job, however, her son Robert was released from
jail. A month before Nora would move into her new high-tech job, I
bumped into her on the streets of Guadalupe and she lamented that
Robert was not eligible for the Farmworker's benefit.

Nora said her son was out of jail now. He'd been in the Central Valley and
they'd let him out and he'd come back to San Jose. Now he was staying with
Nora; he was just getting out of bed at 10:00 a.m. when Nora had left the
house this morning. Robert was twenty-one, and he was at continuation school
and ended up dropping out when he got arrested and put away. He was at
about a tenth-grade level, and now he wanted to continue with his education
and get his GED. Nora said that Robert couldn't get training at JPC because the
program didn't apply to him; it was only for the children of farmworkers. So he
had enrolled at an employment program at the community center over near the

park. This was a small program run by Luis, a park employee who volunteered on the job-training program.

Robert's experience in the small job-training program run out of community center near the park could not have been more different than Nora's experience in JPC just a few blocks away. Robert had no federal government support for his program, and Luis's main responsibility was to the high school and middle school children who congregated in the center after school. Robert and three or four other job seekers came into the center later in the evening and sat in one of the rooms to work on their resumes and look through job listings from the newspaper. The local Catholic parish offered these job seekers the opportunity to work around the parish for minimum wage ten to fifteen hours a week. The organizers of the jobs program at the church hoped to eventually place those who worked steadily in more secure and better-paying jobs in the community by appealing to neighborhood businesses.

Several weeks after Robert had entered the program, he stopped going to the thrice-weekly meetings at the community center. Nora reported that he had dropped out of the job program and was starting to hang around with his old friends. He left her apartment, and she feared he was going to get back into trouble. Luis, the park department employee, was also a Guadalupe resident. I spoke with him one afternoon about the jobs program and Robert's participation in it.

Luis said that the problem with the program in the park was that they [local employers] had promised all these jobs to the kids but then they never came through with them. These kids knew what was going on. There was that big meeting at the church and the kids were made all kinds of promises, but then the jobs never came through. Robert and those other guys weren't going to wait around for them; they saw that it wasn't going to happen and left. But, [Luis said,] I figured that would happen. I figured that first day at the center when we had about ten kids there, I figured that maybe two or three would stay in the program and then if they stayed in long enough it would work for them. But most of them weren't going to stay in.

In contrast, Linda, the teacher at Nora's job-training center, provided the following insights on the students in Nora's class. Over the course of several months, nearly all of the students who had enrolled in her job-training class had completed the course successfully and obtained jobs in Bay Area businesses.

I mention to Linda that all the people who were in the class a few months back completed the program and left. I say that this didn't really surprise me because it seemed that all [the] students were employable. Linda agrees. She says she didn't understand what Marco [one of the most able students] was doing in the class in the first place. Most of the people in her class, she continues, were like Nora—they just fell off the track for a short while, but they were easily employable. Or take the six Mexican ladies who sit at the front of the room—she knew they were going to get jobs. But Linda goes on to say that the class is also getting smaller because the training center oversubscribed to the federal program that supplied most of their operating funds in the first half of the fiscal year. They weren't allowed to admit any more people on that program until September or so.

The experiences of Ben, Manuel, Tina, Nora, and Robert illustrate how finding a job in the low-income barrios unfolded in different ways depending on the resources a job seeker could bring to bear on the problem. Poorly paying, unstable jobs typified by the worker at McDonald's could be easily located, often without any active effort on the part of a job-seeking resident. Unfortunately, for most residents these low-quality jobs were not especially attractive. Finding better-quality jobs depended in large measure on the resources that went into the job search—resources not only of individual time and energy but also of knowledge and power in the workplace. Many barrio residents who held better-quality jobs did not even know when their employers were looking for more workers, and even fewer residents had positions that gave them the power to refer or hire co-residents. For this reason, many of those who found good jobs did so with the aid of employment placement institutions. But here too, level of resources influenced job finding. Larger and well-connected job-placing organizations, such as JPC, had a good track record placing barrio residents in good jobs; smaller organizations had a much more difficult time placing their enrollees. In the quest for a better-quality job, the resources that were brought to the search—whether through family and kin networks or through formal job-finding institutions—were as important as the fashion in which those resources were dispatched.

KEEPING A JOB

Resources from family and friends helped barrio residents find work, and these resources remained important for residents in keeping the jobs they found. Low wages made it impossible for most workers to live, commute, and obtain child care on their own. Residents turned to their social network for the ancillary support that made it possible to survive on low wages. In Guadalupe and Chávez, family, friends, and neighbors shared the rent on apartments and houses, provided each other with child care, and helped out with transportation between home and work.

Housing in San Jose and Los Angeles is expensive. In my explorations in and around Guadalupe and Chávez, it seemed that behind every front door lay overcrowded bedrooms and living rooms that had been converted into sleeping quarters. Sometimes, the overcrowded residents were all workers. Near Guadalupe barrio, I spent one afternoon going door to door with a community outreach worker, and we met six men who lived in a cramped dormitory-style apartment. Cousins, brothers, and friends from Mexico, the men ranged in age from eighteen to thirty. They paid $650 a month for two dark bedrooms that were filled with mattresses, but at least they managed to keep the sleeper in the living room in its sofa configuration. The apartment complex bustled with noise from children playing on small patches of bare ground that no longer grew grass, with residents coming and going to work and on errands at all times of day and night, with peddlers and vendors hollering, ringing bells, and honking horns to attract customers, and with men and women socializing on the streets. The six men all worked as minimum-wage janitors and landscapers, and most of the time one or more were looking for work. Pooling rent through short-term loans was a strategy to keep a roof over their collective heads. Several of the men wished they could afford to move into more pleasant surroundings—at least into a complex where the noise and commotion were less constant—but they had been unable to find other apartments in San Jose renting for less than $800 a month.

In Chávez, regulations required a single family to appear on the public housing lease, so dormitory-style rent splitting was technically impossible. Nevertheless, groups of residents squatted in temporarily vacant units throughout the projects. Two groups moved from unit to unit during 1995. The housing authority discouraged them by nailing plywood over the doors of vacant units and by shutting off the electricity. But they seemed to have little trouble finding their way past the plywood, inconspicuously pulling it away from the back door or scrambling through an unsecured window. Sometimes, squatters paid residents of nearby units to pass an extension cord into an active socket. During the day, the squatter apartments appeared completely vacant, but at night, it was common to see light from candles and flashlights in the windows of vacant units that remained without electricity. The squatters in Chávez faced an even more tenuous financial situation than low-wage workers in Guadalupe. Most of the squatters I knew in Chávez were heroin or alcohol users who ended up on the street when they were unable to find a vacant unit. Their earnings from low-wage jobs, illicit activity, and public aid simply failed to provide enough income to provide for both shelter and their substance of abuse.

Most front doors in Guadalupe and Chávez did not open up onto single-men's dormitories or squatters' apartments but onto families: extended families, multiple families, or families with boarders. In Guadalupe barrio, José Mendoza spent the first part of 1994 as part of an eight-member family household—his mother María Mendoza, her common-law husband Jesús, José's brother Esteban, his sister Rosa, and María and Jesús's two young daughters—who split the $750 monthly rent for a small two-bedroom apartment among the five wage earners. After several months in their apartment, María and Jesús moved to a larger two-bedroom unit nearby. In the new apartment, the rent increased by $75 a month, but María's brother Simón moved into the apartment, which meant there was another earner among whom to split rent. Jesús and María slept in the master bedroom, the three daughters slept in the second bedroom, and the three young men (Simón, José, and Esteban) slept on a daybed and sleeper sofa in the living room. I described a slice of José's work life in Chapter 2. María worked in the same food-processing plant as her son, and the other Mendozas worked in fast-food restaurants scattered around the Silicon Valley and in a nearby corner *tienda*.

In Chávez barrio, the Núñez family paid the rent on a relatively large two-bedroom unit by splitting the rent between two related nuclear families—Teresa Núñez and her common-law husband Sam, Teresa's three children (all under fifteen years old and two from Sam), Teresa's brother Edgar and his girlfriend Natalie, and their toddler daughter. Edgar, Natalie, and their daughter occupied the smaller bedroom in the unit, Teresa and Sam alternated between sleeping in the living room or sleeping in shifts with the three children in the larger bedroom. Sam and Edgar were the primary low-wage earners in the household, working multiple positions in warehouses, security firms, and chemical plants in a one-hour driving radius from Chávez. Teresa and Natalie contributed to household finances by participating in public assistance. As was common in Chávez, Teresa and her children were the only official occupants of the unit, for which they paid $350 a month. Local housing authority officials simply ignored the off-the-lease overcrowding that was nearly universal in Chávez.

Overcrowding provided a home for low-wage workers in San Jose and Los Angeles; getting from home to work constituted another challenge of job keeping in the barrios. Public transportation in both cities was unreliable and inconvenient. In Guadalupe barrio, for example, Esteban Mendoza had to leave an hour and a half to travel to work on public transportation but could make the trip in a private car in thirty minutes. Public transport was merely inconvenient when running smoothly, but it provided notoriously poor service. In Los Angeles, several bus lines passed close to Chávez barrio, and some Chávez residents took advantage of one bus stop conveniently located in the housing development itself. Marty, a Chávez resident who used the bus to get to his job at a mini-mall deli, usually could be found standing at the bus stop an hour before his shift began in order to climb aboard a bus that dropped him off at the mini-mall thirty minutes early. In theory, the next bus through Chávez would have dropped him off at the job site just as his shift began, but experience had taught Marty that if he planned to keep his job, he had to count on delays en route.[6]

For convenience and reliability, residents of Guadalupe and Chávez preferred private transportation to and from work. Many, however, could not afford a car on their own. Because most households had a number of workers—all with complicated and unpredictable schedules—it was difficult to split car expenses in the same way that residents split rent. More typical were the arrangements devised by the Mendoza and Núñez households. In Guadalupe, María and Jesús Mendoza typically spent off-work hours driving each other from one job to another in the household's single car. Jesús dropped off María at 7:00 a.m. and picked her up at the end of her shift at 3:00 p.m. María then shuttled back and forth between home, errands, and multiple fast-food restaurants where Jesús worked often until close to midnight, when Jesús's final shift regularly ended. Other workers in the household such as Esteban were left to their own devices. In the Núñez household, Edgar worked in the same warehouse where an older brother was a supervisor (his brother had helped him obtain the job). Although Edgar had no car of his own, his brother was willing to drive through Chávez on the way to work. The regular ride from his brother was convenient and easy for Edgar, but it did mean a loss of flexibility. One Friday night, for example, Edgar returned home close to 10:00 p.m. frustrated and angry because he had been stuck at the warehouse for hours while his brother took care of some bookkeeping responsibilities. He began planning that night for how to purchase a car of his own.

Barrio residents who managed to pay the rent and get to work with the assistance of members of their social support network often still faced a third hurdle to keeping a job: child care. Figuring out how to take care of young children who required full-time looking after or arranging for after-school supervision presented difficult logistical and social challenges. Logistically, child care providers had to be affordable, reliable, and convenient. Socially, residents wanted child care providers they could trust. In both barrios, parents turned to grandparents, aunts and uncles, and older siblings for child care that provided an acceptable combination of reliability, convenience, and trust.

In Guadalupe, the Mendoza family's move into the larger apartment was motivated not only by the prospect of adding Uncle Simón to the stable of low-wage earners in the household but also by plans to bring María's mother to live in San Jose. The Mendoza children were all school age. After school, they had been going to nearby Mendoza households— one of María's brothers lived in the family's new apartment complex, and another lived in a house approximately three blocks away. On afternoons when he was not working, Uncle Simón also pitched in with child care. Once her mother came to Guadalupe, María expected all of these arrangements to be much easier. Her mother could not contribute to household finances, but she would make the logistics of looking after her daughters much easier. I never heard María complain about how her sisters-in-law looked after the children. But some evenings she expected to find her children at her brother's apartment, only to find out they had gone to the 15th Street house. It was only a few blocks from the Mendoza apartment to her brother's house, but María always went out of her way to give her daughters a ride over, and she worried about the children making the trip on their own. Having her mother around to help provide dependable supervision for the children would also mean fewer demands on her brothers' wives, who already had their hands full with their own young families.

Most workers I knew in Guadalupe and Chávez tried to arrange for family to look after their children when they could not. But few residents I knew in either barrio found child care arrangements that did not require regular compromise. Limited economic resources and hectic work schedules seemed to mitigate against finding stable and satisfactory arrangements. Family was affordable, convenient, reliable, and trusted, but relying on family to take care of children introduced social complications. Paying for child care from a local provider meant avoiding difficult social situations, but many barrio residents mistrusted the motivations of providers and the quality of the care provided under purely economic arrangements.

Family complications descended on the Núñez family in the summer of 1995. Teresa Núñez received $50 to $100 a week, mostly to cover expenses, to provide child care for two sisters who lived nearby and worked full time. This financial relationship tended to reflect—rather than direct—the filial one. During the summer of 1995, a small argument arose between Teresa and her younger sister over how to best take care of Teresa's young nephew. Teresa complained that the child was out of control around his mother and that the mother had to give her the leeway to manage the child's behavior as she saw best. The younger sister took this complaint as an attack on her child and on her own competence as a mother and maintained that Teresa's assessment was incorrect. In response, Teresa announced that she would no longer take care of the child. Teresa's refusal forced her sister to scramble for alternative child care arrangements with a sister-in-law whose house was far less conveniently located and whom she considered less desirable and trustworthy as a child care provider. After only a few days, the argument ran out of the steam, and the child was returned to Teresa's care. In Teresa's view, the younger sister had admitted she was wrong by returning care of her child to Teresa.

Explicitly economic arrangements reduced the social complications of child care arrangements but introduced other problems. In Guadalupe, one enterprising couple took advantage of the husband's home confinement (he was collecting disability payments after an on-the-job injury) to open a small child care center in the house. Several families in Guadalupe took advantage of the service, but the child care center did not have a good reputation in the community. A social gathering at the house where a makeup salesperson presented her wares reinforced this negative view. While the salesperson demonstrated eyeliner and wrinkle remover in the crowded living room, the husband tried to busy the children—an especially large group, thanks to the children of mothers visiting with the makeup salesperson—with toys in the small back yard. Several mothers expressed amazement afterward that the couple was trying to provide child care at all. They called the arrangements a disgrace and agreed among themselves that the child care center was simply a ploy for the greedy couple to make some extra money by taking advantage of the needs of others in the community. All expressed relief that their own children were taken care of through other arrangements.

## THE WORK ETHIC

In everyday life, social networks linked barrio residents to the low-wage labor market. Guadalupe and Chávez residents found low-wage jobs with the help of family, friends, and neighbors, and they kept the jobs they found with the support of these same community networks. These networks composed a structural framework for job finding and job keeping in the low-income barrios. At the same time, the operation of these networks in everyday life reflected a shared cultural understanding in both barrios that working was a worthwhile and important activity. To this point, I have shown how social networks provided structural connections between barrio residents and the labor market. Now I focus on how cultural orientations among barrio residents facilitated the maintenance of these structural connections. These facilitating cultural orientations are the work ethic, and it is fair to say that the work ethic thrived in both Guadalupe and Chávez.

Policy makers, social commentators, and charities have long distinguished the deserving from the undeserving poor by arguing that the former group embraces the work ethic while the latter group rejects it.[7] This history has lent the term normative connotations that many social scientists prefer to avoid in their research.[8] When the controversy surrounding Oscar Lewis's culture-of-poverty theory in the late 1960s forced the work ethic onto the research agenda, social scientists quickly showed that, when asked directly, poor people generally expressed the same sorts of work-affirming orientations as other Americans.[9] But this evidence failed to end the controversy over the work ethic. In the 1980s, policy analysts, suggesting that attitudes toward work were changing in American society generally and that public aid programs offered "perverse incentives" to avoid work among the poor in particular, argued that poor people were not behaving according to their expressed work-affirming values.[10] Some social scientists, using comparative data on employment and public assistance receipt—but not direct measures of cultural orientations toward work—reported results that seemed to hint at an ambivalence toward working among the poor.[11] On the other hand, in his influential research on concentrated urban poverty in African American ghettos, William Julius Wilson called on social scientists to explore the cultural roots of social problems in impoverished neighborhoods even if they harbored suspicions about the intellectual roots of those explanations or found them politically distasteful.[12] Scholars are alert to the potential for abuse when it comes to the work ethic. They know that the term can be used to impugn the reputation of the poor, to depict the poor as undeserving, and to justify cutbacks in efforts to assist or protect them.[13] Scholars also can use the concept of work ethic productively. In a study designed to examine willingness to work, Stephen Petterson examined the self-reported reservation wage—the lowest wage offer they would accept—of white and black youth as well as their actual job-taking behavior. He concluded that reservation wages did not do a good job predicting actual job-taking behavior and suggested that relatively high reservation wages reported by the disadvantaged might reflect a desire "to earn modest but decent wages" rather than a reluctance to take available jobs.[14]

Properly deployed, the notion of the work ethic does not separate the deserving from the undeserving poor but rather references orientations toward work that are sustained within a particular social setting. In this sense, the term *work ethic* can describe orientations toward work in the low-income community in a way that complements the description of work conveyed by the term *unemployment*. Just as the unemployment rate conveys useful information about work opportunities in the structural environment, the work ethic conveys useful information about the meaning of work in the cultural environment. In this usage, the work ethic does not differentiate the deserving poor who want to work from the undeserving poor who want to avoid work. In fact, as Petterson shows, knowing whether people want to work is just one factor—and perhaps not even the most crucial factor—for understanding the meaning of work in the cultural environment of a particular low-income community. For anyone who studies culture, this finding should not come as a surprise. Social scientists recognize that culture does not shape behavior just or even mostly via people's wants and desires. Beyond the ideas or desires that an individual carries around in his or her own head, culture operates through the social conventions and publicly affirmed practices of communities.[15] In the metaphor of Ann Swidler, these practices constitute a public "tool kit" that community members draw on as they manage everyday affairs.[16] Thus, culture is more about *how* people get things done than about what they want to do.

Distinguishing between culture's effects on what poor people say and what they do is particularly important when it comes to the work ethic. Work is a clarion virtue in our society, so it is understandable if Americans usually express enthusiasm for job holding. In Guadalupe and Chávez, residents did more than simply express enthusiasm for work. Their affirmation of work shaped how residents of the barrios lived their everyday lives—not just what they said to an interested outsider but also how they talked to each other, how they interacted with each other, and how they organized everyday household routines. Jobs and working constituted a kind of cultural background noise in both barrios. As the previous discussion has shown, this cultural background did not mean that barrio residents loved their jobs or invested their personal identity in their occupations. One need not be a workaholic to firmly embrace the work ethic, and most residents I knew in the barrios were not workaholics; they did not live to work. But they did take it for granted that economic life revolved around work. I say that the work ethic thrived in Guadalupe and Chávez, therefore, because to the extent that economic life formed one cornerstone of family and community, the residents of Guadalupe and Chávez took it for granted that their lives were grounded in the workplace.

Residents of both barrios invoked and recognized work as an organizing principle for their home or social life, as in a conversation I overheard one Friday afternoon in Chávez. I was chatting with a wheelchair-bound Chávez senior, a fixture of the Chávez street scene known to all as Grandma, while I waited for an acquaintance to come pick me up in his van. Grandma and I were making small talk when a young neighbor of hers drove into the parking lot nearby and walked by us, still in his work clothes, in the direction of the corner *tienda*. Grandma interrupted our conversation to browbeat her young neighbor. "Where have you been?" she complained. "I never see you around the neighborhood anymore." The young man laughed off her complaint. "I'm sorry, Grandma," he said. "But I'm not a kid anymore. I'm a working man. I have my family to take care of." He explained that he put in long hours at his truck-driving job and that when he got off work he came home to see his wife and kids. Right now, he was on his way to pick up some things from the store and then he had to get back to the house. "I don't have time for hanging around the neighborhood anymore," he explained. Grandma let the man go by, quietly endorsing his explanation.

In the conversation that Friday afternoon, the young man pronounced work the primary organizing principle of his life. And in that same conversation, Grandma endorsed the young man's pronouncement without question or challenge—talk that reflected a shared understanding among barrio residents of the importance of embracing work.

Residents of Guadalupe and Chávez also expressed this shared understanding indirectly—in comments that recognized the difficulties and problems that arose from embracing work too tightly. The comments of Teresa, a Guadalupe resident in her mid-thirties, summed up feelings many residents expressed about the problems that could arise from an overcommitment to working. I had gone with her to the corner store to pick up some groceries early on a Monday afternoon, and when I asked after her weekend she described a disastrous party at her brother's on

Saturday night. Everyone had gotten drunk, a fight had broken out, and she had ended up taking her brother-in-law to the emergency room.

Teresa explains that this is not the first time a family get-together has gone bad, and she says that she's definitely not going to any more of these parties where everyone gets drunk. The problem, she tells me, is that everyone in her family works too long and too hard. Her brothers and sisters, uncles and aunts all get worn down and stressed out from spending too many hours at the job and too few hours sleeping, relaxing, and spending time with family. Too much time at work leads to other problems. Wives ask husbands to work less in order to spend more time around the house, and husbands make their wives stay at home. The stress gets worse, and it has to be relieved somehow. Teresa says her relatives use drinking. At family gatherings, it regularly leads to these kinds of fights. She ties it all of it back to the Mexican condition: "As Mexicans," she tells me, "that's our problem as a people. We work too hard; we don't know how to relax."

Teresa cites a problem that residents in both Guadalupe and Chávez could identify with. The residents I spent time with in both barrios shared a similarly strong commitment to work in general, and residents in both barrios worried at times that working too hard created more problems than it solved.

Work, for better or worse, grounded social life in the barrios. Residents in both barrios experienced difficulties in low-wage jobs. When it came to the kinds of frustrations that residents expressed about low-wage work, however, I noted significant differences in Guadalupe and Chávez.

In Guadalupe, recent immigrants objected to specific aspects of lousy jobs—the low pay, unpredictable hours, dangerous working conditions, and mistreatment from bosses or customers—without condemning the desirability or necessity of work per se. The experiences of Orvin—a twenty-five-year-old who had been living in Guadalupe for about five years when I met him in the fall of 1993—exemplified this talk.

Orvin put in long hours for low wages at a local car wash, and while I never heard him speak disparagingly of his hours or earnings, nearly every time I saw him after a shift, he provided an earful about the customers. He described in detail how they treated him and the other people who worked at the car wash. Frequently, he said, customers complained about something on their car after it came out of the wash. They would find some wet spot that the workers had not dried up completely or they would want the windows or dashboard to be rewiped. Orvin generally did what he could to satisfy their complaints. "But," he said, "sometimes they get angry with me about it. I hate it when they do that, and I do my best to ignore them. Even if they scream and yell, I just ignore them. There is nothing to do about that. It is not worth getting upset about." I heard expressions of frustration such as Orvin's regularly when Guadalupe residents talked about the problems of low-wage jobs. These jobs involved significant hardships, and Guadalupe residents hated the hardships and were distressed by them. But these hardships were part of the working experience, so if it was possible, it made sense to let the difficulties slide by.

Chávez residents expressed similar sentiments about the conditions of work at the lowest-quality jobs to a point; like Guadalupe residents, residents in Chávez objected to low pay, unpredictable hours, and the other unpleasant characteristics of these jobs. But many Chávez residents expanded on specific critiques of working conditions in low-wage jobs with talk of how, as U.S.-born Mexican-Americans, they should not have to endure those conditions. The most demeaning and demanding jobs, many in Chávez asserted, were jobs for immigrants.[17] Talking about employment in these lousy jobs, Chávez residents often not only echoed the frustration that I heard in Guadalupe but also could sound angry and resentful—an oppositional orientation that researchers have described among Chicano high-school students and other young people of color who are "involuntary" minorities.[18]

The comments of Henry, an eighteen-year-old Chávez resident, one afternoon in the fall of 1995 exemplified this orientation. A medical emergency involving his brother had pulled the entire family out of bed at 3:00 a.m. that morning, and Henry had been told to go down to the hospital to take care of his brother because his father had to go to work at 4:30. Henry digressed from the story of his brother's injury to talk about his father.

Henry says that he gets along fine with his dad, but he [his father] was never around when he was growing up. "I feel like I barely know him," says Henry. "He was always at work when I was a kid and he's still always at work. He's been getting up at 4:30 to go off to work all his life. So I barely saw him ever. I could never do that. I could never hold a job like that. It's okay if you're like him—if you're just coming here from Mexico—and he supported the whole family that way. I'm grateful for that. But if you're born here, you don't take that kind of job."

Like Henry, other residents in Chávez verbally distanced themselves from poor-quality jobs by asserting that conditions in these jobs was reasonable for immigrants but unacceptable for U.S.-born citizens. This talk referenced an expectation of upward mobility among settled U.S. residents at the same time that it invoked the prospect of rejecting the nation's most significant economic institution, the wage-labor market.

Moreover, among some Chávez residents in some situations, this talk of frustrated expectations and potential rejection informed behavior about employment itself. In Chávez, some workers who abruptly quit jobs following disputes or mistreatment explained these job-quits as an individual decision to stand up to unfair treatment. The following anecdote is a more detailed view of events in the life of Ted Galindo, whose employment experiences I overviewed in Chapter 2. On this late spring afternoon, Ted's outrage at a supervisor's treatment and decision to quit his job exemplified how talk of frustration and rejection expanded into behavior on the labor market.

"The bus was late one day, and so I showed up ten minutes late," relates Ted to a trio of friends. "So my boss starts screaming at me—calling me motherfucker and all that. I always take the early bus and get there twenty minutes before my shift, and one time I take the later bus and it gets me there late, he starts screaming. He never paid me for the time I got there early. So I said fuck it. I just walked out and quit right there."

Stories such as these circulated regularly among Chávez residents—especially among young men—lending an oppositional flavor to decisions about when to quit a job and when to stick it out. And "flavor" is an appropriate metaphor. In Chávez, resentment over frustrated economic expectations and perceived mistreatment in low-wage jobs shaped residents' relationship to work in complex and contingent ways without seeming to dislodge more fundamental relationships among work, family, and community as expressed, for example, in the interchange between Grandma and the young truck driver. I saw that many Chávez residents who angrily quit jobs after disputes soon began working again. Ted, for example, only a few days after angrily quitting his job at the restaurant began an extended stint as a minimum-wage security guard. Thus, Chávez residents expressed and even acted upon resentment, anger, and frustration at particular situations with particular bosses in particular work sites without generalizing those feelings to the relationship between work and social life as a whole. For most of the residents I knew, walking out on a lousy job or rebuffing a particular boss did not reflect an uncompromising rejection of the labor market. Rather, dramatic oppositional outbursts arose during contingent moments. For Ted, arriving at work late one day became a moment of contingency quickly filled with expressions of anger and frustration. Understanding why these moments of contingency occurred more frequently in Chávez than in Guadalupe is the task of the next chapter.

# CHAPTER 5

# Networks and Work

Low-wage jobs assume an inevitable routine. Employers pay low wages to fill positions for which little training is required and in which high turnover can be tolerated. Low-wage workers have little access to the human capital, organizational infrastructure, or political clout that might improve their position in the labor market or their conditions in the workplace. Low-wage work routines thus are shaped primarily by workers' social resources—the orientations, information, and concrete support to which they have access through interactions with the family, friends, and neighbors who make up their residential community. Low-wage workers use these social resources to manage the conundrums that inevitably arise when they are trying to make ends meet on the minimum wage. Backed by family and community, low-wage workers maintain their allegiance to the work ethic, find out about open jobs and how to apply for them, and team up to pay the rent, get to work, and take care of the children.

Lives in Chávez and Guadalupe reflected all of these features of the low-wage labor market, but the inevitable routine of low-wage labor played different roles in the income-generating activities of the two barrios. As I pointed out in Chapter 2, low-wage jobs were the most important source of income in Chávez, but they were by no means the only source of income. In contrast, wage laboring provided nearly all the income in Guadalupe barrio. If wage laboring followed similar routines in the two barrios, why did low-wage jobs play different roles in Chávez and Guadalupe?

This chapter analyzes the different roles of low-wage work in Chávez and Guadalupe. Residents in both communities were devotees of the work ethic—endorsing in others and affirming for themselves the importance of working. Despite this similar devotion to the ideal of work, however, residents of Chávez and Guadalupe often saw working in similar low-wage jobs quite differently. In Chávez, low-wage jobs were fraught with compromises and drawbacks; in Guadalupe, similar jobs represented a difficult but sensible path toward higher status.

These differences in the meaning of work were related to differences in the collective public life of Chávez and Guadalupe.[1] In Chávez, everyday life was stubbornly local.[2] The struggles of residents in low-wage labor markets were seen as an indication that low-wage jobs were futile dead-ends. An active illicit economy and widespread participation in public assistance programs demonstrated alternative ways of earning income.[3] For many Chávez residents, low-wage jobs, illicit activities, and welfare were simply different ways of earning income, and each had its own advantages and disadvantages. The Guadalupe community, in contrast, saw working at low-wage jobs as an integral part of the migration experience between Mexico and the United States, and for many, everyday barrio life revolved around continuing connections to Mexico.[4] In this transnational context, low-wage jobs were part of a difficult path, to be sure, but a path that led to meaningful success.

Different meanings of low-wage work led to the adoption of different economic strategies in the two communities. Residents in Chávez adopted flexible earning strategies that I call *hustling,* in which low-wage jobs played a large but not exclusive role. In Guadalupe, in contrast, residents made ends meet through a strategy of *overwork,* long hours at one or multiple low-wage jobs.

In this chapter, I analyze the place of low-wage work in Chávez and Guadalupe. I show how neighborhood context sustained different understandings of the meaning of low-wage work in everyday life—in the conversations and interactions among friends, family, and neighbors within each community. This meaning developed in the context of observing the economic behaviors of others in the community and through everyday interactions. Because the meaning of low-wage work emerged from the quality of everyday observations and interactions, I analyze this meaning by focusing on whom residents observed, what they saw, and with whom they interacted. I focus, in short, on the social networks that dominated residents' everyday economic lives. Different social networks sustained different meanings of low-wage work, and different meanings of low-wage work, in turn, sustained different kinds of economic strategies.

## WORKING AND EARNING

Outside the shared work routine of child care arrangements, long commutes, long hours, uncertain wages, and unpredictable job tenure, the experiences of low-wage workers in the communities of Chávez and Guadalupe showed further similarities as well as remarkable differences. Residents in both communities accorded jobholders honor as workers. On the other hand, the communities supported different kinds of income-earning activities, and this led to distinct experiences for low-wage workers as earners. Both communities held a positive view of the worker who held a job, but Guadalupe and Chávez held different views of the earner who worked for low wages.

### Workers and Community in Chávez

Low-wage workers in Chávez regularly spent time with family, friends, and neighbors who earned income without holding a job. For workers, interactions with the jobless carried mixed messages. Compared to working in the illicit economy or receiving public assistance, wage work was honorable. On the other hand, the jobless were not exhausted by the draining routine of low-wage work; the jobless who received public assistance had a steady source of income that they could supplement with side work; and the jobless who participated in the illicit economy enjoyed occasional financial windfalls unparalleled in the experiences of low-wage workers.

Working steadily and making work the central priority and organizing principle of one's life was respected in Chávez. For example, working played a crucial role in Chávez residents' understanding of the transition into adulthood. As is the norm in American society, this transition in Chávez was marked by assuming the responsibility of a job. Thus, the young man in Chapter 4 explained how his responsibilities as a "working man" made it impossible for him to hang around the neighborhood anymore—activities that were the province of children and adolescents. This young man was making the transition to responsibility and respectability that Chávez residents expected. A period of youthful wildness could be excused; there was peer pressure to have a period of wildness. But Chávez residents were expected to get a job in order to attain adult membership in the community. Residents noticed when neighbors failed to live up to these expectations, as the following field note illustrates.

> Manny is standing with a group on a stoop near the gym at about 4:00 when Chico, a nineteen-year-old member of the Elm Street gang, rides up on a small bicycle. He excitedly tells Manny, "We just caught a VP [a member of a rival gang] over by the park and got him good. I was over there, and they got after me but I came back with the homies, and we caught that guy. Messed him up real good—I hit him with the phone (demonstrating how he used the receiver of the pay phone as a weapon) bam bam bam! Have you seen Shorty around? I gotta go tell him." Manny tells Chico he saw Shorty up by the store, and Chico pedals off in that direction. Manny says, "He shouldn't be doing that stuff any more. That's okay for the younger guys, but Chico, his old lady just had a kid, and the VPs are gonna mess him up if they catch him, or he'll get locked up. He's got a family to support; he shouldn't be messing around with that stuff anymore."

In Chávez, working ensured a measure of stability for oneself and one's family. Young people were exceptional; without children or other dependents relying on them, they could take chances with their physical safety or their freedom. With age, honorable people changed their behavior by adopting more settled daily routines. Entering the workforce and attaining this reputability and respectability was an accomplishment to be proud of. Tricia, a twenty-two-year-old medical assistant, had grown up in Chávez, moved into private housing after having a child and leaving high school early, and returned to Chávez when the child's father was incarcerated. After receiving public assistance for several years, Tricia entered a job-training program and found employment with a local medical clinic. After several months on the job, Tricia was contemplating an upcoming meeting with her welfare caseworker where they would discuss ending her receipt of public aid. Although uneasy about the prospect of going without steady income from AFDC, when Tricia discussed the upcoming meeting with family, friends, and co-workers in Chávez, she boasted of how far she had come in the months since she began working. "I got my job, I'm off welfare, I'm gonna get out of here in a couple months," she told a cousin one afternoon. "As soon as David gets a construction job, we're going to move out of his mother's house and back into our own place." Moving from AFDC to complete reliance on wages was anxiety provoking, but it was also something to brag about.

Workers' bragging rights in Chávez—to respectability, responsibility, and self-sufficiency—did not blind them to the drawbacks of working in low-wage jobs. Given the long hours devoted to the job and the relatively paltry monetary rewards, low-wage workers at times found themselves making sacrifices that nonworkers avoided. Many workers in Chávez had personally received public assistance or money from illicit activities, and this experience made them acutely aware of the drawbacks and compromises of low-wage jobs. Even residents without personal experience earning income outside the labor force could see that many residents around them made money without working in unrewarding low-wage jobs. The Núñez family provide illustrations of these dynamics.

When Sam Núñez lost his job early in 1995, he spent several weeks looking for a job in companies within walking distance of Chávez while working occasionally as a security guard and at other short-term positions. As the weeks passed and Sam remained unemployed, he felt more and more pressure to expand his job search and begin contributing to the household finances. Soon after beginning to search beyond the local area, Sam found a job in a warehouse. A few days after starting in his new position, a cousin quizzed him about it.

"What are they paying you," the cousin asked, "$4.00 an hour?" Sam replied that he was getting a bit more, $4.25. "And what," came the sarcastic response, "after five years they'll give you a raise to $4.50, right?"

Sam had no adequate reply with which to finish this exchange, and he conceded the obviously disappointing reality. Low-wage workers often confronted these difficult questions. How come the job pays so little? How long are you going to stay in that job without moving up? Look at how many hours a week you work and look how much money it brings you.

These questions bit particularly deep for low-wage workers who understood the benefits of making money outside the labor market—residents who themselves had often participated in illicit activities or public assistance at some point in their lives. Residents with experience in the illicit economy knew that profits, even if short-lived, could be spectacular. Moreover, these profits could quickly be converted into visible signs of prosperity—a sign of prosperity that could outlive in memories and bragging rights whatever fleeting material success the person may have actually enjoyed in the illicit economy. Residents familiar with the routine of public assistance knew that welfare checks arrived with relative certainty, week to week, compared to the paychecks from low-wage jobs, which often fluctuated unpredictably as hours at work rose and fell. Moreover, cashing a check left plenty of time to gain additional income through unreported work. From a certain vantage point, therefore, wage workers faced the worst of both worlds: they had neither the opportunity for financial windfall of the illicit realm nor the reliable easy money of public assistance.

Edgar Núñez's unsuccessful negotiations to buy his younger brother Paul's sports car—negotiations that unfolded over several weeks in May 1995—illustrated the quandary in which low-wage workers in Chávez often found themselves. Paul had bought the car with proceeds from illicit drug sales and a one-time windfall in the legitimate economy in 1993. After two years, he was ready to part with the car, and he offered it first to Edgar, his favorite brother. If Edgar would take over the monthly payments on the car, Paul would sell it to him for $500.

Like Paul, Edgar had experienced windfalls through participation in the illicit economy. At times, he had made extraordinary profits from single drug sales and other transactions, as he recalled one evening as we drove to visit friends in my car.

"One time, I remember, I was going to sell this guy a whole bottle of cools [PCP]. That's gonna get me a couple hundred dollars. He drives in, and I leave him in his car while I go off to get the stuff. At that time, Mundo [a friend of Edgar's] had this police badge. He would come up to people when they were making a buy and pretend to be a cop and take their money. So, I've got this deal going on, and he comes up and he's saying 'You're busted' to this guy who is going to buy the cools. I'm like, 'No no Mundo, knock it off man, be cool, not this guy,' because I want to get rid of the stuff. But Mundo gets on top of the car with a hammer and he's swinging it around, yelling that he's going to bust in this guy's windshield. I'm like 'oh no, he's all fucked up.' But finally he listened to me, and he got down off the car. I sold the guy the bottle and made two hundred bucks right there."

The sale of PCP took place long ago. By the time of the car sale, Edgar had not experienced the windfalls of the illicit economy for several years. He had spent three years in prison for his role in a violent robbery, and he had been released on parole in February. Since his release, as per the conditions of his parole, Edgar had been working full time in a warehouse earning $5 an hour. The $500 Paul wanted for the car—a sum Edgar could conceivably have earned in a few busy days of drug selling—would take months of saving at his current wage. Paul realized this. "Edgar will buy it from me in a year," he told me one day when I asked if they had completed the deal. "When he's had a chance to be working for a while and have the money saved up for it."

There was a sharp contrast between Edgar's past economic life in the illicit economy and his present economic situation in the warehouse. In the illicit economy, Edgar had taken great risks, but he had also enjoyed substantial financial windfalls. Working at the warehouse, Edgar no longer risked going back to prison, but he was guaranteed to experience the frustration of long hours of work for low wages.

These constraints of his low-wage job were thrown into relief not only by contrast to his past life in the illicit economy but also by contrast to the financial position of Chávez residents participating in public assistance. A few weeks after the sale of the car first came up, Edgar, Paul, their sister Teresa, and Edgar's girlfriend Natalie were eating together in Teresa's apartment. Paul had just told the people gathered around the kitchen that he was going to sell his car to Edgar for $500 and that Edgar would pick up the payments, and he added this might happen in a year or so when Edgar was more established in his job and had some money.

Teresa turns to Edgar and jokes, "I can buy that car right now. With my welfare." She looks around the kitchen for confirmation and says, "That's the best pay anyway, right? I can count on those checks, every month." Natalie quickly agrees with her and opens a drawer in the kitchen counter near where she is standing. She pulls out a small stack of envelopes. "Here are my checks," she says and counts out seven checks, each for $100. "I can buy that car right now."

Edgar's situation as he considered buying Paul's car illustrated the dilemma of working and earning in Chávez. Working was respectable. Over the long run, working had distinct advantages. Working carried no stigma like welfare participation, and participation in the labor force gave residents a sense of self-sufficiency and independence. Compared to those active in the illicit economy, wage workers avoided the risks of incarceration and injury. But at any given time, the disadvantages of low-wage working were visible. Welfare and illicit work made less intense demands on time and effort; only wage labor demanded long commutes and long days at $5 an hour. Public assistance provided steadier earnings. Every month, welfare participants received checks in the mail, and at least for a few days they had an extraordinary amount of cash in their control. Illicit work provided more spectacular earnings. Participants in the illicit economy had the experience of making, in a day or a week, what wage workers earned in a month. Chávez residents wanted to be workers rather than participants in welfare or the drug trade. Nevertheless, working had its trade-offs. Chávez residents saw that, as a source of earnings, welfare and illicit activities had clear advantages.

## Workers and Community in Guadalupe

Family, friends, and neighbors in Guadalupe did not participate in welfare or in the illicit economy. Residents' daily rounds rarely brought them into contact with earners who did not work in low-wage jobs. The low-wage labor market's monopoly on economic life meant that Guadalupe residents did not grapple with the same kind of mixed messages that workers encountered in Chávez. There were few residents cashing steadily arriving AFDC checks, and few were enjoying the financial windfalls of illicit activities. Without these income-earning alternatives, working and earning overlapped perfectly for the low-wage jobholder. Many Guadalupe residents, especially recently arrived immigrants, were eager to simply hold a job—any job. The overlap did not indicate, however, that all residents were happy in their jobs and unconcerned by low earnings. In Guadalupe, working was expected and important for all residents. For many recently arrived immigrants, working was the only thing that mattered. But immigrants who had lived in Guadalupe for some time were interested not only in holding a job but also in earning a good living. As immigrants became more settled, the distinction between working and earning became increasingly salient.

Many immigrants in Guadalupe barrio were looking for any kind of paid work. The experiences of Antonio, a twenty-two-year-old newly arrived from the Mexican state of Michoacán in early February 1994, provide a typical example of recent-immigrant engagement with low-wage work. Antonio arrived in San Jose nearly broke and with only a few friends in the area. Through his friends he met Gabriel, a thirty-one-year-old immigrant who had been living in Guadalupe barrio for three years. With only a few years of experience in the States and no facility in English, Gabriel was a recent arrival in some respects, but he had the steady job and the street smarts of an experienced immigrant. Antonio and Gabriel began spending a lot of time together. Gabriel lived in a cramped garage, and Antonio slept in Gabriel's van. Neither man was very comfortable. "The van is better, really," joked Gabriel. "That's right," agreed Antonio. "I have a bigger bed and more room to stand up in there than Gabriel does in his little room." Gabriel and Antonio split the rent for the room ($300 a month), and they paid what they considered an enormous amount on food every month (about $300 each) because they had no access to kitchen facilities.

Familiar with day labor from his home *rancho,* when Antonio arrived in Guadalupe he went to one of the street corners in San Jose where employers picked up casual labor. Antonio worked for whoever was hiring—mostly in landscaping and construction—and at first made only $3 or $4 an hour. His hours varied substantially week to week. During one week in March, Antonio was picked up only on Wednesday; a few weeks later, he treated to tacos one Friday night when he had a good week—he worked every day except Monday when it rained. The first steady work Antonio found was for a Guatemalan family whom he helped with home improvements on weekends. This job provided steady earnings throughout the late winter and into the spring. In May, Antonio began working for a house painter who had picked him up at the day labor market several times. His pay improved to $5 an hour. Between the Guatemalans and the house painter, Antonio had several good months of steady work. Antonio and Gabriel planned to take a visit to Mexico in June. Gabriel was committed to coming back to San Jose, but Antonio's plans were up in the air. Once he got down there, he would see how much money he had saved and decide whether to stay in Mexico or to return with Gabriel to find an apartment to rent in San Jose.

Recently arrived immigrants to Guadalupe often threw themselves into any kind of work—no matter what the pay or conditions of work. Some worked in low-wage jobs for a period of time, saved their money, and returned to the village and neighborhood in Mexico from which they had come. Others hoped that low-wage work would evolve into a better-paying job. How someone worked in the low-wage labor market provided important clues about his or her long-term plans and future financial destiny. Was a recent arrival simply working in a fashion that was familiar and comfortable from his or her experiences in Mexico? Did the person plan to work for a few months and then return to Mexico? Did the person have plans for how to move up into better-paying positions? Did he or she understand how to get a better job in the United States? Rogelio, a friend of Gabriel, was about forty years old and had been in San Jose for more than a decade. His comments reflected the prevailing wisdom on immigration and low-wage work in Guadalupe.

Rogelio said that recent immigrants tend to rely on the day labor markets for work, which Rogelio thinks is a bad idea. He explained that there weren't enough jobs at the day labor markets, so people end up not finding steady enough work to make decent money. Only a small percentage manage to turn day labor jobs into steady work. Many day laborers don't really want to work full time, in his opinion. They use the day labor line as an excuse to hang out with their friends. But most go to the day labor markets because in Mexico that is the way that people work. There is no need to go to job interviews and get real work in Mexico, but in the U.S. you have to find work by learning English, by learning skills in some trade, and by learning the rules of the game. You have to learn not to send your application to just one place and wait for them to offer you a job. A lot of people do that. They don't know that you have to send in many applications.

Over a Sunday lunch in April 1994, Gabriel shared further received wisdom about low-wage work as he discussed Antonio's work experiences in San Jose:

"Antonio has been here for only three months, but he's already learned a lot. Because he had to. Because he couldn't just go with friends and family to get just any job. He's spent time with me, so he's had a good teacher. . . . The person who comes here with family in place is limited in their ambition and their knowledge. If the top wage earner in that family is making $10 an hour somewhere, that's all that the new arrival will strive for or think that is possible. So perhaps they'll start out making $2 to $3 an hour as a day laborer, and after a while they'll finally move up into the $6 to $7 an hour range. They may get a little higher than that, but they'll think that $10 an hour is the best you can hope to make. They'll never realize that they can do a lot better than the top wage earner in their family."

The comments of Rogelio and Gabriel capture the everyday dynamics of immigrant mobility in Guadalupe—both its salience within the community and its practical difficulty. The resources that recent arrivals take advantage of, such as easily found work in day labor markets and family connections to workplaces, are invaluable for finding work. With time, however, a job—any job—becomes less important than the wages earned. The social resources that facilitate job finding can constrain migrants' movement into higher-status and better-paying jobs. Some migrants who continue to tread familiar paths into San Jose's low-wage labor market are lucky enough to find a way into a better-paying job. Others take the pulse of immigrant expectations and find jobs that simply suffice.

Gabriel and Rogelio's views are the settled migrant's view of new arrivals. Both are sympathetic toward recent migrants' struggles to find steady work and achieve steady income. Both express the normative viewpoint in Guadalupe that, with time and effort, better earnings could and should be had on the San Jose labor market. Both point up the difficulty of fulfilling, in practice, prevailing expectations that earnings will increase over time.

If Gabriel and Rogelio's views illustrate settled migrants' opinion of the opportunities and challenges facing recent arrivals, their experiences

illustrate how Guadalupe residents grapple with those challenges in practice. Gabriel had not been in San Jose long, but through what some considered wild chance taking and extraordinary good fortune, he had
found a good job as a maintenance worker at a local private school. The
job paid better than minimum wage and, more importantly, provided
benefits such as health insurance and paid vacation. To get the job,
Gabriel had presented *chuecos*—forged immigration and permission-to-
work documents. Gabriel felt sure that if his employers discovered he
was undocumented, they would immediately fire him, and he worried
that they might even initiate legal proceedings to secure his deportation.
Gabriel's experience was also unconventional in that he had secured his
good job at the school despite very limited English-language skills.

While Rogelio criticized some recent immigrants for not striving for
better-paying jobs, more than a few friends and acquaintances felt that
Rogelio had not done well in the United States. After spending time with
Gabriel and another friend, Pedro, one afternoon, Rogelio drove away in
his sports car and Pedro commented, "After ten years, all he has is that
[sports car]. Do you know where he got the money to buy his house? . . .
His mother in Mexico helped him to buy his house. She cashed in her
pension plan to send him the money to buy the house. It has been hard to
raise his daughter by himself. I know that. But he also spends too much
time chasing after women." Gabriel elaborated on this analysis of
Rogelio's difficulties. "People don't trust him. He is always making sex-
ual jokes. He is always chasing after women. He offends people with the
things he says."

For Pedro and Gabriel, the low earnings of their long-settled friend
needed to be explained. Seeking to explain how Rogelio, a long-settled
immigrant with excellent command of English and many connections in
the local area, had failed to substantially improve his economic position,
friends invoked exceptional circumstances (single parenthood) or character flaws (womanizing).

Rogelio himself acknowledged his modest financial success. In his
view, he had taken risks in his work life in order to accommodate his
responsibilities as a single parent. After many years working as a janitor
for outside contractors, Rogelio started his own janitorial services business. A religiously and politically active member of the Guadalupe community, Rogelio had many selfless reasons to start the business. He felt
Mexican workers in San Jose deserved better wages and working conditions than they currently received from janitorial *contratistas*. Rogelio
planned to pay his workers higher wages than competing contractors; he

set up a worker training designed to encourage economic independence and upward mobility through job training for janitorial work and English-language instruction. Rogelio's foray into entrepreneurialism was also self-interested. Even if he paid his workers a better wage than the competition, Rogelio calculated that his earnings would be higher as a contractor than as a worker and that as an employer he would have a more flexible work schedule. While marketing and selling the fledging business, Rogelio was out of the house close to a regular nine-to-five schedule, so he had time to spend with his daughter in the evening. The business failed to take off, however, and when two early clients left for a lower-priced contractor, Rogelio went back to work as an independent worker-janitor. Rogelio's explanation of his difficult financial position was different from that of his friends Pedro and Gabriel, but all three men felt Rogelio's position needed explanation. All Guadalupe residents expected to work; more settled residents also expected to earn.

HUSTLING AND OVERWORK

Among the poor, working and earning inevitably lead to questions of desire, volition, and constraints.[5] Are the poor impoverished because they do not care to work and increase their standard of living? Are they poor because they do not understand that disciplined work is the only way to emerge from poverty? Or are the poor impoverished because lack of opportunity prevents them from working and increasing their earnings? A way to talk about how desire and volition respond to constraints is to conceptualize poor people's economic behaviors as strategic responses to uncompromising or unforgiving social and economic environments.[6]

    The residents of Chávez and Guadalupe adopted different economic strategies. In Chávez, many sought advancement through hustling, an opportunistic combination of low-wage work and income from other sources. Overwork, the dominant advancement strategy in Guadalupe, involved working as many hours as possible in low-wage jobs.

    These strategies had the feeling of "naturalness" in their respective barrios. In Chávez, common sense dictated that residents take advantage of opportunities to earn a few dollars "on the streets" or to file the paperwork required to receive public assistance or charitable aid. In Guadalupe, a similar "natural" feel surrounded the practice of working hundred-hour weeks at multiple low-wage jobs. To some extent, this apparent "naturalness" reflects the fact that hustling and overwork were consistent with structural opportunities in Chávez and Guadalupe. Yet opportunity is a necessary but not sufficient basis for explaining why different strategies were adopted in the two communities. Neither the structure of opportunity, as I pointed out in Chapter 3, nor the meaning of work, as I argued in Chapter 4, provides a satisfying account of the dynamics of everyday engagement with low-wage jobs in Guadalupe and Chávez. Those chapters emphasized the similarities of opportunity structures and work meanings in the two barrios. Here I show that similar structural circumstances and cultural orientations supported different kinds of practical orientations toward low-wage jobs in the two barrios.

Hustling and overwork represented a positive and active mode of engaging with structural opportunities in a culturally meaningful way. These strategies were not a simple set of rule-driven responses to the structure of income-generating opportunities. Rather, residents of Chávez and Guadalupe adopted different strategies because the social climate in the two barrios made different strategies the most reasonable and accessible means of striving for economic advancement. In this sense, hustling and overwork not only made sense *given* the opportunity structure but also made sense *of* prevailing orientations about the meaning of economic advancement.

### Hustling in Chávez

In Chávez, wage labor was the preferred way to earn income, but most residents combined low-wage jobs with income from illicit activities and public aid. These opportunities were a regular part of everyday life in Chávez. Hustling did not lead to a long-term "life of crime" or "welfare dependency." Hustling was not a "whole way of life"; it was merely the logic behind the everyday decisions that residents made in pursuit of available economic opportunities.[7]

Illegal activities and welfare participation were smoothly interwoven into the everyday social and economic life in Chávez. Depending on age, gender, and personal experience, residents had a variety of reactions to the illicit and welfare activities in their community. Legal, illegal, and welfare economic activities—along with accompanying notions of "decent" and "street"—were intertwined in everyday barrio life.[8] Naive conceptions of unconventional economic activity in low-income communities—exemplified by the twin images of the illicit drug seller who stands outside of and opposes the "community" and the welfare-dependent mother who violates community norms and is blind to her own self-interest—fail to capture the *sensibility* of hustling within the social context of Chávez.[9]

One summer afternoon in 1995, the driver of an eighteen-wheeler parked his rig on a street adjacent to Chávez barrio. The truck was filled with new furniture still sealed in plastic. The events over the next few hours capture the sensibility of hustling in Chávez barrio as some residents sought to take advantage of the opportunity to steal the furniture and other residents simultaneously supported and criticized their activities. Endnotes highlight specific analytical points of interest.

I am with Tina in her living room when two guys come running in, sweating and huffing and slamming the door shut after themselves. They are Frankie and Guillermo. I have seen Frankie around and talked with him to say hello several times. Guillermo looks familiar, but this is the first time I have met him. Tina knows them both, and she asks them what they were doing. "We were just unloading this truck," says Frankie. "The cops came bombing in. They pulled up on the grass and everything, and we just jammed." Tina seems to understand what they mean by "unloading a truck," but I am confused.[10] If they were just "unloading a truck," why are they now running from the cops? I know Frankie is not an Elm Street member, and by all appearances neither is Guillermo.

Frankie and Guillermo are trying to find out where the cops are by calling over to Frankie's mother and sister, who live near where they ran from, as well as by asking passersby to go over see what is going on by his mom's apartment.[11] They finally manage to commandeer little Marielena to take a walk toward where Frankie's mother and sister live and look into things.

I told Señora Lupe I'd come by to see her, and now I wander over to her apartment, which is just a few doors down from Frankie's mother. Earlier this morning, Señora Lupe's doors and windows were wide open, and she had been lying on the couch feeling sick from her diabetes and from the heat. Now her doors and windows are all shut tight, and no one answers when I knock. Two Los Angeles police officers are carrying a large couch, still wrapped in plastic, across the lawn in back of her building towards Maple Street. Half a dozen little kids—five to ten years old—are struggling to carry a matching lounge chair that is also wrapped in plastic. From the doorways and windows, women and girls watch as the police waddle by with the furniture.

When I return to Tina's apartment, Marielena has already returned and made her report. I say to Frankie, "It was a furniture truck?"

FRANKIE: Yeah. It was sitting right there, and it was Guillermo's fault anyway that I was involved.

GUILLERMO: Naw.

FRANKIE: They just left it right there on the street. And we kept looking at it and no one was around or watching it or anything.

DOHAN: An eighteen wheeler?

FRANKIE: No, a smaller one.

DOHAN: No lock on it or anything?

GUILLERMO: Not even. It was completely open. So I just looked in there and it was all full of couches and shit so we just started unloading it. And then they came real fast.[12]

FRANKIE: What were they doing over there? They still picking up the furniture?

DOHAN: I saw them carrying a couch. A bunch of little kids were running around and playing.

FRANKIE: They weren't knocking on doors or anything like that?

DOHAN: I just saw them carrying a couch.

TINA: You guys are stupid.[13] Guillermo, you just got out and they're going to send you back in again for that.

Frankie is still working the phones. He is concerned that the cops are going to knock on his mom's door or on his sister's door. He and Guillermo are too nervous to leave Tina's apartment. Frankie suggests that he and I trade shirts so that he won't be recognized, and Tina says that they should just take off their top shirts and go with their undershirts. Neither is willing to take this suggestion. They sit and wait. Pablo, a forty-five-year-old friend of Tina's, comes into the living room.

FRANKIE: Are the cops still out there?

PABLO: What did you guys do?

GUILLERMO: We were just unloading a truck.

PABLO: That's great, man. That's real smart *ese*. You know what that is? That's commercial burglary, and that will get you seven or eight years in the penitentiary.[14] Think about that. Is that what you want to be doing with yourself?

FRANKIE: It was Guillermo's idea.

PABLO: So you're going to do everything this guy does? If it's stupid? Man, you got to start thinking for yourself. And what were you thinking, Guillermo? You just got out. How come you're not at work now?

GUILLERMO: I had a job, but I quit it. They put me on as a temporary worker, right? And they promised me that after a month or so, they'd make me permanent. But I was in that job for six months, and they never took me off temporary status. So I just quit.[15]

Pablo looks disgusted and leaves the room, and Frankie and Guillermo turn to trying to figure out who snitched on them. They eliminate a number of possibilities. The security people from the nearby businesses won't snitch because they know that they have to get along with the people from the projects or their lives will be miserable. They mention the guard at one food-processing plant who made a deal with Elm Street. He gives the guys free food on his shift, and he told them that he doesn't care what goes on except for at his plant on his shift. As long as his business isn't involved, they know he won't make trouble for anyone. They wonder if one of the people from the projects called, and they worry that the little kids might snitch on them because the kids don't know enough to keep their mouths shut.

After a couple hours Frankie and Guillermo risk leaving Tina's apartment. They walk off toward the store—the opposite direction from where they "unloaded" the truck.

Like Frankie and Guillermo, who said they were just "unloading a truck," many residents in Chávez appeared to stumble into illicit activities or welfare participation. Some Chávez high schoolers supplied marijuana to friends who lived in neighborhoods where the drug was not easily available, and these social relationships seemed to transform of their own accord into an economic exchange. Electronic equipment, building supplies, and toys that some residents "came across" in nearby stores, at the workplace, and through charitable organizations were available for purchase on street corners throughout the barrio. The hodgepodge of items that Chávez residents sold to each other—bicycles, car parts, class rings, gardening equipment, gold chains, pagers, shampoo, socks, telephones, and an all-terrain vehicle—created the impression that the barrio as a whole had "stumbled" into hustling. Hustling in the welfare economy had a similar haphazard feel. Residents traded transferable forms of public assistance—a frozen turkey, baby clothes, and food stamps that "just happened" to be unneeded at the moment. This impression of "stumbling" suggested that it was only "natural" to participate in illicit or welfare activities. They appeared nearly impossible to avoid.

At the same time—just as Frankie and Guillermo scouted the scene, settled on a plan of action to "unload the truck," and were surprised that their activities attracted immediate police attention—closer inspection contradicted the impression that adults "stumbled" into hustling unawares. For the most part, participation in the illicit and welfare economies came after an active consideration of a variety of economic options. It could hardly be otherwise because residents regularly reminded each other of the drawbacks of earning without laboring. They reminded each other that illicit markets were illegal and that welfare offended community norms. They reminded each other that apprehension and severe consequences could follow from illegal activities, and they reminded each other that participating in aid programs was shameful and wrong.

The combination of "stumbling," on the one hand, and planning and reminding, on the other, lent hustling a dual character. There was a market for the gains won through illicit or welfare activities. Markets set the price for stolen goods, and supply and demand in the local market governed exchange. If some Chávez residents rebuffed welfare, few refused to trade or exchange with welfare participants. From the perspective of the market, hustling was simply a way to make money. But Chávez residents also believed and reminded each other that illicit and welfare earnings were different from earnings from a job. The social dynamics surrounding hustling reminded residents that illicit activities were illegal and that participation in welfare was wrong.

For some residents in Chávez, the dual character of hustling disappeared. Residents with few opportunities in legal jobs had a difficult time sustaining the appearance of "stumbling" into illicit or welfare activities. Everyone in Chávez knew that substance-dependent residents panhandled, pilfered, and prostituted to secure alcohol, cocaine, or heroin. Everyone knew mothers who depended on public aid because their companions had died, been imprisoned, or abandoned the family. In contrast, residents in stable legal jobs saw little need to risk hustling. As one stably employed resident watched the police frisk several young men, he remarked, "I just go to my job and come home. . . . That [the scene between the police and young men] is something between them. I don't need to get involved in that." There were residents in Chávez for whom the illicit and welfare economies were a necessity of life, and there were others for whom these economies were irrelevant.

But most of the Chávez residents I knew did not fall into either of these extremes of necessity and irrelevance. They sought to balance opportunity and risk in strategies of hustling oriented toward acquiring items that were otherwise unobtainable. On the day described above, "unloading the truck" struck the balance between opportunity and risk for Frankie and Guillermo. The day after "unloading the truck," Frankie delightedly reported that one item had gone undetected by the police; his mother now had a new couch in her living room. Young Chávez residents converted profits from drug sales and car theft into expensive warm-up jackets, designer jeans, elaborate hairstyles, and silk blouses; with these purchases, young residents used hustling to establish the fashion sensibilities in Chávez. Their material possessions were signs of success—just as they are in most communities in the United States. But in the low-income barrios, residents frequently relied on illicit or welfare income to provide the marginal income that made the purchase of these material signs of success possible.

Hustling also played a role in obtaining the most important success in Chávez—getting out of the projects altogether. For Tricia, the young woman I described earlier who was looking forward to ending her reliance on welfare, hustling meant using her aid check to support her plans to move into private housing with her boyfriend. Until she was securely out of the projects, Tricia continued to participate in welfare as a way to ensure that her income remained as high as possible. Tricia was like most Chávez residents I knew in that she sought substantial advancement through respectable work but saw welfare as a reasonable means to that ultimate end. In a similar fashion, Chávez residents excluded from the labor market due to their age turned to drug selling as a way to secure some limited income. One young man related that when his mother succumbed to crack addiction in his freshman and sophomore years of high school, he had supported himself by selling marijuana on campus. As he neared high school graduation in 1995, he looked back on drug selling as the crucial factor that had allowed him to complete high school. Without the drug selling, he believed, he would not have had the chance to finish high school, get a job, and get himself out of the projects.

Residents further along in the life course also knew how to hustle. "Las Señoras," a group of older Chávez women, occupied an honored position in the community, and among the privileges accorded them was the right to be first in line at the community food bank. By entering the food bank first, the ladies were sure to get the best bags of groceries with the freshest and most desirable items. Once through the food bank line, the ladies traded on the social honor that provided them the best groceries in economic transactions. For some the grocery riches were one element in larger familial economic strategies, others sold the most desirable items to those further back in line, and still others hoarded their windfall in anticipation of times of scarcity in the future.

Hustling was a balancing act that required taking advantage of available opportunities without "messing up" and suffering severe consequences. The income earned outside the wage labor market had to be balanced with the risks of addiction, injury, incarceration, and ostracism that could accompany participation in the illicit and welfare economies. Everyday life in Chávez provided constant reminders of these risks. Every few weeks, new residents appeared on the streets of Chávez following their release from juvenile detention, jail, or prison. The alcoholics who asked for spare change as they passed around bottles of beer near the *tienda* and the squatters who spent all their cash on heroin reminded residents of the toll of substance abuse. It seemed that every household in Chávez had lost family members to violence associated with illegal activities. In 1995, some parents were called to the hospital or police station multiple times to attend to sons who had been shot in altercations over gang turf or picked up while working at the hot spot where drugs were bought and sold in Chávez.

Chávez residents who did find the balance could use hustling in a purposeful way to augment income. Charlie, a twenty-three-year-old lifelong

Chávez resident, exemplified this purposeful balance. On the night I first met Charlie, he drove up to the Chávez gym in a sports car and stepped out wearing a pristine Starter warm-up jacket and Nike sneakers—symbols of material success that most residents understood to be an artifact of drug sales. He instructed a young man standing near him to pick up a case of Budweiser for everyone's enjoyment, and he peeled a bill from a thick roll to finance the purchase. I soon learned that Charlie dated Nina, a woman many Chávez men found extremely attractive. Nina had one child with Charlie, and she was living with her family and supporting the child through public assistance. Nina was pregnant again, and the couple planned to marry at about the same time that Nina bore their second child. Charlie had never been arrested or been to jail, and he had only once suffered a substantial injury as a result of his activities in the illicit economy. He sold illicit drugs cautiously. Several weeks after buying the beer in the gym, he stood in the parking lot of Chávez nearest his apartment and politely refused to sell to one of his regular customers. "Too many *hoota* [police]," he said, waving the man off. "I don't have anything. Check with Topper." Charlie's caution in the illicit economy was due in part to the quality of his day job. After many years working in construction, in 1995 Charlie got his union card. He told me the news one morning late in 1995 when I bumped into him and Nina having breakfast at a restaurant a few miles from Chávez. Charlie was deep in the territory of a rival gang, so the topic of his impending retirement from "the life" came up naturally in the course of our conversation. With a better job, he explained, he could afford to slow down on the drug sales. Nina would shortly be coming off welfare as well. They could take fewer risks and endure less stigma and still buy the things they wanted: cars and clothes, a standard of living consistent with their status, and private housing outside Chávez.

Chávez residents relied on wage labor to make ends meet, and nearly all Chávez residents had worked in low-wage jobs at some point in their lifetimes. At the same time, everyday life in the Chávez community provided predictable opportunities to engage in illicit or welfare activities, and the residents of Chávez barrio regularly took advantage of these opportunities to increase their income. For the most part Chávez residents were not forced into illicit and welfare activities by desperate need, but at the same time few residents were so economically comfortable that they could afford to ignore opportunities to augment their income. Thus, most of the Chávez residents I knew hustled even while they remained acutely aware of the drawbacks of participating in the illicit and welfare economies. Their economic strategy was a daily balancing act.

Hustling took its character from the social context of everyday interactions in the housing projects. Everyday interactions within the community affirmed that clothing, cars, and other material possessions were relevant signs of success and that moving out of the projects and into private housing was success's lasting measure. Local interactions provided meaningful lessons about the opportunities and risks that different kinds of hustling afforded. Project residents sought to balance different kinds of opportunities and risks. On the one hand, they wanted to obtain the signs of success that make them comfortable within their community; on the other hand, available avenues to comfort were fraught with risks to respectability and life chances.

### Overwork in Guadalupe

In Guadalupe barrio, wage labor was essentially the only way that residents supported themselves. Compared to hustling, which involves multiple income sources, Guadalupe's reliance on wage labor appears less in need of analysis, explanation, and understanding. Jobs provide income for the vast majority of Americans, and there is a normative expectation that Americans will turn to the labor market to meet their economic needs. The intense activity in low-wage jobs in Guadalupe—the strategy of overwork—appears to be the "natural" local expression of a broad societal norm.

This "natural" explanation becomes less satisfying, however, as we narrow our analytical focus from the broad context of American society to the local context in which Guadalupe residents actually lived their lives. In Guadalupe, low-wage jobs more predictably created problems and conundrums than opportunity and advancement. Low wages provided meager purchasing power, conditions at work were generally unpleasant and sometimes dangerous, and residents often found themselves hopelessly confined to low-status jobs. In this context, the strategy of overwork was more than simply the local expression of a societal norm; it was something remarkable and "unnatural" that requires explanation and understanding.

In Guadalupe barrio, a remarkable "local" context created by neighborhood social institutions sustained overwork. What was remarkable about the "local" context of Guadalupe was that it encompassed communities thousands of miles away from California. Everyday life revolved around events not only in San Jose but also in the barrios of Mexico City and Guadalajara and in the *ranchos* of Michoacán. Everyday activities such as sending remittances to family abroad, planning for future trips to Mexico to visit family and friends, and reminiscing about past times before migrating to San Jose created transnational connections between Guadalupe and communities abroad.[16] These activities made up the "local" social institutions that sustained the strategy of overwork by addressing three dilemmas of low-wage laboring: the paltry buying power of low wages, the difficult daily routine of working in inhospitable conditions, and the frustrations of confinement to low-status jobs with few prospects for advancement.

Remittances sent to family and communities abroad play an important role in the economic life of immigrant communities.[17] Guadalupe barrio was no exception. Many single men who came to Guadalupe sent much of their earnings back to family who remained in Mexico. Gabriel, the street-smart resident discussed above, sent earnings to family in Sonora to improve their house and to buy land for Gabriel's planned computer business. Twenty-nine-year-old Luis had accumulated a nest egg and business acumen in his years in San Jose. He planned to use the former to buy and the latter to modernize the small packaging business where he had worked in Oaxaca prior to migrating. Other Guadalupe residents sent money to Mexico to support future retirement. One day at a local church that offered adult education, students practiced their English by concocting stories to go along with magazine photographs. Prudentia, in her late twenties, was part of a group that looked at a photograph of a rural field scene—a horse bent to sip water from a small pond foregrounding rolling green hills and scattered trees. Prudentia abandoned her English. "*Ay, qué lindo.* It looks just like the *rancho* in Jalisco. We used to go down to a pond just like that when we were little. We'd swim there every day. That is the kind of place José and I are getting. . . . We almost have enough to buy the land now. Then we just need to save enough to build the house and maybe get some horses. When Rosa and Junior are done with school, we'll go back down there."

Everyday life in Guadalupe was colored by the experiences and plans of people like Gabriel, Luis, and Prudentia. The low wages of the San Jose labor market supported family, fueled investment, and laid the groundwork for future leisure. In this way, transnationality increased the value of the dollar. Social network connections to Mexico gave the dollar a value in Guadalupe that it did not have in Chávez, where dollars were earned and spent exclusively in the United States. Transnational existence thus addressed the first problem of low-wage laboring, the paltry earnings available on the local labor market. In contrast to the economic impotence of low wages in mononational communities, the value of the dollar conferred by transnationality made low wages economically sensible to many residents of immigrant communities.

Transnationality increased the value of the dollar in Guadalupe, but the transnational dollar was a double-edged sword. Transnational connections provided destinations for remittances, but they also made demands on resources.[18] The experiences of Prudentia's husband Fernando Senior, at age thirty-three a relatively prosperous worker in Guadalupe, illustrated the two edges of transnationality. Over the course of several years, Fernando had worked his way into a supervisor's position at a small manufacturing company located about twenty miles south of Guadalupe barrio.[19] Several weeks after Prudentia shared her dream of *rancho*-based retirement in Jalisco, Fernando discussed the burdens of transnational existence. The occasion was a party the couple hosted for about twenty family members and friends in their small two-bedroom apartment. It was early Sunday morning, hours after the conclusion of the pay-per-view boxing match that had motivated the gathering, and Fernando and I were saying good night.

"Remember that our door is always open," Fernando told me as we stood on the sidewalk outside the apartment complex. "I hope that you feel *confianza* with me and my family. You should come over whenever you want—relax, have something to eat, enjoy yourself in our company."

I told him thank you and that I would do that, and he continued.

"I hope we can remain friends. Because the thing is that I sometimes feel alone here. There are not a lot of people around here to be friends with."

"But all the people at the party tonight . . ."

"No, no. Chuco, Jaime, Berto, Gloria, all of them—they are all Prudentia's family. I can't really have *confianza* with them, do you understand? It is hard because I have lived here now for seven years, but we're still in this little apartment. Every time we get some money to move into a house of our own, maybe in a nicer neighborhood, what happens instead is that more of her family arrives. Her sister lived downstairs with us for a long time before they moved upstairs. And now we have her cousin and her two brothers staying with us. It's too many. There are all these people here, but I still feel alone in San Jose."

Fernando's comments reveal both sides of the relationship between transnational networks and the value of earnings in low-wage jobs. Remittance sending to Mexico increases the value of low wages in immigrant communities like Guadalupe relative to U.S.-based communities such as Chávez. Transnational networks also create new demands on those earnings, however. Residents spent months or years sending remittances to improve property in sending communities, to assemble a nest egg, and to bring family to the United States. At the same time, the value of low wages could diminish as immigrants tired of sacrificing to send remittances, as the burden of obligations to children and family in the United States increased, as they became more attuned to signs of material success in the United States, and as they were increasingly expected to acquire domestic signs of prosperity. In any case, the transnational community failed in important respects to reproduce social features of the sending community. In terms of social support, residents did not find that it compared well to the social environment they left behind in Mexico. Fernando's situation—his enjoyment of the initial fruits of economic advancement, the increasing burdens of advancement over time, and his persistent loneliness—illustrated these dynamics.

To visitors, immigrant communities in the United States sometimes feel like a transplanted piece of a foreign country.[20] But, as Fernando's loneliness testifies, these communities could fail to bridge the distance separating residents from their communities of origin. For this reason, among the residents I knew in Guadalupe, there was no substitute for travel, the best bridge between the United States and Mexico.

Every few days in Guadalupe, residents spoke of trips they had taken, trips coming up, or trips being planned for a more distant future. Gabriel left San Jose for ten days in April to check on the progress of his land investments; my landlady Gloria left for El Salvador in June carrying six suitcases of presents and returned two weeks later equally burdened with gifts for family, friends, and compatriots in San Jose; thirty-three-year-old Eustancia packed her husband and four children into a station wagon for a four-week driving excursion to see relatives in northern Mexico. The details of each trip depended on who was going and the primary reason for the visit. No matter the specific reason, however, trips abroad played an important role in the strategy of overwork. These trips addressed the second difficulty of local labor markets by providing a respite from the daily grind of everyday life in low-wage jobs.

In late May 1994, several consecutive hundred-hour workweeks at multiple jobs had taken their toll on Jesús Martinez, whom I introduced in Chapter 3. He was exhausted and frustrated. The final straw nearly came the morning Jesús was scheduled to obtain his California driver's license. Jesús had a 8:00 a.m. appointment to take the test at the Department of Motor Vehicles (DMV). He had not arrived home from work

until nearly 2:00 a.m. the previous night, and his wife María had a difficult time rousing him for his DMV appointment. Then, just as Jesús was
leaving the apartment, one of the fast-food restaurants where he worked
called up and asked him to fill in on a day shift starting at 10 a.m. Jesús
reluctantly agreed. Finally, during the driving test, Jesús turned the
wrong way on a one-way street and the examiner failed him.

> "I think I'll pass it next time," he said afterwards. "I didn't know what they
> wanted so I was a little nervous, and I was half asleep. I'm sure I'll pass it next
> time. But I don't know. I'm thinking maybe I'll go to Mexico for a while. I was
> planning to wait until Christmas and go back with María, but I don't know
> now. I feel like I need a rest now."

Visits to Mexico were an opportunity to see family and friends, to
check on investments and home improvements, and to rest from the
grind of daily work. Visits to Mexico also meant crossing the Mexico-
U.S. border. Some Guadalupe residents found the border crossing imma-
terial. Discussing her family's upcoming trip, Eustancia dismissed
potential problems with immigration officials. "I go to visit family at
least two times a year, and I never have trouble at the border. I am in a
station wagon with my husband and all my children in the back; they
don't bother us." Other Guadalupe residents, however, experienced
hardship at the border. In particular, the border created predictable difficulties for undocumented residents of Guadalupe. Some paid *coyotes* to
guide them while others crossed the border with just a suitcase or two in
order to avoid the appearance of coming to the United States for an
extended stay. The border could cause material difficulties for documented residents as well. Such was the case for Ricardo, a forty-five-year-
old janitor who grew up in Mexico City. When he came to Guadalupe in
1992 on the heels of a new marriage, his teenaged son from a previous
marriage remained in Mexico City. In August, 1993, Ricardo took two
weeks leave from his janitor's job to return to Mexico City and bring his
son north. INS refused to let his son enter the United States, however,
and Ricardo had to return the boy to Mexico City. When Ricardo came
back to San Jose four weeks later, he had lost his job.

The experience of migration—leaving an established community, a
long journey and often difficult border crossing, loneliness in a new
community—facilitated Guadalupe residents' embrace of overwork.
Migration gave residents the experience of movement and mobility, and
these experiences counterbalanced the third problem of local labor markets: the feeling of being stuck in a dead-end job. Remembering and

reminiscing about times past gave Guadalupe residents the feeling of movement and mobility.

An example of this occurred in the Mendoza household one June afternoon after Jesús's work schedule had become less all-consuming. Jesús sat with his eighteen-year-old step-son José and twenty-two-year-old brother-in-law Esteban watching a VCR recording of a cousin's *quinceañera* held in Mexico City two years earlier. The three men commented excitedly about the guests and costumes at the party. At one point in the party, Esteban performed a song dressed as Elvis Presley, and the men's laughter brought María and Rosa into the living room from the back bedroom. The family spent more than an hour reminiscing about the event, identifying the guests to each other and to me, and commenting on the current status of many of the guests.

A few weeks later, the subject of the *quinceañera* guests came up again, this time in a conversation with José. The conversation illustrated the relationship between the experience of international migration and the experience of economic mobility. José had come to San Jose without documents in October 1993, and he began working alongside his mother at a food-packaging company outside San Jose. He earned minimum wage filling in on the assembly line and shrink-wrapping shipping pallets. During slow periods he was sent home before the end of his eight-hour shift. José was frustrated by his irregular hours at the packing company, and he eventually obtained a forged social security card in hopes of moving into a delivery position that provided steadier hours if not higher wages. Toward the end of August 1994, José said he was thinking about making a visit to Mexico to see friends and family, but he said he would have to get more serious about his efforts to learn English.

"When I go back to visit my friends in Mexico, they're going to want to know all about what things are like here. I'll tell them about living here and the work and everything like that. I'll bring some presents. . . . But they'll want to see that I know English. I'll look like a fool if I come back and don't know English after being here for a year. So, I have to learn better English before I go back."

Guadalupe residents such as José felt the expectations of friends and family who remained in Mexico. Family in Mexico expected the remittances and the gifts that U.S. dollars bought, and they also expected stories and worldly knowledge. Low-wage jobs provided the means to send remittances and gifts; they were seen by Guadalupe's immigrants as economically potent. Reminiscing about the past helped combat the daily grind of low-wage work; thinking about the stories that could be told and the worldliness that could be demonstrated also helped. Recalling the setbacks of a difficult trip north or watching a video filled with family still in Mexico underlined the fact that residence and employment in San Jose represented some amount of mobility, no matter what the particulars of living situation or job.

With time and settlement, however, a roof over one's head and holding a job would fail to be sufficient. The experiences of Rogelio, as discussed above, testify to this. The strategy of overwork prevailed in Guadalupe because most residents saw that even a low-wage job had significant value and worth. If individual residents were not entirely satisfied with the daily grind of low-wage work—and few individual residents were—continual reminders of past difficulties in Mexico and on the journey north, continual connections to Mexico through remittances, and continual reinforcement of future expectations nevertheless made commitment to the labor market seem a reasonable way to make ends meet.

## ECONOMIC STRATEGIES AND BARRIO SOCIAL LIFE

Hustling and overwork describe the different economic strategies that linked residents of Chávez and Guadalupe to local labor markets. To understand the nature, causes, and consequences of these strategies, the last three chapters have examined conditions in low-wage labor markets in Los Angeles and San Jose as well as the meaning of work in the social life of Chávez and Guadalupe.

It is important to note, first of all, what hustling and overwork *do not* reflect. During and after two years of fieldwork in Chávez and Guadalupe, I was never able to convince myself that differences in these two barrios' structural circumstances or cultural orientations led to these markedly different strategies. Chávez residents did not turn to hustling in response to a collapse of the labor market or a corrupted work ethic, nor did widely available jobs or an unhealthy attachment to working lure Guadalupe residents into overwork. As I reviewed in Chapters 3 and 4, structural and cultural conditions on the low-wage labor market in the two barrios were, in the main, quite similar. In both communities, the residents with whom I spent time regularly found and kept low-wage jobs but had more difficulty locating better-quality jobs; residents in both barrios generally affirmed the value and legitimacy of wage labor. The puzzle is: How, despite these similarities, did residents of the two barrios come to embrace quite different everyday routines and connections to local jobs?

To understand hustling in Chávez and overwork in Guadalupe, I have used this chapter to look beyond and contextualize the unemployment rate and the work ethic. Hustling and overwork accommodated similarities in structural circumstances and cultural orientations in dynamic and creative ways that reflected differences in the meaning of work and the meaning of low wages in the social life of Chávez and Guadalupe. Low-wage working in the two barrios unfolded within quite different institutional circumstances in the two barrios, with Chávez residents laboring within the confines of local and Guadalupe residents laboring according to transnational definitions of success and prosperity. In short, residents of the two barrios embraced different measures of success. *How* barrio residents worked thus reflected not just local opportunities for jobs and orientations toward work but also the actively constructed meaning of work's rewards.

Poor people often must make ends meet in inhospitable structural-economic circumstances. Low wages entice some to intensify their efforts on the labor market; they cause others to turn to illegal activities and public assistance. Patterns of wage labor in Guadalupe and Chávez show that different responses to limited opportunity do not necessarily reflect differences in individual-level orientations toward work. Legal work, illegal activities, and public assistance inevitably are part of larger strategies for making ends meet. These strategies, in turn, depend more on the public culture of communities than on the private values and norms within individuals' heads. Within the public culture of transnational Guadalupe barrio, a strategy of intense devotion to wage labor—a strategy of overwork—made sense. Within the public culture of U.S.-based Chávez barrio, strategies that combined legal, illegal, and welfare earnings—a strategy of hustling—were a more reasonable path to success. What distinguished the barrios was not the inhospitable structural-economic circumstances they faced or the values and norms to which residents maintained allegiance. It was, rather, the factors shaping community definitions of economic success, how residents communicated this meaning to each other, and how residents combined their own know-how with available resources to develop an economic strategy that offered some chance of attaining that success.

In this sense, hustling and overwork describe broad sensibilities—distinct sets of meanings and practices that characterized income generation in each barrio.[21] These economic strategies served as a social umbrella beneath which other kinds of income-generating activities took place. The barrio residents I knew and spent time with participated in crime and public aid not simply to oppose or reject the low-wage labor market but rather as part of making sense of job opportunities. Thus, connections to the labor market colored residents' participation in crime and welfare.

Economic strategies such as hustling or overwork are often referred to as "survival strategies," but this phrase misleads in Chávez and Guadalupe.[22] *Survival* suggests an economic life oriented toward obtaining basic necessities—food in mouths, clothes on backs, and shelter over heads. There were times when survival was at stake for residents in both barrios. On some days people went hungry, and residents spent some nights in shelters or on the streets. The violence of everyday life—an issue of particular concern for Chávez residents—also meant that barrio residents rarely took survival for granted. As one Chávez resident acknowledged at a party celebrating his thirtieth birthday, "You know, I'm just really grateful to have lived this long. I know a lot of people who didn't make it to their thirtieth birthday." But even as we recognize that survival can be a pressing issue for residents in the barrios—as it can be in all low-income communities—it is also important to note that most residents I knew in Guadalupe and Chávez focused their economic activities on the problem of advancement.

As applied to contemporary urban low-income areas in the United States, researchers and residents often use *survival* metaphorically to reference the salience of economic deprivation in everyday life. But we must be careful not to invoke the survival metaphor too quickly. Compared to the impoverished people in some societies, poor people in the contemporary United States more rarely confront the actual problem of survival.[23] Even when we restrict our view to the contemporary poor of the United States, invoking the metaphor of survival can hide actual differences in the degree of deprivation in different low-income areas. Quantitative measures show that deprivation is more extreme in some communities, such as urban ghettos populated by African Americans or rural reservations populated by Native Americans, than in others, such as areas populated by whites or Asian Americans.[24] Within low-income communities, individual experiences of deprivation also vary considerably.[25] *Survival* is a not just a powerful metaphor for economic struggle; depending on the time and place, it is also a literal reality of deprivation. Invoking the term selectively helps acknowledge this variety.

The term *survival strategy*—with its connotations of entrapped struggle and forced response to necessity—is particularly inappropriate in Guadalupe and Chávez barrios, where contingency and agency shaped everyday economic and social life. I stress contingency and agency here. Chapter 3 shows that unemployment in Guadalupe and Chávez reflects not an automatic response to structural opportunities in local labor markets but also residents' active consideration of the particular jobs that are open, their understanding of what kind of job will help them attain economic goals, and their assessment of the chances that better jobs might be available in the future if they are not available at the moment. Chapter 4 depicts the work ethic as a set of publicly available symbols and practices that residents actively sense, invoke, and manipulate in everyday life rather than as a straightforward behavioral expression of culturally dictated values and norms. The economic strategies of residents of Guadalupe and Chávez reflect contingency and agency no less than the unemployment rate and the work ethic. In embracing advancement strategies, residents of the barrios adopt income-generating activities that inevitably force them to balance uncertainty and risk against personal and variable definitions of success and achievement. They make active decisions about how hard to strive and in which directions, and they constantly assess and reassess their comfort with various kinds and levels of chance taking. To see how strategic action informs and overlays income generation in low-income communities—how overwork and hustling provide an umbrella beneath which poor people made ends meet—we could hardly find a better exemplar than the complex interactions of opportunity, risk, and success facing the low-income Mexican Americans of Guadalupe and Chávez.

# PART III

# Crime

'CRIME' CONNOTES PERSONAL DANGER, DANGEROUS persons, and law-abiding people losing control of their neighborhoods. In low-income areas crime is also an income source, and illegal activities played a conspicuous role in everyday life in both Guadalupe and Chávez. Nearly every day during my barrio fieldwork, I saw residents breaking the law in one way or another in their daily economic rounds. I have just described how wage labor—and the economic strategies of overwork and hustling that framed how residents worked at low-wage jobs—provided the economic foundation of everyday life in the low-income barrios. In the next chapters I examine economic crime, one of the important economic activities that rested upon that foundation. My analysis focuses on how residents of the barrios violated the law, as well as on the role of personal danger, dangerous persons, and loss of control in barrio life more generally.

Overwork and hustling shaped not only how barrio residents earned their hourly wages but also how they broke the law. In Guadalupe, over-working residents participated in the unregulated informal economy, while in Chávez hustling residents more frequently produced and distributed illegal goods and services in the illicit economy. Residents in both communities were aware that their illegal economic activities placed them at risk of apprehension, and understandably this awareness created anxiety among residents in both barrios. In practice, however, illicit work was frequently and aggressively targeted for law enforcement while informal work was not. I noted during fieldwork that these different patterns of suppression coincided with differences in the way residents of Guadalupe and Chávez organized and integrated illegal activities into their everyday economic and social lives. In particular, I observed that the residents I knew shaped the everyday course of barrio crime through their participation in indigenous organizations such as day labor markets, hiring halls, and street gangs. These organizations integrated crime into daily life in Guadalupe and Chávez in different ways by responding to and interacting with local law enforcement officials and with community residents who were not involved in crime. Indigenous organizations, law enforcement, and community created a palpable institutional context within which economic crime worked itself out in the barrios.

In Chapter 2, I showed that patterns of law-breaking differed substantially in Guadalupe and Chávez. In the next two chapters, I explore how these distinct patterns of law-breaking created and reflected the broader institutional context within which barrio crime took place. In Chapter 6, I describe the different kinds of law-breaking that occurred in Guadalupe and Chávez, and I analyze the role of indigenous organizations and law enforcement. Chapter 7 explores the connections between the institutional context surrounding illegal work and social life in Guadalupe and Chávez. I introduce the concepts of "legalizing" and "normalizing" illegal activities to describe the different sensibilities surrounding crime in the two barrios as I examine the complex and contingent relationship between crime and community.

# CHAPTER 6

# Illegal Routines

Moneymaking crosses the line into illegality in two ways. Some economic activities are illegal because they involve goods, services, or activities that are prohibited. As long as marijuana is outlawed, selling the drug is illegal, and robbery requires prohibited forms of coercion. Marijuana selling and robbery—which involve prohibited goods and activities—are part of the *illicit economy.* Other economic activities, in contrast, are illegal because the legal goods, services, or activities they involve are *produced* through illegal means. It is illegal to assemble cloth into dresses if the sewing machine operators do not have permission to work in the United States; serving food is legal only when restaurants comply with local health regulations; CD vendors must have proper permits to sell their wares on the sidewalk. Sweatshops, unsanitary restaurants, and unlicensed street vending—all of which involve licit goods but illegal processes—are part of the *informal economy.*[1]

Not a day passed in either Chávez or Guadalupe without some illegal moneymaking. In Chávez, residents sold illicit drugs on the sidewalk, stripped parts off cars in parking lots, and peddled stolen merchandise door to door. These illicit activities did not dominate the economy of Chávez, but their presence was unmistakable in day-to-day life. In Guadalupe, undocumented immigrants maintained office buildings as janitors and gardeners; provided day care for elders and children; and prepared food in canneries and in restaurant kitchens. Informal mechanics repaired cars in backyards; informal vendors sold burritos off the back of bicycles; informal day laborers waited on street corners to exchange work for cash. These routine informal activities permeated daily life in Guadalupe.

The law differentiates between economic activities that are legal, those that are informal, and those that are illicit. This chapter shows how these legal differences affected routine illegal work in the low-income barrios. Differences in law, by themselves, did not create differences in routine illegal work. The institutions and organizations that enforced the law along with those that defied it created the daily lives of informal workers in Guadalupe and of illicit workers in Chávez. Law-enforcing and law-defying organizations converted the theoretical differences between legal, informal, and illicit work into practical differences in everyday life. To explain the place of illegal work in the low-income barrios, I start with a description of the organizations that patterned informal work in Guadalupe and illicit work in Chávez.

INFORMAL WORK IN GUADALUPE

In Guadalupe, where 40 percent of the working residents I knew lacked proper documents (see Chapter 2), it was often hard to distinguish informal from legal workers. Undocumented immigrants lived and worked side by side with legal residents; only the papers in their pockets or, occasionally, the exact position they held—in restaurant work, for example, undocumented workers seemed to work in less visible positions like dishwasher or table busser rather than as waiters—distinguished undocumented from legal. For many Silicon Valley employers, regulations governing worker documentation appeared to pose little barrier to hiring the undocumented. Many Guadalupe residents I knew said that they found work without presenting any documents at all. Others showed me forged social security cards or other documents that employers readily accepted. Some of these crude forgeries could not possibly have fooled any truly vigilant employer.

The fact that so many employers in the Silicon Valley winked at the law eliminated one potentially formidable barrier facing the undocumented, but other barriers remained. Guadalupe residents seeking to join the informal economy had to find an employer. Many firms hired workers who lacked documents or presented obvious forgeries, but no firm publicly advertised its participation in the informal economy. And employers' willingness to facilitate and condone law-breaking did not extend to law enforcement agencies, the Immigration and Naturalization

Service (INS), and other agencies collectively known as *la migra,* charged
with upholding the laws that regulated economic production. Guadalupe
residents first met *la migra* crossing the border into the United States, and
the threat of *migra* discovery, arrest, and deportation hung over daily life
in the informal economy in San Jose. With rare exceptions, undocumented workers I knew in Guadalupe did not approach employers without some advance assurance that the employer was willing to hire the
undocumented.

Two kinds of local institutions helped informal workers overcome
both of these potential barriers. First, Guadalupe residents turned to
family, friends, and neighbors to locate employers interested in hiring the
undocumented and to avoid employers who might call *la migra.* This
information traveled along the same sorts of social networks that I discussed in Chapter 4.[2] In the informal economy, however, these networks
not only provided information about where to find jobs but also helped
residents manage risks associated with illegal work. Two kinds of indigenous organizations also structured informal income generation.[3] Day
labor markets and hiring halls provided the organizational context in
which informal workers met employers, while flea markets and street
vending provided a direct-sales infrastructure to connect informal sales-
people with buyers.

## Social Networks and Informal Work

Guadalupe residents often turned to social networks within their communities for help negotiating hazy distinctions between legal and informal work. Informal workers turned to their network for "inside"
information about potential employers. Was an employer interested in
hiring undocumented workers? Should an undocumented person approach the employer directly? Were fake documents expected? Barrio
compatriots were the only source of the "inside" answers to these crucial
questions. Guadalupe residents turned to their social networks to manage the everyday risks of working illegally as well as at moments of crisis.

Friends and family steered Guadalupe residents to "comfortable" jobs
quickly and easily. Memo was in his late twenties when he arrived in San
Jose in 1992 as part of the migrations of a large extended family between
Michoacán, Mexico City, and the United States. Memo was one of thirteen children, and his older siblings had been moving between Mexico
and the United States for several years before he followed an elder sister
who settled in Guadalupe. He was a shy man with a boyish appearance,

and it seemed self-evident why he had come to San Jose after his sister had settled there rather than participating in his family's circular migrations to and from the city in the late 1980s and early 1990s. While I knew him, Memo spent a lot of time with his nephews and nieces—most at least a half-dozen years younger than him—and it was only after three months of regularly spending time with his extended family that I learned much of his own income generation experiences and orientations.

Memo's shyness seemed to inform how he worked. Along with many other Guadalupe residents, he had structural reasons to be shy on the labor market because lack of work documents meant potential detainment or deportation. Many in Guadalupe sought "secure" jobs where the danger of detection appeared small, and many, including Memo, turned to social networks to help identify and obtain these secure jobs. Both of the jobs Memo held during the spring and summer of 1993 were in fast-food restaurants not far from the Guadalupe barrio. One restaurant, where he worked as a cleanup and general helper, had employed his uncle for some time before Memo came to Guadalupe. The uncle had become frustrated at the lack of hours at the restaurant and had moved to another branch of the chain further from Guadalupe barrio. But Memo remained at the local branch. He started working at the second restaurant when one of his nieces, who also lacked documents but nevertheless worked as a cashier, passed along the news that there was an opening for a part-time cook's assistant. "Just go and tell them I told you about the job, and if they ask for a *socio* [social security card], tell them you'll bring it next time," instructed his niece. "They won't ask again."

During busy weeks Memo worked only about thirty hours, and he earned little from the minimum wage at both positions. Still, these low-paying jobs offered comfort and security. By following relatives into both work sites, Memo found employers willing to hire the undocumented. His uncle and niece helped him apply for each job. At both restaurants, he worked in back rooms, out of public sight and surrounded by other undocumented workers. Everyone spoke Spanish, and he could relax in the knowledge that these restaurants had employed undocumented workers for many years without problems. For Memo and other informal workers, social networks provided valuable information to minimize risk.

Social networks also helped distribute the risks of illegal work among informal and legal workers in the same household. Informal workers took greater and lesser risks depending on their ability to share resources with family and their responsibilities to provide assistance to others. The experiences of Don Rodríguez, a sixty-five-year-old undocumented migrant liv-

ing near Guadalupe barrio, provide a typical example of how family networks allow individuals to select income-generating activities that protect
them from the risks of informal work. Don Rodríguez lived with a large
extended family in his daughter's household. His son-in-law and several of
his other relatives by marriage supported the household by working jobs
typical of those in the low-wage service sector. Don Rodríguez worked in
the informal economy, usually in odd jobs as a laborer or gardener, but he
was selective in the kinds of work he took on. In Guadalupe barrio's hiring
hall, where employers looking for casual labor found workers looking for
work, Don Rodríguez turned down some jobs that he found too risky.

This afternoon, four positions come up for landscape work for a commercial
firm near one of the heavily immigrant barrios north of Guadalupe. Two of the
slots are quickly filled, but the remaining two remain open. Don Rodríguez is
one of the few men in the hiring hall at the time, and the job coordinator knows
that he has taken gardening work in the past.
"Don Rodríguez," she calls out. "What about you? This is a good job. You
want to work, don't you?"
"Yes, I want to work," Don Rodríguez replies. "But I don't want this job."
Later, Don Rodríguez and I are talking, and I ask if he's feeling okay and is
that why he was not interested in the landscaping job. He says that he's feeling
fine, and that he didn't want the job for other reasons.
"Where that job is, there are too many *migra* over there. I don't want to take
that job because maybe they'll pick me up and send me back to Mexico. . . . I
can wait for a better one. I'm not like these *muchachos* who have to take whatever comes. My daughter takes care of me at home, so I'll go home and come
back tomorrow and maybe there will be something better."

Because of his social support at home, Don Rodríguez felt he could be
more selective in the illegal economy compared to the young men who
had arrived in San Jose without a support system or whose household
depended more centrally on their earnings. Don Rodríguez had not
retired, nor did he seem content to live off the resources provided by his
daughter and son-in-law. He frequently took difficult jobs to contribute
to household finances, to stay active and busy, and because he became
bored at home. At the same time, his position in the family network
allowed him to participate in informal activities in a manner that balanced his desire to contribute to the household with an understandable
interest in avoiding risks of detection and apprehension.

Household networks frequently shaped how aggressively residents
pursued opportunities in the informal economy, while community networks facilitated work routines. Chela was a mother of two who lived
with her husband in a small cottage in the northern corner of Guadalupe

barrio. Her husband was a carpenter's assistant in a job that paid well but inconsistently during the months I knew the family. The family finances depended on the cash Chela earned under the table cleaning private homes. When her husband was busy, Chela worked less and spent more time with her children and as an enthusiastic participant in the English-language classes at the Guadalupe community center, which is where I first met her in the early spring of 1994.

But a few weeks after I met her, Chela began to come by the center less frequently. Work had slowed down for her husband, and she began to spend more time cleaning houses to help the family make ends meet. Unable to afford a car, Chela bicycled to her cleaning assignments, sometimes covering ten miles round-trip. And she frequently brought along her four-year-old daughter in a seat mounted on the back of the bicycle. Chela's legs bore the scrapes of falls, and her self-deprecatingly dramatic tales of close encounters with inattentive motorists could be hilariously hair-raising. Some weeks, she careened on her bicycle from job to job from early morning until late afternoon, but other weeks she found few jobs at all. More than once, she bicycled across town to find no one home at the appointed time or to discover that the key she had been given failed to open the front door. One afternoon she spent hours pushing her daughter and bicycle home after the latter suffered a flat tire.

Chela found jobs from a variety of sources. Before I met her, she cleaned houses with a partner who had a car. But the partnership ended when she began working less in the winter of 1994. Now, as Chela sought more work, the partner provided some referrals. Her friends at the community center also heard about people looking for cleaners and passed on the tips. Chela put some photocopied notices in her backpack and posted them on telephone poles in the middle-class areas she biked through. When her husband found work again later in the spring, Chela became more selective in her domestic work. She passed up far-away jobs and did not follow up tips for jobs with vaguely described duties or from less reliable contacts. She spent more time at the community center socializing and working on her English, and she made a trip to visit family in central California. But when her husband lost his job in the summer, Chela resumed the long bicycle commutes and unpleasant cleaning jobs for several hot weeks in July.

Many households in Guadalupe included individuals with complementary income-generating strategies. Memo's low-risk strategy of working only part time in close-by and well-known restaurants was balanced by his uncle Eduardo's hundred-hour weeks in far-flung establishments.

Don Rodríguez was acutely aware of how his children's earnings facilitated his more selective engagement with informality. Chela moved out of and back in to the informal economy as her husband's fortunes rose and fell. Many households of Guadalupe tended toward these zero-sum income-earning activities. Memos in a family balanced Eduardos; more economic activity or risk taking by one person in the household stemmed from the economic misfortunes of another. In this sense, even if particular individuals drew on network resources to avoid the risks of the informal economy, it was much harder for entire households to do the same.[4]

Household networks in Guadalupe had the beneficial effect of supporting individual efforts in the informal economy. They also had the downside that untoward events such as illness, job loss or, more rarely, deportation could disrupt the lives of everyone in the network.[5] The risks Chela took on her bicycle reflected her husband's misfortunes on the job market. Francisco and his family experienced more extreme consequences. An undocumented worker, Francisco had been in San Jose for about a year and a half along with his wife and two children. His excellent set of fake documents included a driver's license. Driving to his job at an auto repair shop one morning, he lost control of his car and crashed into the median divider of one of the larger throughways of San Jose. The police cited him for a moving violation, and he was required to appear in court in a few weeks to determine what extent of reparations he would be forced to pay for the damage done to city property in the accident.

As his court day approached, Francisco became more and more nervous about his situation. He was afraid that the fake driver's license would be discovered and that he would be imprisoned. Two days before he was due to appear, he decided he could not risk the court appearance and he would have to return to Mexico for a short time to regroup. He sold his stereo system and some other valuable possessions to raise money for the trip and left the next day. His plan was to return after the situation had cooled down and then to obtain new documents.

After his accident and abrupt departure from San Jose, Francisco expected his extended family in and around Guadalupe to step up and help support his wife and children while he was away, and the extended family did its part. Francisco's brothers helped pay the bills at his apartment, and already enmeshed household routines became even more so. When Francisco returned three weeks later, he had lost his job at the auto body shop, but he found a position in a recycling plant. After a few weeks, he had managed to pay back his brothers and the consequences of the auto accident had worked their way through the family.

*Street Corner Day Labor and Hiring Halls*

Many informal-realm workers, especially those who were recent arrivals to Guadalupe barrio and those with less well-developed social networks, turned to day labor markets and hiring halls, the two most active hiring organizations in Guadalupe during my fieldwork. Street corner day labor markets and hiring halls connected workers and employers in no-questions-asked arrangements. Some of these arrangements led to long-term employment, but many employers were looking for temporary help or labor for one specific job. For undocumented workers, these institutions offered a way of earning cash income without incurring much risk of discovery; for other workers in the informal realm, these institutions provided the opportunity to earn some cash in a flexible way without long-term obligation; and for employers, these institutions provided a temporary and flexible workforce.

Street corner day labor markets were scattered throughout San Jose and in other communities in the Silicon Valley.[6] Most of the designated street corners were located near the low-income barrios where recent immigrants lived. These workers often did not have access to a car, and bus fare was not an insignificant expense, so the location of the day labor markets near the low-income barrios meant that many workers could walk to work. Most Guadalupe residents walked to the active day labor market at Strong Road, where workers gathered along several contiguous corners from early morning until midafternoon to find informal jobs in construction, gardening, and building maintenance.

Workers turned to day labor markets at different times. Some used the day labor markets as a way to find work when circumstances kept them from holding a more permanent position. Thus, Antonio, the recent arrival discussed in Chapter 5, first entered the informal economy via the Strong Road day labor market when he arrived in San Jose after migrating from Mexico. Henry, a thirty-year-old documented immigrant who moved to San Jose from Los Angeles, found work through Strong Road for several weeks after he was laid off his job in the legal economy. "I didn't really have to work there," he explained. "I was getting unemployment, and the extra money came in handy because it was tough to support myself and my wife and kid just on unemployment. And it got boring at home—just watching TV all day. So I used to go down to Strong Road just to have something to do." For workers such as Antonio and Henry, the day labor market was a place to go on a temporary basis to find work when other opportunities were not available.

Other workers returned again and again to the day labor markets. For circular migrants, who came to San Jose for only a few months or weeks, the day labor market offered several important advantages. Compared to other informal work, day labor demanded more modest individual investment and social network support. Day laborers could walk to the street corner, where employers would transport them to the work site at the beginning of the workday and from the work site when there was no more work to do. Paid in cash, day laborers did not need any sort of documents to cash checks before making purchases. Spanish was the lingua franca at the day labor street corner, and circular migrants were familiar with the routines of the day labor market from similar institutions in Mexico. Guadalupe barrio was home to quite a few workers who worked at Strong Road day labor as their primary income-generating activity. Eduardo, a twenty-year-old, found a variety of jobs in construction and landscaping during his repeated visits to Strong Road between March and June 1994. Some jobs lasted just a few days, while others kept him busy for two weeks or more. Eduardo also attended school graduations and *quinceañeras* in pursuit of his real ambition—to become a professional photographer. After the high school graduations and proms, Eduardo reassessed his photography business. Day laboring at Strong Road had kept him supplied in film, but he had not made much progress in the photography business. Most of his photographs documented the graduations and parties of family and friends, and he was frustrated that the time, effort, and money he put into producing proof shots rarely led to sales. After running out of money to buy film in June, he decided that instead of returning to Strong Road he would leave Guadalupe barrio for an extended visit with friends and relatives in Mexico.

Many Guadalupe residents felt that Strong Road had become less attractive in recent years. Macario was a twenty-six-year-old migrant to San Jose from Jalisco. When he first arrived in San Jose without documents in the mid-1980s, he had worked at Strong Road, but then he took advantage of amnesty laws for undocumented immigrants to adjust his status. By the time I met him in late 1993, he was working in the formal economy, and he felt that things had gotten more difficult at Strong Road compared to the 1980s. "Back in those days it was okay at Strong Road," he said. "There weren't so many people as there are now. So you could always get some work, and the cops and *migra* didn't bother anyone over there." Other Guadalupe residents agreed with Macario that opportunities at Strong Road had deteriorated. Roberto, Gonzalo, and Jaime were recent arrivals to San Jose who were splitting expenses in one bedroom of a small two-bedroom apartment just a few blocks off of Strong Road. They had been in the United States for only a few months, having crossed the border together and come to San Jose on the advice of friends from home who said that work was easier to find there than in Los Angeles. But upon arriving in San Jose, they had been unable to find work. "We go to the corner every morning, but there isn't much to do these days," said Roberto one afternoon as we sat in their nearly unfurnished apartment. "Do you know of anybody looking for workers? We're willing to do anything. Gonzalo found some janitor work but then they didn't need him any more."

In 1993 and 1994, some local opposition developed to the day labor markets. On some mornings, officers from the San Jose police monitored activities at Strong Road, ensuring that workers did not block the entrances to stores near the day labor markets and occasionally breaking up the games of cards and dice that some day workers used to pass the time. Friends and family of Guadalupe residents reported that other day labor markets nearby had been raided by *la migra,* some undocumented immigrants had been repatriated to Mexico, and some U.S. citizens had been mistakenly detained. Simultaneously, support for the day laborers developed among community groups. Strong Road became the site of a day laborer education center, providing a space indoors where job seekers could sign up for work and employers willing to adhere to preset rules (such as a minimum wage) could recruit workers the center certified as experienced and reliable. While waiting to go out on jobs or on days when work was not available, day laborers at Strong Road could learn English, computers, or garment skills. The center provided limited child care, making the day laborer center a much more attractive place for women than most street corners, which tended to be male-only affairs.

The Strong Road Day Laborer Center moved some way toward transforming day labor street corner into a different kind of informal organization, the hiring hall. There were hiring halls in several low-income barrios in San Jose, including Guadalupe. Many informal workers used hiring halls in the same ways as day labor markets, but hiring halls were less conspicuous than their outdoor counterparts. Hiring hall staff mediated contact between employer and employees. Workers at the hiring halls were interviewed and given job leads that had been called in to the hall by employers seeking workers. Typical employers at the hiring hall serving many Guadalupe workers included restaurants and private homeowners looking for gardeners, home health workers, domestics, or child care workers.

Less conspicuous and more bureaucratic, hiring halls attracted fewer green arrivals and more undocumented immigrants with some experience in the San Jose labor market. Because the jobs they offered were less likely to involve hard labor, because they seemed safer than the outdoor day labor markets, and because they were less oriented toward providing work for circular migrants, hiring halls had more women applicants and workers. In Guadalupe, the hiring hall run by volunteers from a variety of Catholic and Protestant churches was the largest and most active in the area. In contrast to the seven-mornings-a-week operation of the day labor market, the hiring hall was open during regular business hours— 10:00 to 4:00 Monday through Friday.

Elena's experience at the Guadalupe hiring hall were typical. A two-year resident of San Jose, the twenty-eight-year-old Elena had moved north from Mexico City with her husband Enrique and their eight- and ten-year-old children. Enrique spent an hour a day commuting to jobs at two restaurants, and this left Elena home alone for most of the day. For most of her residence in San Jose, Enrique had prohibited Elena from working outside the home, but Elena argued that the family could use the extra money and that she was bored at home. Most of her U.S.-based family had settled in Chicago, and Elena felt isolated in Guadalupe. Once Enrique relented in his insistence that Elena stay home, she began coming to the Guadalupe hiring hall in search of child care jobs. After a few months of coming to the hiring hall, Elena had become more particular about the kinds of jobs she would take. She was happy to take child care jobs located close to Guadalupe whose employers paid the going rate of $100 to $130 for a six-day week of full-time child care. But she was also willing to walk away from a job that fell short of her expectations. After only two days, she left one child care arrangement she had found through the hiring hall. "That woman was crazy," she said. "She had twins, three months old, and a three-year-old. And she said they could *never* be left alone. I couldn't go to the store or anything. That's crazy! How can someone take care of children like that, without relief or help or a break of any kind?" Elena found a more reasonable child care position through the hiring hall only a few days later.

## Flea Markets and Vending

Day labor markets and hiring halls organized exchanges of labor between informal workers and informal employers. Flea markets and street vending organized exchanges of goods between informal sellers and informal buyers. Many residents of Guadalupe barrio attended one of two large weekend flea markets, which featured products ranging from cars to fruit to books. Much of the commerce in the flea markets occurred in the formal economy. Vendors and customers bargained over price, and completed transactions took place entirely within the law— cash or credit cards exchanged, taxes paid, receipts issued. But the flea markets also housed a substantial amount of informal commerce.

During visits to the flea markets—sometimes on my own, sometimes with Guadalupe buyers, and sometimes to spend time with sellers—I noticed two kinds of informal activity. The first kind involved established vendors who ostensibly used the flea market to display wares for passing shoppers but spent considerable time at the markets working out informal exchanges with steady customers. The experiences of Jesús, a regular seller, and Henry, the occasional day laborer I mentioned above, exemplified these latter relationships.

Jesús had a regular stall in a large flea market where he mostly sold leather goods imported by his father from Mexico. His clientele were mostly Mexican immigrants who came to his stall to purchase boots or vests or, especially, intricately tooled belts in the distinct *ranchera* style. The belts cost $100 to $150 apiece, and they could be seen on the waists of men throughout Guadalupe and the other Mexican immigrant barrios of San Jose. Henry began as one of Jesús's customers, purchasing boots and a belt for himself as well as several additional belts for family members. Henry also had relatives in Mexico who occasionally sent him leather goods, and Jesús became interested in the belts Henry received from his relatives. The two worked out an arrangement. Jesús supplied Henry with leather goods to peddle to friends and neighbors, and in exchange Jesús sold Henry's merchandise at his stall in the flea market. For Jesús, this informal arrangement brought distinctive goods into his shop that helped set him apart from the many other leather goods vendors at the market. For Henry, who was unemployed and occasionally working at Strong Road, the arrangement gave him another way of earning some cash under the table. He kept one of Jesús's belts in his car and showed it to people he met in the neighborhood, at parties and other social gatherings, and at the job-training center that he attended as part of his receipt of unemployment compensation. During the fall of 1993 and into the winter of 1994, the flow of goods between the two men expanded. Henry offered Jesús some stereo equipment he had purchased at a yard sale in exchange for a higher percentage of the selling price of a few belts. Jesús sold the stereo equipment through another vendor at the flea market, and Henry sold the belts to friends at the job-training center, giving Jesús a fixed amount for each belt and keeping the remainder for himself.

The flea market provided the organizational context in which these informal transactions took place. The presence of a variety of vendors made it possible to market and sell all kinds of barter goods, and the market's permanence provided a stable base for economic activities. It was only after they met in the context of a legal economic transactions and went through some weeks of trust building that Henry and Jesús expanded their activities into the informal economy. The flea market gave the two men a chance to interact as business partners and test each other's reliability.

The second kind of informal activity I noticed tended to occur in flea markets smaller in scale and less professionalized than the one where Jesús worked. At these markets, many vendors rented space to sell household items on a one-time-only informal basis. While Jesús and other established merchants rented regular space week after week in the flea markets and constructed fairly elaborate stalls, the informal vendors of the smaller markets generally sold merchandise from the back of their car, off folding tables, or off blankets laid out on the ground.[7] While the professional sellers at the large markets established fixed or nearly fixed prices for merchandise, accepted credit cards, and issued receipts, the informal sellers in the smaller markets often set prices through haggling and accepted only cash. For example, Esteban, a Guadalupe resident in his forties, came to a small market near Guadalupe one Saturday in November to sell several sets of wrenches and other small tools. As he laid out the tools on a blanket laid out on the ground in back of his car, Esteban told me that he had been storing some old tools in his house for a long time but that he picked up most of the tools at yard sales.[8] He had wrenches from a variety of sets, some of them desirable American brand names and others with Asian brand names that were considered of inferior quality; some were brand new and others had seen heavy use. Esteban attracted a steady flow of customers during the busy hours of the market from early morning until midafternoon. He quoted prices ranging from twenty-five cents to one dollar for an individual wrench depending on the size and quality, and he offered discounts to buyers who were willing to purchase a complete set. Generally, buyers expressed interest in one tool or another, received a quote, and then bargained for a lower price. Many customers attempted to lower the effective price by supplementing their original request with other items. Everyone paid cash. By midafternoon, his blanket picked nearly clean, Esteban packed

up his car for the day. After several weeks browsing yard sales, Esteban
returned to the flea market with a fresh set of tools to lay out.

As it did for professionals, the flea market provided occasional informal sellers such as Esteban a permanent site for economic activity.
Informal sellers did not establish bargaining or bartering with other vendors in the markets the way professionals did, but they did benefit from
the presence of a variety of informal vendors in the same space. In
essence, the flea markets served as sites for common yard sales—saving
customers the trouble of moving from house to house, neighborhood to
neighborhood. Informal vendors did pay a price for this privilege. The
flea market charged for the rental of the space where they worked, and in
theory the vendors paid sales tax on all they sold. However, I did not see
informal vendors at smaller flea markets charge customers sales tax the
way professionals at the larger markets regularly did.

Outside the flea markets, the streets of Guadalupe served as a sales
floor for informal vendors who sold goods door to door or from carts
they pushed through neighborhood streets or placed at a strategic street
corner. Some vendors were formally employed. María and Rosa, for example, provided fresh produce such as *nopales* and squash to households in Guadalupe and other low-income barrios. The two women,
friends in their mid-twenties, were part of larger team that included
another team of door-to-door sellers and a central supply van operated
by the owner of the enterprise. In exchange for the bulk of their gross
receipts, the van driver supplied the two women with convenient-sized
quantities of vegetables to sell, transported them from one neighborhood
to the next so that they could sell widely, and provided for their physical
security on the job. María and Rosa particularly appreciated the protection. They said that working as a team and having the van nearby made
going door to door in many neighborhoods a safer business enterprise.[9]

Just as the flea markets included "professionals" such as Jesús and
"casuals" such as Esteban, not all vendors in the barrio were full-time
sellers such as María and Rosa. Some vending was done by residents
who cooked burritos, tamales, and other food in their home kitchens
and sold it out of food coolers mounted on bicycles, in cars or simply
carried to the street corner. Geraldo, a Guadalupe immigrant from
northern Mexico in his mid-fifties, earned income in one of the typical
patterns for this kind of "casual" vendor. In the morning, his wife prepared twenty to forty burritos of various kinds—pork, chicken, or
beef—and loaded them into the small cooler attached to the back of a

bicycle. Salsa, hot sauce, peppers, and napkins filled the basket at the front. Geraldo rode to several places around the Guadalupe neighborhood at lunch time. Two or three times a week, he parked his bike by a corner where day laborers gathered, in a car dealership lot, and on the sidewalk next to a job-training facility and stood at the back handing out burritos for $2 apiece. He had competitors. A large, full-service, shiny lunch wagon frequented one of "his" spots in Guadalupe, but he beat them on price. Their burritos were a bit larger but usually cost $3 to $4 apiece. He also had to deal with competition from other small-scale food vendors. One day at the car dealership, he confronted a competing vendor who had arrived before him. After a few words, the other vendor left. "I told her that this was my spot, that I always sold here, and that she would just have to move on to a different place. She didn't like it, but she moved on," he explained. But he did not always win these direct battles. In early June 1994, a couple in their mid-thirties began parking their small hatchback station wagon near the job-training facility loading dock where Geraldo usually stood with his bicycle. In the back of the wagon were two large coolers—one containing hot burritos and tamales and the other containing cold drinks. Geraldo's business at the center dropped off precipitously, but after a few weeks the couple stopped appearing, and Geraldo and his bicycle regained control of commerce in the spot.

Another pattern of casual vending involved less foresight and planning than Geraldo's burrito business. Manuela's vending near her apartment proved a typical example of this kind of income generation. She was a thirty-year-old homemaker whose husband was employed in a legal job at a warehouse. They lived in one of the most overcrowded apartment complexes in Guadalupe barrio, and theirs was one of the more prosperous households. Manuela nearly always kept a supply of easily sold foodstuffs on hand, including cans of soda and beer in the refrigerator and packages of popsicles in the freezer. Neighbors regularly came to her kitchen window to purchase a can of soda or a six-pack of beer late at night after nearby *tiendas* closed. Children were her most reliable customers, taking advantage of her supply when they were able to scrape together fifty cents for a treat. The earnings from this vending were not substantial. For Manuela, much of the appeal of the economic activity appeared related to the chance to interact with friends and neighbors. She enjoyed how the vending contributed to making her household the center of attention and activity in the apartment complex.

## ILLICIT WORK IN CHÁVEZ

A remarkable feature of illegal activity in Guadalupe was the absence of law enforcement. As my descriptions of everyday informality show, aside from the occasional interruption of business at Strong Road and other day labor markets, informal workers went about their business undisturbed by law enforcement. The routines of illicit activities in Chávez could not have been more different.

Of the many social service, charitable, and religious organizations that maintained a presence in Chávez, only the housing authority itself, which owned and managed the projects, had a more notable presence in everyday life than the police. Five different law enforcement agencies patrolled Chávez: the California Highway Patrol (CHP), Los Angeles County sheriffs and deputies, officers from citywide Community Resistance Against Street Hoodlums (CRASH) tactical antigang units, officers and detectives from the local precinct of the City of Los Angeles Police Department (LAPD), and officers of the housing authority's own police force. Officers patrolled on foot, in cars, and from helicopters. In the Appendix, I described how police officers detained me, along with four other young men, for sidewalk questioning only a few days after I had begun fieldwork in Chávez. During my time in Chávez, roundups similar to this occurred three to five times a week, with the majority conducted by officers from antigang CRASH units. In addition to patrol officers, drug rehabilitation counselors, parole officers, and police-sponsored outreach workers played a role in Chávez residents' everyday affairs.

Despite this law enforcement presence, illicit activities remained common in Chávez, and I find it useful to distinguish between three different kinds of routine illicit activities. First, Chávez residents occasionally took advantage of illicit opportunities that presented themselves. Frankie and Guillermo's experiences "unloading a truck," which I described in Chapter 5, exemplified this kind of casual, disorganized, and unsophisticated participation in the illicit economy.

A second kind of illicit activities occurred when Chávez residents actively sought out opportunities for petty crime. In their relative lack of organization and sophistication, these activities resembled Frankie and Guillermo's "unloading a truck." They differed, however, because people actively sought out these opportunities, turned to these petty crimes for income again and again, and relied on the income they gained as a way to make ends meet. One afternoon in Chávez, for example, two men spent several hours walking door to door in the projects trying to sell a weed-whacker and lawnmower that they had stolen from the garage of a nearby home. "We got it out of a garage up on the other side of the hill," the man with the weed-whacker said. "It was open, so we just went in and took it out. You want to buy it? How much? It's in pretty good shape. You can cut through anything with this thing." Theirs was the typical method for selling hot merchandise in Chávez. The seller presented merchandise to a group of people, interested customers sometimes inquired about the merchandise's origin, the seller usually provided a general explanation that failed to qualify as incriminating, and buyer and seller attempted to negotiate a price. The weed-whacker peddling was atypical in that yard tools had a smaller potential customer base than most of the hot merchandise that circulated through Chávez. Residents who relied on petty crime usually peddled watches, gold chains, or other luxury items that were easily stolen, widely sought after by Chávez residents, and easily passed around from hand to hand for customers' inspection.

Finally, Chávez residents participated in more organized and sophisticated illicit enterprises such as car theft and drug selling. Thieves brought some stolen cars to nearby garages to be sold intact while other cars were parked in out-of-the-way lots and playing fields in Chávez to be stripped of parts. After several days, police often towed away the carcasses of these stripped cars. The drug sales I observed in Chávez mostly involved $5 to $20 sales of cocaine, PCP, and marijuana. Residents of Chávez and of nearby neighborhoods provided some business to the Chávez drug sellers, and drug buyers also came from outside the neighborhood. The Chávez barrio was conveniently located near freeway exits, and residents were sure that many drug buyers took the freeway to Chávez specifically to buy drugs. "There's this white lady sitting in her Mustang out by the gym," reported forty-three-year-old Art as he entered a Chávez apartment one night. "She's got her cigarette with that little wet tip [PCP was often ingested by smoking such a dipped cigarette]. You know she just drove over here to get high before she gets back on the freeway to see her boyfriend."

Illicit activities of all types—casual burglary, petty-criminal careers, and illicit economic enterprises—persisted despite law enforcement suppression efforts. I noticed several local institutions that helped foil these suppression efforts, including local social networks, public marketplaces devoted to illicit activities, and the operations of the local street gang.

Just as information about informal employers was passed through social networks in Guadalupe, information that mattered for illicit activities was disseminated by networks in Chávez. Residents learned from each other who was trustworthy and who might snitch or steal, who was dependable under pressure and who might "snap" at an inopportune moment, and which police officers were reasonable and which were best to avoid.

Flea markets and street vending in Guadalupe were the direct sales organizations of the informal economy; in Chávez, shooting galleries and the hot spot provided illicit counterparts. In the two shooting galleries of Chávez, residents prepared and injected heroin and other drugs. Some residents hated the galleries. The comments of Linda, a Chávez mother in her early forties who lived in an apartment building next to one shooting gallery, captured the feelings of residents who wished the galleries would go away. "They're always making a mess up there," she complained. "And they leave their trash all over place—needles all over. Some day, one of my kids is going to get hurt by one of those things. And I don't like my kids to see that every day."

For the most part, police and residents adopted a "don't ask-don't tell" policy toward the galleries. From patrolling the projects, police knew of the galleries, but they rarely intervened to end the use of drugs there. Even residents who frequently complained about the galleries in the community did not press police officers for their eradication—certain that the galleries would reemerge in a different spot in the projects or fearful that gallery users might take retribution. A similar live-and-let-live policy protected the hot spot, whose name reflected the illicit transactions such as drug sales that occurred there. Many Chávez residents resigned themselves to the hot spot's existence, despite the fact that it was the most frequent target of CRASH raids. Residents told me that community and police pressure did force the hot spot to move occasionally. Every year or two, the exact spot where drugs were bought and sold in Chávez moved a few blocks one way or another. But like the street vending, the business of the hot spot continued no matter its exact geographic location.

Street gangs provided a third response to attempts at suppressing illicit economic activities. In Chávez, the Elm Street gang played an important role in economic life, especially for residents engaged in sophisticated illicit activities such as car theft and drug selling. The gang was a source of instruction in specialized skills as well as a source of social contacts that facilitated participation in illicit work. In addition to its role in economic life, Elm Street played an important social and cultural role in the Chávez community.

## Police and Illicit Work

Illicit workers kept an eye out for the police. They noted which agency officers represented, assessed their probable business in the projects, and shared information about the personalities of officers who commonly patrolled Chávez. Police made similar observations about illicit workers—their routine illicit activities, their behavior at any particular moment, and their personality in general. Mutual surveillance created an intimate relationship between illicit workers and police, with illicit workers and police sometimes monitoring each other like boxers in the ring. Informal rules governed how officers should patrol, which illicit activities to suppress and which to ignore, and how to handle relationships with illicit workers at leisure. Illicit workers understood the rules of getting along with police: how to behave while being searched or questioned, which insults police considered "fighting words," and which actions would provoke physical retaliation.

The experiences of Paco, a Chávez resident in his late thirties, show how illicit workers kept an eye out for the police. Paco participated in petty crime and illicit enterprises, and in June and early July, he spent two weeks selling M80s and other prohibited fireworks. He began by selling small amounts that he carried with him on his person. As his business picked up closer to July 4, Paco filled the trunk of his car and drove from group to group in the projects selling cartons of fireworks. An experienced illicit worker, Paco kept an eye out for police. As he told a group of men outside one of the shooting galleries, "I don't take any chances with these guys. When I see a cop, I just go. I'll just keep on going by and not even stop." Paco's desire to minimize his exposure to the police meant that for several weeks after I first observed him in the projects, he curtailed all of his activities if I was around. Only after I was introduced as "okay" by an acquaintance did Paco continue his normal moneymaking routines in my presence. Similarly, while selling fireworks one evening, he urged the boys and young men inspecting the merchandise in his open car trunk to hurry up because he was nervous about police in the projects. "Let's go, let's go," he said. "Make your choices and get going here. Norton's in the area." Norton was a CRASH officer who patrolled Chávez regularly. He was well known among illicit workers for his aggressive demeanor, his disrespectful attitude, and his occasionally brutal law enforcement tactics.

Residents familiar with the informal rules governing the relationships between police and illicit workers predicted an unhappy fate for Officer Norton. They were convinced that Norton had overstepped these informal rules. Norton detained residents several times a week, sweeping up illicit workers at leisure and residents who had no involvement with the illicit economy at all. One afternoon in September, several young men watched Norton search some Chávez residents and predicted that if he did not become less aggressive, someone would shoot him. "That's what happened to that guy over where I live in Garden Homes," said a young man who lived in a nearby housing project. "The homeboys got sick of that guy's disrespectful attitude, and they took him out."

The tense relations with Norton were exceptional. For the most part, police and residents accommodated each other's daily routines, even when these daily routines involved illicit activities. This accommodation meant ignoring, for the most part, law-breaking in the shooting galleries or the hot spot. At times, officers actively attempted to connect with illicit workers. For example, twenty-four-year-old Ron spoke highly of two LAPD officers who attended him after he had been shot two years previously. The officers appeared in Chávez one afternoon, parked near the hot spot, and brought out a thick spiral-ring notebook that contained examples of gang *placas*—graffiti and tattoos unique to a gang. Ron greeted the two officers warmly when he saw them. "These two were the only cops who were decent to me when I got shot," he said to the group. "The other guys were all, 'Ron who shot you? Who shot you?' But I wasn't gonna tell them nothing. But these guys came and visited me in the hospital and brought things from my family and everything." As they looked over the *placas* with several residents, it was clear that the officers had established some degree of trust and comfort even with the several members of the group who were involved in the illicit economy.

Informal rules also governed how Chávez residents treated police, as the story of Gonzalo—told to me by his friend Ernie—illustrates.

"Did you hear they shot Gonzalo? LAPD and CRASH were in the projects, and Gonzalo was there. He was really drunk, and when they tried to rack him up, he pulled a knife and started waving it around. They got behind the cruiser and pulled their guns on him, but he wouldn't put the knife down and finally they shot him. He knew what he was doing; he knew that they were going to shoot him. . . . Really, he just committed suicide. His girlfriend broke up with him, and he was depressed about that. That's why he did it, I think. It was just tragic."

In general, the police represented a problem to be overcome for illicit workers in Chávez. Workers knew which officers created problems and which were unlikely to interfere with their activities. For their part, the police were expected to observe unspoken rules about how to deal with illicit activities in Chávez. When the activities were well confined to certain physical areas, officers usually adopted a live-and-let-live attitude. Those officers who failed to adhere to this standard or who were considered too aggressive risked retaliation by illicit workers, who maintained that they were prepared to force more reasonable behavior. Most officers seemed happy to forge casual relationships even with residents who participated in the illicit economy, as long as the law-breaking remained appropriately inconspicuous.

## The Gang and Illicit Work

In the low-income barrios, residents frequently found that the police were a repressive force as much as a protective one.[10] Young male residents were stopped and searched on the East LA streets—often, they reported, while just "minding my own business." While police searched residents, cars and pedestrians were held up behind their squad car roadblocks. At night, sleepers were awakened by the noise of police helicopters passing only five hundred feet overhead or by the light of the "midnight sun" searchlight that police used to track suspects. Older barrio residents complained that police were "never around when you need them" and were slow to arrive when called. Artists painted murals throughout East LA that celebrated the memories of young residents killed by police bullets during "legal interventions." As much as any event of everyday life, these well-remembered killings lent police forces the air of outside occupiers rather than community protectors.

East LA street gangs were a visible opponent of police, and residents who felt oppressed by police often had sympathy for the gangs. Residents embraced a range of positions in ongoing police-gang conflict. Gang support ranged from active assistance to reluctant sympathy; some residents cursed gangs and police equally; and still others wished the police would sweep the gangs out of the barrios. This variety of orientations reflected the multifaceted relationship between gang and community.[11] Residents objected to police brutality, but they also opposed gang-associated violence. Residents wanted safe streets and a law-abiding citizenry, but history taught them—and daily life reminded them—that unconstrained police officers could be both disruptive and dangerous.

The relationship between gang and community differed from barrio to barrio and from time to time. In 1995, for example, intergang violence in

East LA's Lawndale Court housing project killed four young people in
less than two weeks. In these circumstances, one young resident's opinion
of the Lawndale gangs was typical. "Every night they [members of rival
gangs] get drunk and start shooting. Bam bam bam. I hear them outside
my apartment all night long. I get up in the morning and there are bullet
holes in the outside wall. I hate them." Lawndale residents welcomed
police intervention to quell the violence. On the other hand, in another
barrio near Chávez, a community activist sought to end the tagging of
neighborhood residences. Local gang members thought the activist too
aggressive, and their viewpoint gained support from the community.
Over the course of two months, negotiations between the local organization heading the antitagging campaign and the gang became increasingly
tense. Finally the gang forced the activist to abandon the antitagging
campaign and resign from the organization, and a gang leader assumed
the vacant position on the organization's board.

Chávez barrio had only one gang, or *varrio,* which I call Elm Street.
The Elm Street *varrio* traced its history back to the 1930s, when Mexican
Americans first began settling in the private homes that would later be
torn down to construct the Chávez housing project. After Chávez Homes
was built, Elm Street reestablished itself in the development. In 1995,
Chávez was peaceful compared to Lawndale Court because Elm Street
had firm control of the projects. Rachel, a lifelong Chávez resident in her
early forties, expressed the gratitude that many residents felt when she
said, "One thing about Chávez that is good is that there is only one gang
here. That means we don't have the problems, like they do at Lawndale
Court, where the project is cut up into so many different little territories.
Over there, there is fighting all the time and violence is a big problem."
In the 1990s, Elm Street had extended its control to "natural" social bor-
ders in East LA—freeways, large parks, and industrial areas—by establishing itself in two neighborhoods of private housing adjoining Chávez.
Beyond East LA, Elm Street members who had moved out of Chávez had
established affiliated gangs in distant communities.[12] Elm Street members
attributed the gang's strength to its political stability (their historic rival
gang in East LA, several residents said, was paralyzed by leadership quar-
rels) and to a positive relationship with the Chávez community.

The presence of Elm Street in Chávez had both positive and negative
effects on illicit economic activity. The presence of *varrio* members and
affiliates on the sidewalks of Chávez at nearly all times of day and night
discouraged some kinds of illicit economic activities in the Chávez community. Residents "hanging out" noted who entered the projects in cars

and confronted strangers passing through on foot. Their presence created lively and populated streets that reduced opportunities for street crime.[13] Their preeminence in public meant that many people strongly identified Elm Street the *varrio* with Chávez the barrio. By maintaining a public presence on the streets of Chávez and in the "staging areas" of Los Angeles, the Elm Street *varrio* represented the whole community to the outside world.[14]

The strong identification between Elm Street the *varrio* and Chávez the barrio facilitated illicit work by interfering with law enforcement efforts at suppressing illicit activities in the projects. The entrance of the police into the projects was announced by warning shouts from residents hanging out on the sidewalks, and news of police arrival often spread through the projects more quickly than the police themselves were able to drive from one side of the development to the other. Sometimes these warnings came from illicit workers, gang members, or gang affiliates who had a specific reason to fear police presence. But as frequently "civilians"—Chávez residents without involvement in either illicit activities or Elm Street—issued warnings.

Advance notice was particularly valuable for residents selling illicit drugs. Gato was an Elm Street member who made most of his income selling illicit drugs on the streets of Chávez. Like the other drug sellers, Gato was most vulnerable to arrest when he actually had drugs in his possession, so Gato maintained stashes near the hot spot. When he heard warning shouts, Gato would put whatever he was holding in a hollow spot near the base of a small tree or he would jump onto the handrail of a nearby unit's stoop and jam the drugs into a rain gutter. Anyone on the streets could see where Gato had stashed the drugs, so he had to keep an eye out for thieves. At the same time, hiding places could not be too obvious, as police often raked nearby bushes or turned over garbage cans looking for stashes.

The relationship between illicit work and the *varrio* was also affected by the social capital conferred by gang membership.[15] This social capital both constrained and facilitated activities in the illicit economy. Membership was a liability because police often focused on residents dressed in the distinctive *varrio* style—young people in baggy pants and carefully selected sneakers who displayed tattoos and hand signals; young men who shaved their heads; and a smaller number of young women who carefully plucked their eyebrows and applied makeup in distinctive styles—when they patrolled the projects. Looking like a gang member was an important component of *varrio* membership. Residents who were merely affiliated with a gang often dressed in the *varrio* style, and street-wise residents of East LA prided themselves on their ability to distinguish the "wannabe" poser from the legitimate "OG" or "original gangster."[16] On the other hand, as one Elm Street member complained, "The cops hassle us just because we wear baggy pants and we're baldy. Half the time we're not even doing anything when they rack us up." Police also focused on Chávez "civilians" who dressed in the fashionable "baldy" style. For example, Chuck was an eighteen-year-old Chávez resident who was not affiliated with Elm Street but did dress in the "baldy" style. He was hanging out with friends one afternoon in Chávez when CRASH came into the projects. He was searched and questioned and, a half hour later, cited for drinking in public. Chuck, who was unemployed, considered the $100 citation a disaster. "There's no way I can pay that, and there's no way I'm going to go to court and get put in jail for a couple days. They're going to put a warrant out for me. I guess the next time I get picked up, they're going to arrest me."

Gang membership also facilitated illicit work—especially for residents engaged in the relatively sophisticated activities of illicit enterprises. Older Elm Street members taught younger members the skills needed to participate in these enterprises. For example, Ron, the twenty-four-year-old Chávez resident mentioned above, learned how to steal cars from going on "missions" with older Elm Street members soon after he became active in Elm Street at age thirteen and fourteen. Older members of the gang had taught him which cars were valuable to steal, how to enter and start up the car, and what to do if problems arose during the commission of the theft. His first thefts, Ron said, were mostly just for joy-riding. He remembered the horrible day he broke into his father's car and ended up steering it into a telephone pole, and he recalled with bravado the day he and three homeboys in a hot car successfully eluded the police in a wild circuit through the alleyways, lawns, and playing fields of Chávez. But with time, Ron began to steal cars for economic reasons. At that time, gang membership again proved valuable. Through members, Ron was introduced to a mechanic at a nearby garage who bought stolen cars and parts. By his late teens, Ron said he had become a confident and competent car thief. At times, he patrolled parking lots and residential streets not far from Chávez looking for attractive cars to steal, and at other times he filled orders for particular parts or cars from the garage mechanic.

Elm Street provided the social support needed for illicit enterprises. Following a drive-by shooting late one afternoon in Chávez, Beto, a twenty-six-year-old Elm Street member, explained the techniques involved:

"There are a couple different kinds of drive-bys. Some of them, like the one today, are pretty disorganized. They just had one car come in. They just grabbed a car and came at us. . . . . . A more organized one, you get two cars and you get a whole bunch of homeboys in the front one. They come in and they get all the attention. Everyone's worried about that car because they can see all the homeboys. But the second car is the one with the shooter. . . . Sometimes, they'd have a kid do the shooting so that if they got caught it wouldn't be as bad."

Supporting illicit activities need not be offered up voluntarily. Beto's own experience with drive-by shootings provide an example of how Elm Street members could be coerced into participating as crime partners in illicit activities. "The first one I was in, I was terrified," he recalled. "I was fifteen or sixteen years old, and they wanted me to do the shooting. I didn't want to do it, but the older homeboys put a lot of pressure on me, and finally I did it. They really didn't give me a choice." Unaffiliated residents of Chávez could be compelled to provide social support for illicit activities as well. When Elm Street members became convinced that the adolescent boy in one family had provided police with information about a recent robbery, they retaliated against him and his family. After receiving threats, the boy and his family hastily left Chávez and moved in with relatives who lived some distance away. Their apartment was broken into, its contents burned, and its walls emblazoned with Elm Street tags. Many residents understood the burnt-out apartment—soon boarded up by housing authority officials—as a reminder of what Elm Street could do to defend itself against threats from within the community.

A final way in which the social capital of *varrio* membership facilitated illicit activities was by mitigating the consequences of police apprehension and imprisonment. Elm Street was a large enough *varrio* that its membership was represented inside penal establishments including the Los Angeles County Jail and California state work camps and prisons. Illicit workers who were affiliated with Elm Street benefited from the protection of the gang if they spent time in prison. The experiences of Stinger, a twenty-one-year-old member of Elm Street, illustrated this dynamic. Stinger was implicated in an auto theft that several members of Elm Street participated in. Because his firearm was used in the incident, he received a longer prison sentence than the other participants in the robbery, and he spent about two years in state prison. "Prison wasn't too bad," he said. "I had all my homeboys in there, and they help you out a lot. They get you what you need and teach you how to deal with the prison and everything, and they make sure that other people don't fuck with you or anything like that. I mean, it wasn't too different in there from out here except it was really boring."

Shorty described how Elm Street membership affected a short stay in county jail for armed robbery. "I was really scared going in," he confided.

"Because I'd heard all this stuff about how they treat you so bad. But because I was in Elm Street they put me in the special gang unit. So I only had to share my room with one other guy. He was from some other neighborhood— some *negro*. We didn't really talk much or anything. It was better where we were than in general population where you have to deal with all the drunks and all that stuff."

Whether they were incarcerated or not, the gang played an important role for illicit workers in Chávez. Against the background of tense police-community relations, many residents of the low-income barrios sympathized with local street gangs even if they had little affection for violent intergang wars. Gang wars were not as pressing a problem in Chávez as in other nearby barrios because the Elm Street gang had consolidated the physical territory of the barrio. In the neighborhood, gang membership had some important advantages as well as some drawbacks for illicit workers. One drawback was that police recognized the signs of gang membership. They targeted enforcement efforts against residents who looked like "gangsters"—even if a "baldy" hairstyle, baggy pants, or distinctive makeup was adopted as a fashion statement more than in accordance with the requirements of membership. On the positive side, gang membership provided access to specialized training and introduction to valuable social contacts for those who participated in more sophisticated illicit enterprises. In addition, membership was a form of social capital that could prove especially valuable to illicit workers who spent time in jail or prison.


ROUTINE CRIME

In some ways, routine illicit activities in Guadalupe and Chávez differed little from legal moneymaking activities. Some illegal work was nearly identical to legal counterparts. The day-to-day routine of a job bussing restaurant tables in a downtown San Jose hotel did not differ much for jobholders with or without green cards in their wallets. Social networks connected illegal workers to illegal jobs in much the same way that they connected legal workers to legal jobs. These similarities aside, however, illegal work remained illegal, and law enforcement suppression inevitably affected income-generating routines.

Law enforcement did not target all illegal activities with identical intensity or tactics. When it came to enforcing the letter of the law regarding how economic activities were undertaken, police suppression efforts were relatively temperate. In Guadalupe barrio, the illegal activities of the informal economy could not take place completely out in the open, but *la migra* rarely disrupted the daily routines of everyday life. Illegal economic transactions took place in specialized informal institutions: street corner day labor markets and local hiring halls matched undocumented workers to informal employers, while flea markets and street vending were outlets for informal buying and selling. When it came to illicit goods and services, however, law enforcement assumed a much more aggressive stance. Police turned a blind eye to some illicit activities that were confined to special settings, such as heroin shooting galleries, but in general the five different police forces that patrolled Chávez played an important role in the daily routines of Chávez residents. The Elm Street gang, like other East LA street gangs, had a complex relationship to the Chávez barrio that housed it. Of importance here, however, is the fact that Elm Street was an illicit institution that stood in opposition to the police. By providing training, contacts, and social capital, the gang organized illicit work routines and facilitated the economic activities of illicit workers.

Different kinds of illegal moneymaking lead to different kinds of illegal work routines. Law enforcement attempts to suppress illegal activities, and illegal organizations counterbalance those suppression efforts. Without illegal institutions such as the day labor market or the street gang, illegal income generating could not persist for long in the face of suppression efforts. Thus, the illegal institutions of the low-income barrios play an important role in the everyday lives of illegal workers. But what about residents who do not break the law? How do illegal institutions affect legal workers in Guadalupe or residents of Chávez who only occasionally dabble in illegal activities, residents such as Frankie and Guillermo? In the next chapter, I turn to these questions.

# CHAPTER 7

# The Consequences of Illegal Work

Of the social problems in low-income neighborhoods, few excite more concern and consternation than crime. Concern often centers on violent crime, which is said to plague street corners, apartment buildings, and neighborhoods in America's big cities.[1] The consternation focuses on economic crime, which appears to have a sadly necessary place in neighborhoods whose economic vitality has been undercut by deindustrialization and among individuals, such as single mothers, teenagers or recent immigrants, who are marginalized in the legal economy.[2] Often we interpret the concern and consternation as a reflection of the difficulty of controlling crime. Sometimes the urban poor find they are unable to stop violent crime in their neighborhood, and they instead are forced to adopt a range of strategies such as avoiding certain areas of the neighborhood, staying inside the apartment, or even staying away from windows to guard their own safety as well as that of their children and family.[3] In other neighborhoods, lack of opportunity in the legitimate economy appears to thrust residents into illegal work.[4]

Violent crime concerned residents in both Chávez and Guadalupe. In an ironic testimony to that concern, many Chávez residents, as Rachel described in Chapter 6, were grateful that Elm Street controlled the barrio and spared the community intense intergang conflict. Violence less frequently interrupted public life in the barrios of San Jose than in East Los Angeles, but Guadalupe residents were still concerned about it. When staffers at a community center heard rumors that a group of

*Mexicano* teenagers was planning to attack a group of young Chicanos in a Guadalupe park, they quickly called in the San Jose police to head off the confrontation. Two patrol cars were dispatched toward the Guadalupe corner where the Mexican youth, supposedly armed with shotguns, were said to be assembling. Specially trained mediators escorted the unarmed Chicano youth in the opposite direction—taking them out of the community center and across a busy thoroughfare to "safe" territory in an adjoining neighborhood.

Economic crime caused consternation in both barrios. As I described in Chapters 3 through 5, barrio residents faced a legal labor market that created as many problems as opportunities. Depending on how they valued its opportunities and managed its problems, the legal job market could push residents into economic crime.[5] Some residents I met in both Guadalupe and Chávez had intense difficulties generating income on the job market, and they turned to economic crime as a survival strategy. More frequently, the residents I knew who broke the law did so in pursuit of economic advancement. In Guadalupe, for example, I observed a substantial amount of economic crime undertaken by undocumented immigrants who came to San Jose to pursue a financial nest egg, although other undocumented migrants were fleeing indigence-threatening economic dislocation or life-threatening political upheaval.[6] Whatever their motivation, these migrants broke the law simply by taking a job. In Chávez, many residents involved in hustling used illegally gained income to purchase material signs of success.[7] Barrio residents were troubled when lack of legal jobs forced residents into economic crime as a matter of survival. Economic crime also evoked consternation in more subtle ways, such as when it reflected a lack of legal pathways for advancement or when it appeared a reasonable way of garnering important symbols of economic success.

As in other low-income urban communities, residents of Guadalupe and Chávez barrios struggled with violence and with economic crime by adopting a variety of protective measures in everyday life. They expressed frustration when crime in their neighborhood seemed to spin out of control. At the same time, fieldwork in the two barrios revealed substantial differences in the place of crime in the everyday worlds of the two barrios. In Chapter 6, I discussed how illegal activities were economically integrated into daily life in Guadalupe and Chávez by a variety of indigenous organizations and institutions. I focused on how particular institutions in the two barrios—*la migra* and police that sought to suppress illegality; social networks, hiring halls, flea markets, shooting galleries, and gangs that encouraged its persistence—shaped illegal income generation. In this chapter, I examine how these illegal organizations and institutions affected social life in the barrios.

Illegal institutions and organizations shaped the social fabric of everyday life in both barrios in different ways. In Guadalupe, indigenous organizations made illegal work in the informal economy seem like a legal undertaking. Thus, I refer to the social integration of informal work in Guadalupe as *legalization*. Legalization of informal activities did not relieve Guadalupe residents of the private anxieties associated with breaking the law, but it did mean that these private anxieties tended not to erupt into public troubles. In Chávez, on the other hand, indigenous organizations made illegal work in the illicit economy seem like a normal event. I refer to the social integration of illicit work in Chávez as *normalization*. Indigenous institutions created a social context in Chávez barrio within which the private anxieties and public troubles of the illicit economy became an expected and accepted part of everyday life.

Residents of low-income areas oppose crime and prefer a peaceful and law-abiding community.[8] My comparative analysis of crime and social life in the barrios confirms this general view but also reveals its limitations. In Guadalupe and Chávez, residents experienced different struggles, frustrations, and compromises when it came to crime. Comparative analysis shows that these differences reflected the fact that indigenous organizations integrated crime into barrio social life in quite distinct ways. Thus, my fieldwork in the barrios suggests that the low-income community does not simply oppose crime but rather dynamically engages with it. This chapter analyzes how the institutions of Guadalupe and Chávez integrated informal and illicit activities into daily barrio routines and, in the process, addresses the broader question of the relationship between crime and community.

## "LEGALIZING" INFORMAL WORK IN GUADALUPE

There was a gray area, not a sharp line, between legal and illegal work in Guadalupe barrio. Many workers lived out day-to-day life within it, entering the gray area in a number of ways: through illegal work that was sanctioned by legal employers; by using illegal means to create the appearance of legal employment; and by undertaking the long and uncertain process of adjusting to legal status. In the workplace, the institutions and organizations of San Jose's informal economy sustained this gray area. Informal networks, hiring halls, day labor and flea markets, and street vending facilitated residents' participation in the informal economy, as the previous chapter has shown. The public appearance of legality in the everyday activities of the informal economy helped create the ambiguity surrounding informal work in Guadalupe. Publicly and objectively, it could be hard to distinguish legal from informal workers even through close observation. Privately and subjectively, however, informal workers' concerns over legal status and legal jeopardy made it impossible to ignore the gray area surrounding informal work "Legal" law-breaking shaped public life in Guadalupe barrio but not the private lives of informal workers.

In this section, I show how informal institutions created the ambiguous gray area between legal and informal work in Guadalupe barrio. I see this gray area as the outcome of processes within the informal economy—not inevitable distinctions that flow from distinctions in law. I use the term *legalization* to describe how informal institutions created a "legal-like" public order around illegal work routines without, however, altering the meaning of illegality within the private lives of Guadalupe residents.

## Legalizing at Work

Having walked across the border without documents, José Mendoza was consigned to work in the gray areas of the informal economy. In Silicon Valley, José found work through informal networks. Acting on information supplied by his mother, he was hired by the manager of the food-packing plant where she worked to work the assembly line. After a few months, José was frustrated at the food-packing plant. His hours were irregular, and frequently he was sent home before the end of his eight-hour shift. José said that the manager of the plant liked him and wanted to send José out on the plant's delivery truck—a promotion in a sense because the work hours were more dependable even if the hourly wage was no higher than on the assembly line. But the manager wanted José to present some documents first. "When you're on the truck," José said, explaining the manager's thought process, "you go out and deal with all the people all over. They could ask for some ID, or you could get pulled over by the police for going through a red light." José understood his boss's position. To work on the truck, he would need some ID.

José consulted with his mother's brother, Alberto, who was considered the most streetwise member of the family. Alberto told José to go to the Strong Road day labor market and buy a social security card, a false document or *chueco*. According to Alberto, the logistics were easy. You tell them which kind of ID you want, what name to appear on the card, and the desired ID number (it cost extra if they had to make up the number for you). You negotiate a price, and a week later you return to Strong Road to pay and pick up the *chueco*.

The logistics were easy, but a failure of nerve stopped José from going to Strong Road. He heard that *la migra* patrolled Strong Road intensively and that there was a good chance he would be picked up and deported if he even went to shop at the stores near where the day laborers gathered. It was several weeks later, after another frustrating week of truncated hours at the food-processing plant, before José decided to go to Strong Road. He asked Alberto to accompany him and help him negotiate with the *chueco* sellers, but his uncle refused. Anxious for any kind of company, José turned to his uncle Simón, the youngest of his mother's brothers and much less streetwise than Alberto. The trip to Strong Road was a success. In a week, José had only to return with $30 and he would have his social security card.

The next week, I joined José and Simón on their trip to pick up the *chueco*. José was nervous, and he insisted that I drive because, he pointed out, this would reduce our chances of apprehension if *la migra* stopped us. Simón was even more nervous than José, and when we entered the parking lot at Strong Road, he slid off the rear seat of the car onto the floor to hide himself below the level of the rear window. We circled the parking lot, and José spotted his *chueco* seller. Leaving Simón in the car, José and I walked over to meet the seller. José handed off his $30, the seller walked out of sight around a building, and when he returned a few minutes later he had José's *chueco*. Less than fifteen minutes after entering the Strong Road parking lot, we were on our way back to the Mendoza apartment.

The *chueco* was a poorly made copy of a social security card with José's name and his chosen social security number clumsily typed in the appropriate places. The quality of the forgery seemed appropriate given the price, but it was hard to imagine the card could fool anyone. Nevertheless, the next week José was working on the truck at the food-processing plant. As promised, his hours increased and became regular, and his take-home pay soared.

The experiences of José illustrate three features of legalization in Guadalupe barrio. First, in his original position at the food-processing plant, José's experiences illustrate how legal employers sanctioned informal work. José had crossed the border into the United States without any documents, but when informal networks led him to the food-processing plant, the manager hired him anyway. Second, the steps he took to secure his "promotion" show how informal institutions allowed illegal workers to create the appearance of legality. José depended on the advice of his uncle Alberto and the resources of Strong Road to obtain the *chueco* his employer demanded. These events also provide a further example of employer complicity in illegal work; the *chueco* could not have fooled any employer who viewed it with a skeptical eye. Third, his experiences illustrate that neither the routinization of illegal work in informal institutions nor the legitimacy granted informality by employers who turned a blind eye to law-breaking assuaged the private anxiety of Guadalupe's informal workers. It required substantial economic pressure for José to go to Strong Road for his *chueco,* and even though Guadalupe residents routinely spent time at the Strong Road day labor market, José and Simón still worried about *la migra.* The experiences of José illustrate how informal institutions—informal networks linking workers to employers, informal institutions such as the street-vending *chueco* sellers, and continuing threat of law enforcement suppression by *la migra*—allowed residents to subvert the law and maintain the appearance of legal employment even as they failed to address private feelings of vulnerability.

## Legalizing and Status Adjustment

Informal institutions that facilitated law-breaking were not the only legalizing mechanism in Guadalupe. The process of adjusting one's status from undocumented to legal resident also sustained the public appearances of legality and the private sense of vulnerability. In Guadalupe several organizations—for-profit businesses, church-based charities, and activist-based nonprofits—helped residents apply for legalized status. For Guadalupe residents, this status adjustment was a huge gamble. The decision meant leaving the relatively safe confines of informal institutions and willingly exposing oneself to state scrutiny. Scrutiny was an ongoing process that endured as long as the adjustment process, which typically took a year or two. And, until the last *i* was dotted and last *t* crossed, the outcome remained in doubt. To be "in process" meant to be in doubt, as illustrated by the trials experienced by my landlady Gloria as she attempted to adjust the status of her family.

One of the first things I noticed when I moved into Gloria's house in October, 1993, was that her younger son was in trouble. Javier never left the house except to go to his busboy job at a chain restaurant on the other side of San Jose, and he always had a small black box strapped to his right ankle. After several weeks, I learned from Gloria that the family had moved to Guadalupe, at least in part, to get Javier into a new social environment. Some of the kids he used to go to school with had used drugs, she explained, and she wanted to get him away from their influence. Javier explained that he and some friends were hanging out near his car when the San Jose police came up and asked to look through the vehicle. They found marijuana hidden in the car—the first Javier knew that his friends were involved with drugs. None of the friends would admit to owning the drugs. The stupid lawyer that the family retained had recommended he plead guilty in return for a suspended sentence, but the judge had reneged on the deal and sentenced him to house arrest.

In March 1994, the problems with Javier's guilty plea suddenly become much more serious than six months of court-imposed boredom. Soon after moving to San Jose from San Francisco, Gloria had retained an immigration lawyer to help facilitate the family's adjustment to legal residency in the United States. Gloria, Manuel, and Javier had all, technically, been living and working in the United States legally while their case slowly meandered its way through the INS. In March, the immigration lawyer learned of Javier's conviction. The conviction, he reported to Gloria, meant that Javier could not gain legal residency. In fact, at the conclusion of house arrest, deportation proceedings could begin against him. Gloria was distraught at the thought of Javier's deportation and furious that the lawyer to whom she had already paid thousands of dollars said there was nothing he could do to keep her son in the country. Friends suggested she dismiss the lawyer and take her case to a local nonprofit agency that helped undocumented residents negotiate the process of adjustment for nominal fees. Gloria took her friends' advice. She dismissed the lawyer and brought home the enormous stack of documents from her case. A few days later, she took a day off work, and she and Javier walked the stack of documents to the local agency. The workers in the center secured an extension on her case. The criminal lawyer, they told Gloria, had made a huge blunder by allowing Javier to plead guilty, but they gave her some hope that he would avoid deportation and that his adjustment could go through.

Gloria and Javier's experiences illustrate the effects of status adjustment on private life. After his house arrest ended, normal public life resumed for Javier—working, spending time with friends, seeing his girlfriend. But the uncertainty of his adjustment case dominated life at home. In the tension immediately following the news of Javier's adjustment problems, there were fights between Javier and Gloria, and Gloria spent several nights crying over the phone with friends and relatives. One night, after I confessed I had no idea how to facilitate Javier's entrance into college, she angrily accused me of standing in the way of his obtaining a student visa.

The fact that immigrants were not allowed to leave the country while their cases were pending exacerbated the difficulties of adjustment. A huge break in the tension at home came in June when Gloria, after years of INS-enforced exile from El Salvador, finally returned home to visit relatives and friends (I mentioned this trip in Chapter 5). The restriction on travel was one of the most hated conditions of status adjustment among Guadalupe residents, and some residents defied it by surreptitiously crossing the border *into* Mexico. In short, the nature of the bureaucratic process meant that status adjustment had implications far beyond the workplace.

The for-profit businesses and nonprofit agencies of Guadalupe barrio lent an orderly public progression to the private turmoil of status adjustment. The specific turmoil varied. For Javier and Gloria, the problem was the criminal courts; for Ricardo, the forty-five-year-old janitor mentioned in Chapter 5, the problem was the Border Patrol that would not allow his stepson to cross into the United States with him; for nearly everyone in Guadalupe, the problem was the expense of the process, the reams of paperwork, and the restrictions on travel. The specifics of each case varied, but the lines of people outside the nonprofit adjustment office testified to the fact that many families in Guadalupe knew the difficulties firsthand.

Illegal work shaped everyday life in Guadalupe barrio through public order and private turmoil. The public order came from barrio institutions such as social networks that linked undocumented workers to informal employers, day labor and flea markets that publicly winked at state regulation, *chuecos* that circulated among the undocumented, and organizations that facilitated status adjustment. These institutions "legalized" informal work. None of these institutions, however, assuaged the private turmoil of informality. Following the letter of the law—presenting an employer with a *chueco* or meeting the criteria for legal residency—did not necessarily reduce the private price of informality. The *chueco* satisfied the employer's legal obligation, but in the process it settled responsibility for law-breaking on the shoulders of the employee. Moreover, obtaining the *chueco* entailed further risks. The adjustment process left hanging, for months at least, the question of whether the myriad documents were really in order, and residents in the midst of adjustment were on tenterhooks; one inadvertent misstep or piece of bad luck could ruin years of planning, work, and sacrifice. Even when adjustment went smoothly, it extracted its pound of flesh in restrictions on foreign travel.

"Legalized" law-breaking characterized the public appearances but not the private realities of informal work. Thanks to informal institutions, the daily lives of workers and the barrio routines of working differed little, whether a resident carried documents in his or her pocket or not. But the "legality" of informal work was not complete. Informal institutions failed to address residents' feelings of vulnerability to *migra* raids and to vagaries of the adjustment process.

## "NORMALIZING" ILLICIT WORK IN CHÁVEZ

A clear line separated legal from illegal work in Chávez. Illicit workers knew—even as they took advantage of opportunities to burgle, relied on petty crime to make ends meet, and participated in sophisticated illicit enterprises—that they were breaking the law, risking imprisonment, and exposing themselves to violence. Even with a clear line separating legal from illicit work, however, the illegal economy played a paradoxical role in the lives of Chávez residents. This section addresses how these paradoxes arose in everyday life and how they characterized the lives not only of those who earned income illegally but also of those who did not.

It is tempting to dismiss the ambiguity surrounding economic crime in Chávez as inevitable. In cities where deindustrialization has undercut the economic vitality of whole neighborhoods, residents may rely on economic crime to survive. Single mothers, young people, and others who lack power in the legitimate economy may turn to economic crime as a way to make ends meet.[9] When law-breaking is necessary to survive— when it is the only way to provide food for the table or a roof over one's head—its role in the community is understandably ambiguous. In the face of extreme economic exclusion, lack of alternatives means that residents are not freely choosing to break the law; circumstances are forcing them to do so. As noted in the Chapter 5, however, residents of Chávez turned to economic crime as a means of advancement more often than as a means of survival. In Chávez, many residents turned to illegal activities for the marginal income to purchase material signs of success rather than as a day-to-day means of economic survival. In Chávez, illegal activities were socially ambiguous but not because they played a necessary role in local survival strategies.

The social ambiguity of economic crime in Chávez arose from the routines and institutions of the illicit economy itself. In their daily rounds, Chávez residents had to deal with the shooting galleries, the hot spot, the gang, and the rest of the illicit infrastructure. Most residents disapproved of the activities that took place in these institutions; they wanted less crime and fewer criminals in their neighborhood; and they saw policing as a good career that allowed a person to help low-income communities and enjoy personal advancement. But even residents who wanted less crime in their barrio had mixed feeling about the police officers charged with enforcing the law. Their support of crime fighting was tempered by the fact that police too frequently detained innocent bystanders and too often failed to protect vulnerable "civilians" during their raids. Residents also had mixed feelings about the police due to the endemic conflict between Elm Street and police departments. Many residents identified with Elm Street. Young people often identified with the gang, which represented them in the public staging areas of East LA, even if they were not themselves members. Older residents often had a personal connection with members who were family members, friends, and neighbors. And everyone in Chávez recognized that gang members wore many hats in the community; in addition to its illegal economic activities, Elm Street played important social and cultural roles.

The paradoxes surrounding illicit work in Chávez stemmed from the way illicit institutions integrated law-breaking into everyday barrio life. Interactions *between* different illicit institutions and *within* locally controlled illicit institutions produced contradictory attitudes and behaviors toward the illegal economy in three ways. First, even though most Chávez residents obeyed the law, they supported locally controlled institutions even when those institutions were involved in illegal activities, and they attacked institutions controlled by outsiders even when those institutions were committed to law enforcement. Second, even residents who had no interest in illegal activities were familiar with the dynamics of the illegal economy because illicit institutions "schooled" all residents in the skills and orientations needed to participate in and understand the routine procedures of illicit work. Finally, residents had to make sense of the fact that many of their friends, family members, and neighbors were involved in high-risk illicit activities; they came to see participating in illegal activities as a personal decision made with an understanding of the risks and drawbacks involved. Supporting local illicit institutions against outside institutions, "schooling" residents inside local institutions, and focusing on the individual decision to become involved in illicit institutions "normalized" illicit activities in Chávez in different ways: by normalizing illicit activities for outsiders, by normalizing the routines of illicit work, and by normalizing the decision to become involved in illicit activities.

## The Outward Face of Normalizing

One of the ironies of the illicit economy in Chávez was that relationships *between* illicit institutions created the impression that Chávez residents embraced and endorsed the illegal economy. This impression dominated my first visits to the barrio, as it did the visits of many others.

Armed with an introduction from a neighborhood priest, I met during one of my first visits to the barrio with forty-five-year-old Ana-Berta, a longtime Chávez resident and minor bureaucrat in the offices of the housing authority. Like many residents, Ana-Berta assumed I was interested in writing about violence, drug dealing, or other problems in the housing development, so as we chatted in the community center, she took care to emphasize that Chávez was a pleasant place to live, that the neighborhood was relatively free from violence because Elm Street controlled the streets, and that there was a greater sense of community there than in other places she had lived. Of course, there were some problems, just as in any community. "I don't really like the gang much myself," Ana-Berta confessed. "But they do their thing, and I do mine. It's just live and let live." Most of the serious problems in Chávez could be traced to the influence of outsiders, such as the school system that treated children poorly just because they were from the projects. And Ana-Berta reserved her harshest criticism for the police department. They purposely rotated officers out of Chávez just as they began to establish trusting relationships with residents, she charged, and although no fan of Elm Street, she nevertheless condemned how police treated gang members. She cited several examples of their brutality, saving for last the story of how they shot and killed Ramón, an unarmed member of Elm Street, two summers ago. With funds raised door to door and labor from Elm Street members, a mural had been erected in Ramón's memory, and Ana-Berta walked me to the far side of the development to see it. The mural showed the young victim amid a border of roses and crucifixes, and a poem recalled how he had lived (peacefully and happily) and how he had died (in a hail of

unjustified bullets). As we stood in front of it, Ana-Berta recalled how
her then sixteen-year-old son had lost a friend in a shooting.

"It was the day of the funeral, and he was at home just sitting in his room.
Not dressed up or anything. So I said to him, 'Aren't you going to the funeral?'
And he said no. He said, 'Mama, I counted it up and I have gone to twenty-
three funerals in the last couple of years for friends who got killed one way
or another. I'm not going today. I just can't take it anymore.' "

The mural to Ramón and Ana-Berta's identification with it despite her
ambivalence toward Elm Street illustrate how interactions between institutions in the illicit economy shaped the public culture of Chávez. Ana-
Berta had no kind words for those who sold drugs or stole cars. Elm
Street members identified her as someone who had to be dealt with carefully—a powerful figure in the community due to her position in the
housing authority but one not terribly sympathetic to gang members.
Her own son never joined Elm Street. "My mother would kill me if I ever
tried," he explained (and Ana-Berta agreed with him). Nevertheless, after
meeting me, an outsider, and taking the measure of my interest in her
community, Ana-Berta guided me to the memorial to Ramón, a member
of the gang struck down by the police.

Residents' embrace of the mural to Ramón illustrated one way in
which illicit activities were socially integrated into the Chávez community.
For Ana-Berta and other Chávez residents, the story of Ramón exemplified how the barrio was mistreated by outside institutions and how
the community, in solidarity, confronted these injustices. During my time
in Chávez, many residents brought me to the mural or took care to direct
my attention toward it as we walked or drove by, and they told the story
of how the police had unjustly cut the young man down. The mural and
the stories surrounding it represented community solidarity in conflicts
with outsiders. In Chávez, the illicit economy inevitably meant conflict
with police. Police-gang conflict was endemic, and residents had to take
sides. Nearly all, even those who had deep misgivings about the gang and
did not want themselves or their family involved in it, sided with Elm
Street. Reflecting this side taking, residents of Chávez told stories that normalized and explained their side of the conflict. Often, as the mural to
Ramón and the stories residents told about it exemplify, these explanations took the form of "bad cop" stories that normalized illicit activities.[10]

"Bad cop" stories reflected residents' attitude toward outside institutions, but these stories were not the final word on residents' attitude
toward the illicit economy. "Bad cop" stories reflect endemic conflict

between illicit institutions—between gang and police in particular—and they show that Chávez residents prefer the illicit institutions they control to the illicit institutions controlled by outsiders. But this preference is only one part of the place of illicit work in Chávez. "Bad cop" stories said little about the place of illicit institutions in everyday life *inside* the barrio.

### Normalizing Illicit Routines

Education in the classroom teaches students the skills and orientations to participate in the legal economy; "schooling" in the streets teaches what is needed to participate in the illicit economy.[11] Illicit institutions provided a forum in which residents learned the skills to participate in the illicit economy, and in the process these institutions normalized illicit work inside Chávez. Schooling was not just for residents who earned money illegally. Chávez residents who did not earn any income illegally nevertheless learned the basic social and job-specific skills needed to participate in the illicit economy. Many had little choice in the matter because illicit institutions dominated the public spaces of Chávez and residents who spent time in public learned the rules and norms that governed everyday life in these institutions. For most residents, this schooling carried positive benefits. The social skills used in the illicit economy constituted a foundation for street wisdom, the understandings and practices that helped smooth residents' everyday interactions in Chávez and the wider barrio community.[12]

Young Chávez residents began their schooling at the feet of older siblings and other family members. During 1995, Blondie, an eighteen-year-old Chávez resident, was schooling his five-year-old brother Ernesto. School was in session one spring day when the boys' mother gave Ernesto a few dollars to buy some groceries and told Blondie to walk his brother to the corner store. The brothers lived with their parents and siblings in a large apartment on the far side of Chávez from the hot spot. Ernesto spent most of his time in the apartment, in the playground area that served the half-dozen buildings in his corner of the housing development, and in the parking lot in back of his building that opened up onto a moderately busy street. Residents injected heroin a hundred yards away in a shooting gallery across an open field from Ernesto's playground. This was the closest Ernesto came to the illicit institutions of Chávez, and the shooting gallery was barely noticeable from his playground. The hot spot was not too far from the shooting gallery; it faced a small street that ran nearly through the center of the housing project and led to the corner store. Blondie and Ernesto's route to the corner store took them along a pathway that started at their apartment and ran past the shooting gallery. Their route then passed by the hot spot and crossed the final block to the corner store.

Blondie knew the hot spot. His older brother was an active affiliate of Elm Street who often hung out there. In the fall of 1995, his brother was shot in the leg at the hot spot, although it was never clear whether the shooting was an intentional attack or an accidental discharge. The hot spot was also Blondie's preferred hangout for several years while he made money selling cocaine to friends at middle school. He said that he was a more serious user of cocaine than seller, and in 1994, he was sick—"all shrunk up"—from heavy use. Like other Chávez residents, he sought support from local spiritual organizations for help managing his substance use. During 1995, Blondie still spent time at the hot spot. But often he was there coaxing a friend to go with him to a Narcotics Anonymous meeting or waiting to be picked up by members of a local evangelical church. Sometimes his presence at the hot spot was incongruous. In the midst of the drinking, socializing, and business activities of Elm Street members and associates, Blondie seemed perfectly at ease adding a well-worn Bible to the "baldy" uniform of shaved head, baggy pants, and gold chains.

On the day of Ernesto's trip to the corner store, the two brothers emerged from the path by the shooting gallery and stopped to chat at the hot spot.

Blondie and Ernesto are walking by on their way to the *tienda,* and Blondie greets several of the guys at the hot spot. CJ shakes up with Blondie—going through all four steps of the ritual: shake with thumbs clasped, shake with palms clasped, shake with fingers joined, and then "snap" as hands flew apart. CJ then crouches over and offers his hand to Ernesto. Blondie encourages his brother to "shake up" and then helps Ernesto move his fingers into the right positions. Blondie and CJ laboriously talk Ernesto through the ritual, molding his hand at each step. At the conclusion, CJ gives a cheer, and Ernesto looks a bit baffled but very happy to have participated.

Blondie then goes to chat with some other guys and leaves CJ and Ernesto alone. CJ asks what he is doing there, and Ernesto explains, in baby Spanish, that his mother told him to go to the store to get something [neither CJ nor I can make out the names of the exact groceries Ernesto has been sent for]. He opens his fist to show CJ the few crumpled dollar bills that his mother gave him to make his purchases, and as he does this Blondie returns from his conversation with the other guys.

"Look," says Blondie when he sees how Ernesto has shown CJ the money. "You have to learn how to carry that money properly. See you take it like this and you fold it up and put it in your shoe, like this, see?"

"Like this?" Ernesto responds, still speaking in Spanish. "You fold it and put it in here? In your shoe?"

"That's right," says Blondie. "That way it's safe, and no one knows you got it there. So they're not going to take it from you. But you have to talk English, okay Ernie? You have to learn how to talk English." Blondie turns to CJ and says loudly enough for several others at the hot spot to hear. "You see. I'm going to turn him into a homeboy yet. He's going to learn how to carry his money right. I just got to get him out of the house more so he can learn some English."

Ernesto was learning street smarts that fit some Chávez residents like an old shoe. Blondie and CJ knew how to present themselves in public—the clothes to wear, how to handle money and other valuables, how to greet people and shake hands, when to use English or Spanish or *Caló,* the English-Spanish argot of East LA. Most residents in Chávez had some rudimentary grasp of street smarts. For some, street smarts consisted of knowing how to schedule a day so as to avoid the hot spot or the shooting galleries at certain times. In Chávez, some older women preferred to go to the store in the early morning—before people began socializing at the hot spot.[13] One group of high school athletes typically gathered inside the Chávez gym to play basketball in the early evening. They cleared the floor of the younger children who played there after school and began intense half-court games. Elm Street members regularly socialized inside the Chávez gym after dark, and when Elm Street began to gather, the high school athletes often quickly wrapped up their own game. Sometimes they played a game or two with Elm Street members. These games were not a particularly difficult athletic challenge for the experienced high school players. But they could be a social challenge. Elm Street played a physical game; hard fouls were common, and rough tactics neutralized much of the athletes' advantage in basketball skills. Occasionally, games between the athletes and the homeboys ended with the threat of violence and an abrupt departure from the gym (usually, gang members who threatened violence were escorted out of the gym by other members). At other times, the athletes had difficulty retrieving their basketball from Elm Street members when they wanted to go home. On these occasions, the athletes sometimes defused the situation with help from Elm Street-affiliated family members.

Chávez street smarts were not a set of rules to be followed but rather a sense of how to interact.[14] Playing basketball in the evening or shopping in the morning arose from this sense, not merely from rule-based decisions to avoid the illicit institutions of Chávez. The basketball players did not simply flee the gym when Elm Street members came inside. Their decision to play in the afternoon was a strategic decision to minimize the chance of problems, but it was not a concession of public space. Similarly, the older women in Chávez could not, and did not, always avoid the hot spot. They went to the store in the afternoon if they needed to, and sometimes they bumped into young people drinking and socializing or doing business at the hot spot during morning trips. At these times, the younger streetwise residents of Chávez shared the public space of the barrio with the older residents they respectfully referred to as *las señoras.* Like the basketball players, the sensible decision to go to the market in the morning did not mean that *las señoras* had conceded control of public space to illicit institutions. One older resident who lived near the hot spot regularly admonished the young people there to pick up their empty beer bottles, and Elm Street members often interrupted their socializing and business dealings temporarily when a *señora* approached along the sidewalk. Most times, *las señoras* did not cross the street or go more than a few steps out of their way to avoid the hot spot because they counted on people gathered there to have the sense to show respect. What the older residents hoped to avoid by shopping in the morning was being inadvertently caught up in the routine activities of the hot spot that they usually avoided—a fight or a police raid, for example. Older residents also knew that while most of the time they would be treated civilly in public, problems would inevitably occur. For example, one afternoon a group of young men was gathered at the hot spot drinking beer when Mrs. Rodríguez came along the sidewalk heading toward the corner *tienda.* Several of the men greeted her with a "How are you, Mrs. Rodríguez," but Mario had his back to the sidewalk. Mario was a nineteen-year-old Elm Street member who was a bit more than six feet tall and weighed well more than two hundred pounds. He was telling his friends a story as Mrs. Rodríguez came along the sidewalk, and he did not notice her approach or his friends' greetings to her. Stepping back and waving his arms to emphasize a point, he was on the verge of knocking the much smaller Mrs. Rodríguez to the ground when one of his friends grabbed him just before the moment of impact. He apologized and Mrs. Rodríguez continued on her way. Her trip home from the store proceeded without incident, and she took advantage of the opportunity to stop at the hot spot, admonish the drinkers there that they shouldn't be drinking beer there, admonish the nondrinkers that they shouldn't be hanging out with the drinkers, and admonish everyone to pick up the empty bottles scattered on the lawn. Mrs. Rodríguez did not invite trouble by planning afternoon shopping trips, but shopping in the morning did not mean that she had conceded the public spaces of Chávez to the illicit institutions of the neighborhood. She had the sense to avoid trouble at the hot spot if she could, and she also had the sense to maintain the respect of the people who hung out at the hot spot by confronting them when problems occurred.

Learning the habits and skills of the streets did not mean that Ernesto, or other young people in Chávez, were destined for work in the illicit economy. In Chávez, it was important to know how to handle oneself in public no matter what one's interest or attitude toward illicit work. An illustration of this concerns Gloria, a thirty-three-year-old resident of Chávez whose youngest child, Daisy was ten years old and attended the local elementary school. Gloria and her friend Laura were discussing how their children were doing at school one evening in Laura's living room.

Gloria said that Daisy was having some problems with a group of boys at school. Some of them were picking on her. They would take things from her lunch, and on the walk home from school they teased her. One day, she came home from school in tears because the kids had been picking on her. "She came home and she was crying and she asked me to go over to the boy's house and tell his mother about it and get him to stop. I told her that she had to stick up for herself. I told her, I'm not going to go over there and fight your fights for you. If he is picking on you, you go up to him and you hit him in the stomach. So, the next time he picked on her, that's what she did. She went right up and hit the kid in the stomach a couple of times, and he has not bothered her since." Gloria tells the story with pride, and Laura endorses Gloria's analysis of the situation, saying that you have to learn how to stick up for yourself, and she knows her children—one a toddler and the other in diapers—are going to have to learn the same lesson.

Certainly neither Gloria nor Laura hoped their children would partic- ipate in illicit activities. Gloria was raising Daisy and her brother largely on her own because their father was in prison serving a long sentence fol- lowing a drug conviction; Laura's partner had also spent time in jail. Laura was sympathetic toward Elm Street; on one occasion she had even helped several members escape from police after a botched armed rob- bery. But Gloria had no kind words for the gang or other illicit institu- tions in the barrio, and in private she regularly cursed the gang and the drug sellers and the police and wished they all would leave the neighbor- hood in peace. Nevertheless, she recognized that her daughter had to fight her own fights on the streets of Chávez. Handling oneself in public was simply a necessity of life in the barrios. Even for young children, this meant learning, understanding, and following habits and skills that were taught and practiced in the illicit institutions of Chávez.

Street smarts is a sense that includes knowing how to carry your money, how to shake hands, what language to speak, how to retrieve your basketball, and how to handle yourself on the way to the corner store, as well as knowing that fighting is inevitable and necessary. This sense so dominated the day-to-day public culture of the barrio that it appeared to float in the air. Of course, the residents who spent more time on the streets were more street savvy, but nearly all residents had mastered the basic skill set and acquired at least a rudimentary sense of how to get along in public. Like Ernesto, many residents learned the sense of the streets in illicit institutions, which were the schools of the streets. Continual interactions with these institutions—with the gang in the gym and with the hot spot on the way to the store, for example—kept the street skills of all residents at the ready.

## Normalizing Illicit Involvement

Outsiders could and often did interpret the barrio's embrace of its local illicit institutions as an embrace of illicit activities by Chávez residents. Inside Chávez, most residents had at least a rudimentary sense of how to carry themselves on the streets. But embracing illicit institutions and mastering street smarts did not necessary lead to participation in the illicit economy. Inside Chávez, residents were familiar with everyday life in the illicit economy, they knew the drawbacks of illegal activities, and they mostly disapproved of individual or gang-organized law-breaking. Nevertheless, residents had to make sense of how illicit activities fit into their everyday life. Thus, residents normalized illicit activities in Chávez by assessing how family, friends, and neighbors became *involved* in illicit activities and institutions.

In Chávez, the decision to involve oneself in illicit activities was a personal decision, with the risks and drawbacks of illicit activities personally assumed. Thus, even as residents sided with their neighbors and their institutions against nonresidents and outside institutions, they also distanced themselves from illicit activities and institutions inside their community by analyzing who was involved in illicit activities and how they got into that position.

Residents normalized involvement in illegal activities by noting that groups and individuals involved in the illicit economy often "knew what they were doing," "understood the risks they were taking," or were "living the life." No one participated in illicit activities without understanding the potential price to be paid in life and limb, and many in Chávez had paid a heavy price. Ron, a twenty-five-year-old resident of Chávez with five brothers and four sisters, calculated that, in addition to his younger brother who was shot and killed, half of his brothers had been shot and lived, half had spent time in prison, and three were still young and active enough in illicit affairs that shooting and jail could not be ruled out of their future. There was no memorial in Chávez to Ron's younger brother. He had been in a car full of Elm Street members when a rival gang member shot him in the chest through an open window. It was only after several months that I even learned of the family's loss when Ron's mother explained that she and her husband had dressed up one morning to go visit the boy in the cemetery. Another brother, twenty-three-year-old Rodrigo, was currently involved in illicit activities—selling drugs and participating in robberies throughout the latter half of 1995. Ron said of his brother:

"I remember, he went into this liquor store and pulled a gun on the owner. He was doing this right there on Center Street, in hostile territory, and there were a couple of guys from Goldtown [a local gang] in the store. They started firing away at Rodrigo, and he just turned right on them and blasted back. Then he ran out of the store, and the owner, he had those automatic doors that slam shut when there's trouble. So, he hit the button and the door closed right after Rodrigo got outside, otherwise those other homeboys would've got him. He's crazy. He's never been hurt bad so he doesn't know what it's like. I was like that, too, before I got shot. . . . I talk to him. Trying to get him out of the life. I talk to him, but it doesn't do any good. I mean, he knows what he's doing. He knows what he's getting into. He just keeps on doing it, though. No one can tell him what to do."

For Ron and his family, the risks of participating in the illicit economy were a normal part of "living the life." Regular encounters with violence—often with relatively minor consequences given the weaponry involved but sometimes crippling or fatal—were understood to be one's lot in life if you decided to become involved in illicit activities. Family and homeboys remembered those who died. The injured often spent time on the streets of Chávez. Most of the imprisoned eventually came back out to tell of their experiences. These rituals ensured that people who became involved in illicit activities knew what they were getting into. They allowed Chávez residents to normalize the suffering of illicit workers as a personal decision to be made on the basis of an individual's understanding of the rewards and drawbacks involved.

Of course, the illicit economy needed customers as well as workers, and illicit customers also took risks. The normalizing logic that explained illicit workers' risks also applied to illicit customers. The experiences and attitudes of Sandra, a thirty-two-year-old resident who regularly patronized the hot spot drug market, illustrate this logic.

> Sandra is walking across the field, and I call to her. She calls back to me and I call to her, and she finally walks over. She introduces herself and I remind her that we know each other. She apologizes, saying that he doesn't recognize people sometimes. "I get so fucked up on the booze and the drugs and stuff that I don't know where I am half the time or who I'm talking to. Everyone looks the same to me when I'm on that stuff, and I meet a lot of people. So I don't recognize people a lot. I'm always afraid that someone is going to fuck with me when I'm like that. The beer isn't so bad; I mean that's a natural thing and you just piss it out. But the drugs, who knows what that stuff is made out of, you know? That stuff really fucks you up. You don't know what's going on half the time with that stuff, the cools [PCP]. And the rock [cocaine] is even worse. Some people do that, but it just makes you all crazy and shit—all twitchy like that. It makes you feel like you're the top, but it makes you too nervous and everything. So I stay away from that stuff. You don't know what's in that stuff. That's why I keep my hair like this because that way everyone recognizes me."

Customers believed that illicit drugs caused bad health and social vulnerability, and they wanted to minimize these negative side effects of consumption. Customers shunned drugs (in words if not always in deed) that seemed "unnatural" and particularly unhealthy. Customers also tried to reduce the problems that inevitably resulted from being disorientated and socially vulnerable. Sandra's hair, which formed a striking thick braid down her back, ensured that people recognized her and, she hoped, looked out for her well-being. The public spaces of Chávez also afforded illicit customers some social protection as Don, a resident in his mid-thirties who often hung out on the sidewalks of Chávez, explained. "Everyone knows me here," he said one evening as we sat drinking on the curb. "I feel safe because everyone knows me. So even if I'm fucked up, no one's gonna fuck with me." Like illicit workers, illicit customers were "living the life." By seeing their patronage of the illicit drug markets as a personal decision and then taking specific steps to reduce the risks of that patronage, customers normalized their participation in the illicit economy.

In Chávez, the decision to become involved with the illicit economy was meaningful in part because all residents were seen as eligible for participation. Illicit institutions were so visible in everyday life that residents assumed that if family members, friends, or neighbors wanted to get involved in illegal activities, they could. The question was, would they do it?

## CRIME AND COMMUNITY

Crime is often said to plague low-income communities. In this image, the low-income community is depicted as an unwitting victim of crime in the same way that a sick person is the unwitting host of a disease. Social conservatives, for example, argue for harsher punishment for supposed "superpredators" who prey on the innocent.[15] Scholars draw on the language of infection when they use epidemiological models to help describe the spread of social problems from one neighborhood to another.[16] More often, however, scholars speak of criminal infection metaphorically. There are a variety of different social organisms that may invade and infect. Elijah Anderson shows how a culture of violence may invade and establish itself in an impoverished community.[17] Gangs are frequently cast as invading organisms that prey on a community by recruiting youth to participate in illicit activities.[18]

We can extend the metaphor of criminal infection further. Social scientists concerned about crime and interested in better understanding its dynamics—particularly those with an eye toward reducing the human tragedy associated with crime—adopt the disease metaphor to examine what makes particular communities vulnerable to criminal infection. Robert Sampson has focused analytical attention on the characteristics of a community that lower its collective efficacy and impede its ability to fight off infections of crime.[19] Opportunistic criminals find it easier to operate in these sorts of socially disorganized, and hence socially vulnerable, communities.[20] They find that better organized communities can more readily muster the collective resources to repulse invading criminal infections. In the communities where crime establishes itself, residents may find that their everyday lives are completely altered by violence; they may feel as embattled as patients grappling with serious illnesses.[21] Social circumstances in low-income areas can even force residents to be unwitting carriers of the disease of crime. In economically marginalized communities or groups, crime may be the only available way to make ends meet.[22]

It is easy to apply the metaphor of crime as infection in Guadalupe and Chávez. In Guadalupe barrio, many recent immigrants could not obtain legal permission to work. These residents seemed to unwittingly engage in crime because they broke the law simply by taking a job and trying to make ends meet. In Chávez, residents did not like the shooting galleries and the drug dealing in their neighborhood, but they appeared to lack the collective will to force them out. Host-disease models—crime as infection or plague—do appear to capture something about the everyday dynamics of crime in these barrios.

For the most part, however, comparative fieldwork highlights the limitations of the infection-of-crime metaphor. Crime in these communities had different consequences for community social life. In Guadalupe, criminal and legal work were barely distinguishable in everyday life. Neither the employers who hired illegal workers nor the law enforcement officers charged with suppressing illegal work made much of an effort to discourage informal work in Guadalupe. Privately, undocumented status and working illegally caused residents anxiety and discomfort. But publicly, residents faced little public pressure to desist from a life of informal crime. The indigenous organizations of Guadalupe barrio—ranging from the groups of young men who sold forged social security cards to the Fortune-500 subcontractors who accepted them—legalized participation in the informal economy by allowing informal workers to follow the same kinds of daily routines as legal workers. But these institutions did not erase the distinction between legal and illegal. No matter how similar the daily routines of informal and legal workers, the former felt vulnerable to apprehension and deportation. Adjusting one's status by seeking legal residence was one way to address these private anxieties. But adjustment was a long and difficult process with an uncertain outcome. The effects of the adjustment process and of informal institutions in Guadalupe reinforced each other. They both created the public appearance of legality without resolving private feelings of anxiety.

In Chávez, the vigorous suppression of illicit activities by police made the public appearance of legality impossible. Chávez residents involved in the illicit economy had their own institutions, and these locally controlled institutions were in near-constant conflict with the police. These institutions normalized illicit activities in Chávez in two important ways. First, even Chávez residents who had little interest or sympathy in illicit activities identified with illicit institutions such as the gang. This identification was the outward-looking face of normalization in Chávez. In conflicts between gang and police, Chávez residents usually sided with the gang not because they liked what the gang did but because the gang represented their community against the institutions of the outside world. Second, Chávez residents who had no interest in participating in illicit activities nevertheless learned the basic skills and habits of illicit workers. Illicit institutions dominated the public spaces of Chávez. From child-hood, residents learned how to interact with these institutions. As adults, residents developed strategies to selectively engage with and avoid the illicit institutions of Chávez. By setting the tone of the public spaces, the illicit institutions of Chávez normalized the routine of illegality inside Chávez barrio. Local institutions normalized illicit activities in Chávez. Residents knew that these institutions constituted the barrio's outward-looking face to the world, and they knew what was involved, in a basic sense, in moneymaking in the illicit economy. Even if residents did not embrace the illicit economy, they also did not see it as an invading out-side organism over which they had no control. The final way in which Chávez residents integrated illicit activities in their community was by normalizing the process by which family, friends, and neighbors became involved in the illicit economy. Involvement was seen as a voluntary choice, made with an understanding of the benefits and drawbacks of that choice.

The infection metaphor postulates that criminals and community stand apart from each other and oppose each other—just as viruses stand apart from and then invade their animal hosts. But my experiences in Guadalupe and Chávez are at odds with this imagery of infection. As a rule, residents in Guadalupe and Chávez had good connections with their friends, relatives, and neighbors who were involved in criminal activities in the barrios. Complaints about neighbors' out-of-control criminal behavior were the exceptions that proved this rule. Nearly all the residents I met had a fairly concrete idea of how indigenous organi-zations regulated criminal activities. Many even participated in these organizations in some capacity at one time or another. In short, the rela-tionship between crime and community that I observed was more com-plex than a host-disease interaction. Though crime was ubiquitous in the barrios, the criminals did not seem opposed to the community, and they did not seem to have overwhelmed it.

Many barrio residents I knew seemed to feel better connected to and better able to control the criminals than they did the police. Certainly, residents in Guadalupe and Chávez—just like residents of any commu-nity—preferred to avoid getting tangled up with law enforcement. And just like many residents of low-income communities, many residents in the barrios spoke with frustration of the difficulty of getting police help when they wanted it.[23] For both of these reasons, police-community rela-tionships could be tense. But I also found that a simple conflict model seemed as inadequate a characterization of community-police relations as it did the criminal-community relationship. In Guadalupe and Chávez, as in other low-income communities, lines of communication connected residents and police.[24] Most surprisingly, residents of the barrios who often became entangled with the police—or who had a history of entanglement—maintained important lines of communication between police and community.

The disease-host metaphor suggests a clear and compelling story about the relationship between crime and the low-income community, but my experiences in Guadalupe and Chávez contradicted its central tenets. In the disease-host model, criminals stand outside the community, and the community attempts—and low-income communities have more difficulty with these attempts—to resist invasion by partnering with the police. In Guadalupe and Chávez, however, relationships among criminals, community, and law-enforcement were marked by communication and nuance as well as conflict and confrontation. Crime did not infect these communities; rather, it was integrated into them by local institutions over which residents had relatively substantial control. Crime thus did not always force itself upon residents. Repeatedly, I saw residents make an active decision to participate in crime or to interact with criminals. Often these decisions were based on firsthand experience about what it was like to be involved in local illegal institutions. In short, Guadalupe and Chávez did not lack the social organization to rebuff crime; rather, their social organization included crime and its associated institutions.

PART IV

# Welfare

LIKE MOST AMERICANS, GUADALUPE AND Chávez residents disapproved of welfare and those who used it. In both communities, nevertheless, some residents used public assistance to generate income. In Guadalupe, residents generally turned to aid during short periods of acute financial crisis, and in Chávez a substantial number of residents collected public aid during extended periods of financial dislocation. The dollar amounts provided by public assistance were small in Chávez and even smaller in Guadalupe. Small amounts could be significant, however. Consider, for example, what might happen if the income from one source—work, crime or welfare—suddenly disappeared from either barrio. Clearly, loss of income from work would be most devastating, and considering how many households relied on the informal or illicit economy, losing income from crime would also be highly disruptive. For most residents, losing welfare income would be the least disruptive, but in the limited number of households that relied on aid to make ends meet, the disappearance of aid would entail serious hardship. To understand the significance of welfare in the low-income barrios, we need to recognize that residents did not like aid and that welfare made up a small proportion of total income generation. But we also need to know who received aid, what kinds of aid they received, and how they received it in order to appreciate when welfare really mattered. I take up these tasks in Chapter 8.

Welfare has a relatively small financial role in the barrio economy, but it plays an outsized role in barrio social and cultural life. Comparing how aid shaped community life in Guadalupe and Chávez proves instructive. In both barrios, residents disapproved of public assistance, especially participation in the Aid to Families with Dependent Children (AFDC) and General Assistance (GA) programs. AFDC and GA were more common in Chávez, so it is not surprising that welfare stigma played a particularly important role in that community. But even in Guadalupe, where AFDC and GA were rare, residents regularly invoked welfare stigma. Policy makers and social scientists have worried for decades that the increasing size of public assistance expenditures reflects a growing acceptance of welfare among poor Americans.[1] Obviously, my observations in Guadalupe and Chávez cannot directly address this concern. These observations do show, however, complex social and cultural attitudes, opinions, and practices surrounding stigma in these two communities. Residents in both communities fundamentally disapproved of aid receipt. Beyond this baseline similarity, welfare stigma played out in a wide variety of ways in the two communities depending on who was stigmatizing whom and why.

Chapter 9 analyzes the social and cultural dynamics surrounding welfare stigma, with a focus on how the stigma that surrounds public assistance in America played out in the low-income barrios. Welfare stigma thrived in the barrios, and my observations suggest that the *use* of welfare does not directly reflect an *approval* of welfare. In my analysis I focus on the relationship between the everyday use of welfare and its local meanings. My observations, particularly in Guadalupe, revealed connections between the local culture of the two barrios and a national ethos of welfare stigma. I noted that welfare stigma was alive and well in Guadalupe and Chávez but that residents nevertheless regularly violated its proscriptions. These widespread violations provided an opportunity to *use* culture—by expressing and deploying welfare disapproval and stigma in creative, instrumental, and even strategic ways.

Thus, fieldwork in the barrios revealed welfare subcultures in action. I argue that welfare subcultures are one of the institutions of poverty because they reflect broad themes of our national symbolic life at the same time that they make sense of the specific exigencies of everyday life in poverty. Social scientists have described similar subcultures in a variety of low-income communities.[2] In the chapters of this section, I describe the welfare subcultures of the barrios, and I analyze the institutional dynamics of residents' sense-making and culture-creating activities.

# CHAPTER 8

# Making Ends Meet

For the last four decades, the face of welfare in America has been that of a black single mother receiving Aid to Families with Dependent Children (AFDC).[1] During these decades, caseworkers, journalists, and social scientists have become increasingly interested in her answer to two simple questions: How long? and How much? Has a mother received aid for a few months, or is she raising her children during decades of aid receipt? Has she abandoned work and marriage in favor of dependence on public assistance? Are public funds subsidizing voluntary unemployment or instigating family breakup? Concern with these questions provided the political energy to replace the AFDC program with Temporary Assistance to Needy Families (TANF), a program that centers on imposing time limits on aid receipt and training recipients to join the workforce.[2] As I write, results from TANF are encouraging. Welfare roles have shrunk, single mothers are enrolling in job-training programs, and an increasing number are working. But these positive results have occurred during an era of vigorous economic growth; given the substantial challenges of moving from aid to work, some wonder whether TANF has really addressed problems associated with poverty and single motherhood.[3] Journalists have noted that day-to-day life for single mothers under TANF, which promised to improve poor people's quality of life by fostering self-reliance and upward mobility, either has not changed much or has gotten more difficult.[4] Focusing on "how much" and "how long" may not capture the complex dynamics of aid in the day-to-day lives of the poor.

The change from AFDC to TANF occurred after I had left Guadalupe and Chávez barrios, so I cannot discuss how this policy change affected everyday life in the low-income barrios. What was clear during my time in the barrios, however, was that the pitfalls of welfare—the issues of "how much?" and "how long?"—were a concern not only for policy makers in Washington, D.C., but also among residents of Guadalupe and Chávez. As in Washington, the problems of dependence, laziness, and family breakup aroused concern in the barrios. But discussions of welfare in the nation's capital failed to reflect the realities of welfare in the low-income barrios in at least two important respects. First, the policy debates overlook the fact that public assistance includes a wide variety of activities. Residents in the barrios saw public aid as any resource that was obtained by participating in a public or semipublic agency without working for that agency, and I adopt their definition here.[5] According to this broad definition, public aid includes means-tested welfare programs, such as General Assistance (GA) or food stamps; social insurance programs, such as unemployment insurance or Supplemental Security Income (SSI); semipublic aid agencies, such as food banks; and private charities that open their doors to all comers, such as church-based soup kitchens. In Guadalupe and Chávez, AFDC was only one of the many sources of public aid income and in-kind support, and the single mother who relied on AFDC was only one of a diverse group of welfare users. The figures in Chapter 2 paint the picture. In the barrios the "standard" face of welfare in America—even leaving aside the fact that aid recipients in Guadalupe and Chávez were Mexican American and not black—captured a stereotype, not a reality.

The second difference between welfare in the barrios and welfare policy in the capital was related to the first: not only was there no "standard" face of welfare, but also there was no "standard" way of using public aid. A variety of economic strategies included public aid. Some residents used aid as a way to navigate short-term financial distress, others used aid as a marginal supplement to other sources of income, and still others relied on aid as a primary source of support for an extended period of time. I observed that these different ways of using aid corresponded to different kinds of aid programs. For example, in both Guadalupe and Chávez, local charities distributed free food and clothing, and some residents depended on the resources they garnered from their weekly visits to these charities. This kind of assistance could be helpful for residents navigating a period of short-term financial distress or as a supplement to other sources of income, but residents did not rely on local charities as a primary source of income. In contrast, a number of residents who received monthly AFDC or GA checks relied on that income as their primary source of income. Focusing on the issues of "how much" or "how long" obscures the variety of ways in which residents of the low-income barrios used public assistance in everyday life.

Amid these complex realities of public aid receipt in the barrios, residents of Guadalupe and Chávez focused on the same rhetorical questions as policy makers and social scientists. In this sense, a common culture pervades welfare receipt in the United States, and policy makers and the poor share a similar orientation toward public assistance. In Chapter 9, I show how this common cultural framework worked itself out in everyday barrio life. Before turning to that analysis, however, it is important to understand specifically what residents meant when they asked, "How much?" or "How long?" Even if policy makers in Washington and residents in the barrios asked the same questions, the local context within which they did so differed considerably. This chapter describes and analyzes the barrio context.

There were many faces of welfare in the barrios. Public aid played different roles in residents' economic strategies, and in the next section of this chapter, I describe and analyze the different ways that residents of the barrios used public assistance as part of their larger economic strategies. Of the different ways of using public assistance, one in particular— the long-term reliance on aid as a primary source of income—has been most troubling for policy makers and was most troubling for residents in the barrios. In the second section of this chapter, I focus on the experiences of residents who relied on aid as a primary source of income. In that section, I analyze the use of aid in Chávez, where reliance was much more common than in Guadalupe. I describe and analyze the different pathways that residents traveled to reliance, and I describe and analyze the different ways that reliance unfolded in residents' everyday lives. Together, the sections of this chapter introduce the everyday reality of welfare use in Guadalupe and Chávez barrios.

## PUBLIC AID AND ECONOMIC STRATEGIES

In Guadalupe and Chávez, some aid programs provided in-kind aid such as food stamps to use for groceries or community food and clothing "banks" from which residents made periodic withdrawals. AFDC, GA, unemployment insurance, and SSI programs, among others, provided direct cash assistance. Residents participated in these different aid programs in different ways, with some turning to aid during short periods of acute financial distress and others using aid to supplement other income sources. Residents also could come to rely on aid for most of their income for an extended period of time, and this third way of using aid attracts much of the public and scholarly attention. These distinct ways of using aid were not mutually exclusive, and many residents combined public assistance in different ways. As Chapter 2 shows, public aid played a larger role in the economic life of the residents I knew in Chávez than in Guadalupe. Here I show that even though the amount of aid in the two barrios differed, the three ways that residents used aid in everyday economic life were remarkably similar.

*Short-Term Aid during Acute Financial Distress*

In June 1994, soon after the governor of California gave his vocal support to California's Proposition 187 (which proposed eliminating all forms of state support, including public schooling, medical care, food stamps, and welfare, for undocumented migrants to California), a group of Guadalupe women I knew had crammed themselves around the small table in Verónica's kitchen. The women were all mothers, were all married, and were all recent arrivals to Guadalupe. They had met at a local English as a second language (ESL) program, and after a few weeks they began to meet outside class, rotating from house to house and apartment to apartment, to eat lunch, socialize, and let their children play together. The ESL class ended in May 1994, but the get-togethers—the *convives*—continued throughout the summer. The conversation that afternoon at Verónica's turned into an exploration of how the women used and thought about public aid.

Chela, a housecleaner from Veracruz who had lived in Guadalupe for about three years, and Rosa, who kept house and occasionally did some informal street vending, often shared the role of instigator at the *convives*. This day, Chela took the lead. Chela had followed her Mexican husband to the United States, but the marriage ended soon after she arrived. She met her current husband in San Jose—a man she playfully referred to as a *gringo* and claimed refused to speak a word of Spanish. When I first met Chela she exclaimed that she had to enroll in the ESL class because the only way she could communicate with her husband at the moment was with grunts. At the summer *convive*, Chela ignited the conversation around the table by saying that her husband supported Governor Pete Wilson's position on Proposition 187.

"When we're in the store and there is a Mexican person using food stamps at the checkout counter, he'll say to me, 'There goes my taxes.' That's a terrible thing to say!"

Others at the table agree that it was a terrible thing for her husband to say. But some also suggest that he has a point. Some people do come across the border just to receive welfare. "You know it is a problem," says Verónica. "Not for most people. But there are some people who come here illegally and get welfare. And that's not right."

Doña Lupe, sitting across the table from Chela, takes the floor to offer her perspective. "All the people on my street are Mexican. They don't have papers. But none of them are getting welfare. And they don't get MediCal [California's version of federal Medicaid], and they don't get food stamps. They are all working—my barrio is full of janitors! They didn't come here to get welfare."

The other women around the table agree, and sentiment around the table turns toward Doña Lupe. Carmen, María, and Chela are nodding their heads. Most immigrants, they agree, came from Mexico to get work, not to go on welfare; Wilson's initiative is misguided. After a few minutes even Verónica concedes that not all immigrants should be punished because some abuse the system.

Throughout the discussion, Rosa's voice has been conspicuously absent. She is a small woman who has been living in a two-bedroom Guadalupe apartment with her husband, two children, and a rotating group of extended family for six years. She is one of the more streetwise members of the group—only Chela, who quickly became streetwise when her first husband abandoned her, matches her in this regard—and she is one of the group leaders. She initiated most of the springtime *convives,* kept track of whose turn it was to host, dealt out potluck assignments, and decided who would bring home the leftovers. She often set the gossipy lunch table agenda. But today, Rosa seems to have little to say about Governor Wilson, Proposition 187, immigration, and welfare. As the women continue to discuss hard-working Mexican immigrants, Rosa finally steps in and gently redirects the conversation.

"Sometimes, it is necessary to get some help," she says quietly, and the ladies direct their attention to her. "After Junior was born, we were short of money because it cost us $5,000 to cover all the hospital expenses. So David [her husband] borrowed the money from his boss, and they took it out of his paycheck. We already had the two babies and [David] wasn't making good money, so we had to get some help. So we got food stamps for a while—just a year—while we paid the debt. As soon as we paid off all the debt to David's boss, we stopped getting the food stamps."

As soon as Rosa stops talking, Chela and Doña Lupe jump in to offer their own welfare stories. Chela received AFDC and food stamps for a few months after her first husband left her, and Doña Lupe recently signed up for food stamps to supplement the meager disability income the household had been collecting since her husband injured his back at work. Both women recoil as they relive the shame they feel paying for groceries with the stamps. That is the worst part of receiving them, Rosa agrees. It is terrible to take them out of her purse at the corner store. She always hopes her neighbors will not see her. "But we never abused them," adds Rosa. "People I see in the store use food stamps to buy beer. Or they buy their food with stamps so that they can spend their money on alcohol. But I never did that. I used the stamps only for food—and mostly food for the babies."

As the participants at the *convive* discovered, a number of Guadalupe residents found themselves turning to aid to get through a period of temporary fiscal crisis. Some temporary crises were brought on by an unexpected need for income, not a disruption in income-generating activities. For Rosa, a huge medical bill meant the household had to suddenly produce $5,000. Rosa and David had little choice but to use food stamps for as long as it took them to repay David's boss. In other cases, disrupted social relationships created a crisis. Fortunately for Chela, the economic crisis that followed the end of her marriage proved temporary; she went off AFDC as soon as housecleaning and a new husband got her back onto her financial feet. For Doña Lupe, the disruption that motivated her turn to aid was an economic and social shock, and in the summer of 1994, the crisis had not yet been resolved. Doña Lupe expected that her husband would soon be back on his feet and back at work, but uncertainty remained.[6]

When all three women signed up for aid, they did so in the expectation that their use of aid and the shame associated with that use would quickly end. Their economic plans were not built on the foundation of a steady aid check. They knew that in the not-too-distant future—a few months, a year at most—they would no longer need the checks or the food stamps. They had turned to aid after some unexpected event with negative economic consequences such as a huge medical bill, abandonment, or injury, and they would turn away from aid as soon as they could.

In these ways, the *convive* women used aid like other residents I knew in Guadalupe and Chávez who experienced a short period of acute financial difficulty. Few preferred aid as a way to manage financial crisis. Most first turned to family for help with unexpected bills, and these family networks helped. But tight household budgets meant that large bills could overwhelm family network resources, and Guadalupe and Chávez, like other low-income Mexican American communities, lacked indigenous credit sources such as rotating associations that might provide larger amounts of cash at short notice.[7] Thus, in both barrios, residents who prided themselves on their economic self-sufficiency turned to food stamps, local charities, and other aid sources when they were hit with large bills without advance warning.

Residents collected both in-kind and cash assistance. In-kind support could free up cash to pay off a creditor, but it required reorganizing household finances. New priorities had to be set, and new daily routines had to be adopted. Someone had to invest time at the local thrift store or church in order to collect the "free" clothes or food. Residents using food stamps for the first time or for a short period of time often changed their shopping habits at local grocery stores, for reasons I discuss below. In-kind support could help pay off an unexpected bill, but it did not solve economic problems brought on by an interruption in income generation. In those cases, in-kind support simply did not provide the right resources or enough of them to get through a period of short-term distress. Residents turned to cash programs such as AFDC, unemployment, or disability insurance to replace income they lost through misfortune. When the monetary shortfall was not too large, when it did not last too long, and when it had a predictable end point, aid programs in both barrios helped residents navigate through these periods of short-term financial distress.

*Aid on the Margin*

For some barrio residents, public aid helped stave off financial collapse following an unexpected economic shock. For other residents, public aid acted as a safety net by providing small but regular infusions of in-kind resources that provided the marginal support they needed to make ends meet day to day. Many residents who used aid on the margin expected to and did receive aid for a long period of time. In-kind assistance such as food or clothing commonly played this long-term marginal role, and in both Guadalupe and Chávez charitable organizations—operating in many cases with support from local and state government—were the most important source of this form of public assistance.

In Guadalupe and Chávez, residents did not rely on the food bank or the charitable thrift store as a primary source of support, but the quality of life in many households rose and fell depending on how successful residents were in securing resources from these local institutions. Success in securing aid on the margin involved relatively small stakes—a grocery bag filled with name-brand food was preferable to one full of generic government surplus products, for example, and securing a relatively new pair of pants was a success while locating a pair with only a few months of life left was nothing to become excited about. But small differences mattered a great deal in the barrios, and competition for these resources could be keen. The organizations that distributed in-kind aid in the barrios needed the support and active participation of residents to operate. A small number of residents put in a substantial amount of work to operate the barrios' charitable organizations. A larger group of residents made some contribution of time or effort and in exchange improved their chances of garnering a better selection of goods. Because marginal aid was publicly visible and locally controlled, the limited economic resources at stake created and reflected important social dynamics in the community. The Chávez food bank exemplifies all of these characteristics of long-term aid on the margin.

The Chávez food bank was a cooperative effort. The Department of Housing opened the doors of the Chávez gym to the food bank once or twice a month. Santa Margarita, the local Catholic parish, provided a secure room in its social hall to store dry goods as well as access to its freezers for perishables. Mike Gonzales, who had attended twelve-step Narcotics Anonymous meetings with several Chávez residents, helped out by driving the food on his flatbed truck from the food bank warehouse in South Central Los Angeles to the East LA Chávez gym. And most of the heavy lifting was done by resident-volunteers, who unloaded boxes of food from Mike's truck, who attempted to prevent nonresidents from participating in the food bank, who organized Chávez residents to ensure that food was fairly distributed, and who collected donations to defray the nominal cost of participating in LA's food bank network.

In theory, the food bank equitably distributed available food to Chávez residents on the basis of need. In practice, need was an important criterion for distribution, but local control over the food bank meant that the distribution of foods also reflected political relationships in the barrio. In late 1994 and early 1995, political infighting in Chávez paralyzed the food bank. Three residents elected as Chávez's official resident representatives had been running the food bank, but elections in January 1995 toppled this trio from office, and a new group took the official reins of the projects. Paul, who I knew well, sided with the newcomers, and he assumed responsibility for the food bank. He soon found out that the just unseated trio had damaged Chávez's relationship with the bank by failing to provide documents proving that donations were going to needy community members. Several weeks passed while Paul recreated the missing paperwork, and it was two more weeks before he could secure the cooperation of Mike Gonzales and his flatbed. Finally, in March 1995, Paul went to the food bank to present the missing documents.

Ring binder in hand, Paul asks to see the food bank director, but the supervisor on the warehouse floor says that the director won't meet him. "She's too busy to meet you today, and she already gave you her no," says the supervisor. Paul persists, "I have all the documents right here. Just let me get in to see her, and I can get things straightened out." Paul pleads and flatters the supervisor until she agrees to call up to the director. "She's going to come down and say hello," says the supervisor as she hangs up the phone. "But she already gave you her no, and now she's just going to come down here and give it to you again."

After fifteen nervous minutes, the director enters the warehouse. She is clearly annoyed, and she reluctantly shakes Paul's hand. She says that she is too busy to even glance at his documents, and she chastises Paul, saying that the food bank is under no obligation to give out food without proper documentation—she had been doing Chávez a favor by continuing to provide food for weeks. "Now you come in here without even making an appointment and ask for food immediately? I'm too busy to deal with this today." Eventually, the director makes an appointment to go over the documents with Paul next week in Chávez, but she remains angry and hastily brushes Paul's hand when he tries to shake. A Chicano forklift operator witnesses the whole scene. "Sometimes, people forget why they are doing this," he says.

The next week, a calmer food bank director met Paul at Santa Margarita to go over his documents, and the Chávez food bank resumed the following week.

Bringing the food bank back to Chávez had required some deft maneuvering on Paul's part—constructing the documentation, securing Mike Gonzales's cooperation, flattering the food bank supervisor, and dealing with the director's anger without responding in kind. The announcement of the bank's resumption prompted Chávez residents to begin their own maneuvering to corner the benefits of the food bank's largesse. At the community meeting announcing the resumed food bank, Señora López—a Chávez resident who relied on social security to make ends meet—argued that older residents should be first in line at the food bank. Without the food bank the last few months, she had been running out of beans and other staples at the end of the month, and she was sure that others were in the same position as her. Paul assured Señora López that seniors would be granted first entrance to the Chávez gym once the food bank was set up next week. He also said that he would need volunteers to get up early in the morning to prepare the gym; volunteers, Paul said, would get to go through the food bank line before anyone else. After the meeting, Linda asked Paul if she could volunteer. Linda was in her late twenties and a mother of three children from ages two to seven years. She had moved to Chávez a year earlier, after her husband was imprisoned on a drug possessions charge, and she turned to AFDC to make ends meet. "I'm not usually up that early," she told Paul. "I usually just get up and get the kids off to school and then go back to bed. But my wallet got stolen this month, so I really need the help. I'll set my alarm and drop the baby off at my mother's so that I can be there."

When food bank day arrived, Linda showed up at the appointed time. So too did Blanca and Gladis, two-thirds of the trio who had formerly been Chávez's official representatives. "We want to make sure that Paul does this right and fair," explained Blanca. "If we don't keep an eye out, he might just give everything out to his friends and family."

While Linda, Blanca, Gladis, and two other volunteers started setting up the gym, I joined Paul, Mike Gonzales, and two other men for the drive to the South Central food warehouse. Mike was a tall, thin, fiftyish-looking man with a full beard and a smattering of tattoos on his forearms. He had been attending an evangelical church in nearby El Sereno, he said, and during the drive to South Central he recounted how his experiences in Vietnam, three decades ago, had left him with a deep and unshakable faith. "Some kind of larger power was looking out for me; people would shoot from seven or eight feet away and miss, and well-trained and experienced fighters would run away from me. How can you explain that? It was some kind of miracle."

At the food bank, the flatbed was loaded with boxes of bread and cases of tortillas. There were enormous plastic jars of avocado dip and peanut butter, boxes of frozen pastry dough and potato chips, cases of *frijoles* and rice, cookies and juice boxes, yogurt and ice cream. The truck groaned when the forklift operator dropped the pallets of food onto it, and it bottomed out as we left the warehouse parking lot.

Halfway back to Chávez, Mike pulled the truck into the parking lot of an abandoned factory and stopped next to a mid-1970s American sedan. Mike introduced the driver of the car, a man in his late fifties, as his Narcotics Anonymous sponsor, and he put three boxes of food into the sedan's large trunk. Next, we stopped at Santa Margarita, where Paul and I unloaded some of the most desirable food, including most of the peanut butter, half of the potato chips, and a third of the cookies. Later in the day, Paul and Mike would return and bring this food home to their own friends and family. Finally, we drove the remaining blocks to the Chávez gym, where a crowd of about eighty residents greeted our arrival.

While Paul and Mike held the residents at bay, a bucket brigade of volunteers moved the food into the gym. Linda, Blanca, Gladis, and the other volunteers assembled boxes of food for themselves and stashed them out of sight on one side of the gym. Then Linda opened the front doors of the gym, and Señora López and a dozen other seniors entered the gym. The volunteers put tortillas, dip, pastry dough, beans, rice, cookies, yogurt, ice cream, and drinks into plastic grocery bags, and young men from Elm Street appeared to carry the heavy bags of food home for *las señoras*. Several Elm Street members took advantage of their early access to the food bank to put together choice bags of food for themselves, and Paul unsuccessfully chased after one young man who stole two cases of yogurt.

Once *las señoras* had passed through the gym, other residents were allowed in. Linda had handed out numbers on a first-come-first-served basis, and now she stood outside the entrance to the gym calling out five numbers at a time. Each resident signed in—Paul had emphasized that the paperwork had to be up to date to keep the food bank open, and he checked throughout the day to make sure the sign-in proceeded smoothly—but several people who lived outside Chávez nevertheless went through the food bank line. Linda stopped one woman who had given a non-Chávez address. "I just live across Birch Street," pleaded the woman. "And my sister lives in Chávez. I came to all the food banks before. Just ask Gladis." Linda relented, but only after the woman agreed to sign in using her sister's address.

Less than an hour after the truck arrived at the gym, the more desirable cookies, chips, and ice cream were gone. The seniors had received most of this "good" food. Linda's numbering system had begun to break down as residents scrambled to grab what was left of the desirable goodies. Streetwise residents propped open the gym's back door, a pickup basketball game started up, and Paul found himself besieged by residents, mostly Elm Street members, who pleaded with him to "give up" the food that remained to be distributed. The volunteers, fearful that their own food stashes would disappear in the increasing chaos, wanted to go home. Residents who had stood in line for hours complained as the food line was overrun by homeboys, homegirls, and basketball players sneaking in through the back door. Finally, Paul intervened. He stepped in front of Greg, a nineteen-year-old homeboy who was walking toward the back door of the gym with a bag of groceries and ordered him to "put it down and get out!" Greg protested and the two squared up to fight, but then Greg backed down (Paul said later, "I would have kicked his ass, and he knew it"); he dropped the bag of groceries and walked out of the gym. Everyone saw the confrontation with Greg, and Paul took advantage of the momentum to sweep the food bank raiders and the basketball players out the rear door and to assign Ronnie, a well-respected twenty-eight-year-old Elm Street member, the task of preventing their reentry. With order restored, the volunteers quietly and quickly distributed the final cases of beans, rice, tortillas, and other staples.

For the next few days, the kitchens of Chávez were filled with supplies from the food bank. The snack foods and desserts disappeared quickly. The evening of the food bank, it seemed there was a bag of chips at every street corner, and everyone was eating ice cream. Over the next day or two, some children discovered that yogurts stored in the freezer could be eaten like ice cream, and they quickly disappeared. The staples showed up at meal time and were eaten off stove tops in soups and out of fry pans.

The food bank never provided enough to alter household economics greatly or for long, but it was still an important institution in the barrio. The practice of allowing the volunteers and *las señoras* to pass through the food bank first and the numbering system lent the distribution of food bank goodies fairness and legitimacy. But even the volunteers and *las señoras,* who received the best the food bank had to offer, valued the food bank more for the treats it provided—the chips and ice cream— than for the savings it made possible in the weekly grocery bill. The food bank mattered because it supplied goodies on the margin, not because residents counted on it for the staples of everyday life. Thus, while the distribution of food ostensibly was determined by the relative need and vulnerability of local households, in fact the food bank mattered as much for local politics as it did for household economics.

In the barrios, residents themselves controlled aid on the margin and thus distributed it along the lines of local politics. When the political leadership of the projects changed hands, the new leaders, represented by Paul, had to reestablish their relationship with the food bank administration and organize a distribution system. Mike Gonzales and his flatbed were crucial. Mike participated in the food bank because he thought it was a good cause and he wanted to help out, but he also made sure that some food bank goodies went to his NA sponsor, a person with whom he had a personal relationship. Inside Chávez, local politics and food bank goodies were crucial in the distribution system. Residents such as Linda volunteered to help Paul because in the short term they wanted to gain access to the resources of the food bank and in the long term they wanted to be part of the group that had political control of the Chávez barrio. Residents such as Blanca and Gladis, who had been recently ousted as the elected resident-leaders of the projects, volunteered for the food bank in order to keep an eye on the new leadership.

The food bank largesse benefited residents who had some power in the projects. It benefited residents with formal political power such as Paul, Linda, Blanca, and Gladis. It benefited residents with power derived from access to resources, such as Mike Gonzales. It benefited residents such as Señora López and the other seniors who were able to make a legitimate claim on the food bank resources. And it benefited streetwise residents, such as the Elm Street members whose power on the streets meant that they would not be stopped when they opened the gym's rear door and walked off with choice items.

The marginal aid provided by the food bank in Chávez and other indigenous charitable organizations had its own social dynamics. Participation was a highly visible public act. Long-term receipt of marginal aid rarely escaped the notice and comment of relatives, friends, and neighbors—more so, for example, than receiving food stamps, which the *convive* women in Guadalupe described using with such embarrassment. Marginal aid programs were also distinct in that they were often locally controlled. Local activists worked with city and county bureaucracies to bring in-kind aid into the neighborhood, and barrio volunteers often staffed the programs that handed out the food and clothing. Public visibility and local control meant that among some residents with whom I spent time, marginal aid became fodder in local politics, while for others it served as a source of stigma and shame—social consequences of aid that I explore in greater detail in the next chapter.

*Relying on Aid*

For some residents, aid was the primary means to support themselves or their families. Nothing appeared more simple than relying on aid—just take the monthly check out of the mailbox and cash it. But among the residents I knew, the experience of relying on aid rarely ended up being this simple. The experiences of Guadalupe residents Henry and his common-law wife Tanya illustrate both the simplicity and the complexity of public aid in the barrios. In Chapter 6, I described the informal income-generating activities of Henry. For a few weeks in the fall of 1993, Henry worked as a day laborer at Strong Road near Guadalupe barrio. Then, during the first few months of 1994, he earned money on the side selling intricately tooled Mexican leather belts in cooperation with his partner,

Jesús, who had a permanent stall at one of the San Jose flea markets.
During this time, Henry and Tanya also participated in public assistance.
The way they did so illustrates how residents of the barrios used aid as a
primary means of support.

The first public aid that Henry received was unemployment insurance, which he received for about six months after he left a warehouse
job where, he said, "the boss treated us like animals." Of the six employees at the firm—three men, three women, all Mexican immigrants—
Henry was the only one with documents. "I was the only one who talked
back," he said. "All the wetbacks were afraid of losing their job, and
they told me that the boss was going to fire me as soon as I became eligible for benefits. He kept the illegals on because he didn't have to give
them benefits."

Henry and Tanya lived in a room they rented in Tanya's sister's house,
which they shared with the sister and a boarder. Like many women in
Guadalupe, Tanya worked seasonally in the canneries and received
unemployment insurance when she was laid off in the fall.[8] In the fall of
1993, the timing of Tanya's layoff could not have been better; she was
pregnant, and she left the cannery only a couple weeks before her due
date. As Henry described in Chapter 6, life at home in the months after
he left the warehouse and Tanya was laid off were pretty dull. After a few
weeks in front of the TV, he went to Strong Road, where he worked for
a few weeks as a day laborer just to have something to do. When his
caseworker at the California Employment Development Department suggested he get some job training at a center near Guadalupe, Henry enthusiastically enrolled. For three months, Henry and Tanya combined their
welfare incomes—hers from cannery unemployment and his from a job-
training stipend—and they did pretty well. The checks came in the mail;
they cashed them, paid the rent and the bills, and had a little left over to
finance Henry's side-business dealings at the flea markets.

As was the case for many people in the barrios, however, Henry and
Tanya were not able to sustain themselves for long simply cashing public
assistance checks. After the birth of their son, their economic life changed
slowly but dramatically, and so did their use of public assistance. As the
weather turned colder in the winter of 1994, Tanya's sister raised the
rent. With the baby at home, the heating bill had shot through the roof,
and Tanya's sister said she needed more rent to pay it. Henry said that the
heating bill was simply an excuse. He was sure that Tanya's sister did not
like having an additional noisy tenant in her house, and he began to ask
around about a new place to live. At around the same time, Henry's job-

training stipend decreased—a program feature designed to encourage trainees to return to the labor force. With less income coming from job training, Henry began focusing more time and energy on his flea market side job. His stipend income decreased further because the training center docked his pay every time he skipped class to go hustle leather belts. In February 1994, as the financial pressure mounted, Tanya returned from a trip showing off the baby to relatives in Mexico and signed up for AFDC. Henry was relieved. With AFDC money, Henry and Tanya could pay the rent on the house for at least a couple of months; that would provide enough time for Henry to get a job and for the couple to figure out a more stable living arrangement.

AFDC soon proved as unstable as unemployment, however. In March, a few weeks after Tanya signed up for aid, Henry received a notice from the welfare office, directing him to come down for an interview. "I went down and they started asking me about Junior," he explained.

"They asked me if I was the father, and I said yes. Then, they ask," and he pauses to assume a deep *basso profundo* tone that mocks the welfare worker's serious Anglo-accented English. "Are you willing to take responsibility? And I said"—another pause while he mocks himself, the humble *Mexicano* shifting uncomfortably from one foot to the other and maintaining his gaze on the floor—"yes. So they say that I have to make support payments for the kid. They're going to take the money out of my stipend and give it to her, but they keep her AFDC the same. They just keep the stipend money for themselves."

For the household, it seems to me, this is a financial disaster. The net loss of income is going to make it difficult to make ends meet. Once they pay the rent and the bills, there is not going to be enough left enough to buy food. I think of policy makers' theories that AFDC participants, rationally calculating the costs and benefits of program participation, manipulate the program's rules to make aid dependence pay off. Henry's behavior does not seem to fit this theory; his honest replies to the caseworker have caused him enormous problems. I ask, "Why did you say yes? You could have just said that it wasn't your kid or that it was your kid but you wouldn't take responsibility. Didn't you see what they were going to do?"

"I knew what was going on, and I thought about it. But I decided not to. The feelings inside that would have created" and Henry grabs his chest—his heart—to show where those feeling would have struck him. "I couldn't live with myself. Also, if something happened to the baby, I could have no say in it if I did that now. I wanted to have something to say about his life. So, I guess pride was my first reason and then the other things came second."

Henry and Tanya muddled through the remainder of the spring. Henry attended job training long enough to collect the substantial one-time award for finishing out the program, but he also stayed active in his flea-market side business. Eventually, he ended up in a new warehouse job. Tanya stayed at home, but as soon as the baby was old enough to be looked after by her sister, she planned to go out and look for cannery work. The two also kept looking for a new apartment. Paying less rent would be another way to address their economic problems.

As was the case for Henry and Tanya, most of the barrio residents I knew found that public aid by itself did not provide enough income to support a household, and most combined public assistance with income from other sources.[9] Relying on aid meant managing the public aid bureaucracies. Recipients had to present themselves and their household as an eligible category of aid recipient, and they had to manage the consequences, often unintended and unanticipated, of exposure to the bureaucracies. Thus, while nothing seems easier than receiving an aid check in the mail and cashing it at the corner store, the experience of relying on aid rarely resembled this picture.

PATHWAYS TO RELIANCE

In both Guadalupe and Chávez I spent time with many residents who used aid to get through short periods of financial distress or as a way to increase income at the margin. When it came to long-term reliance on aid, however, experiences in the two barrios diverged. Guadalupe and Chávez did not differ in the experience of aid reliance; the experiences of Henry and Tanya, who happened to live in Guadalupe, typified the course of aid reliance among residents in both barrios. The difference was that experiences such as Henry and Tanya's were relatively rare in Guadalupe and fairly common in Chávez.

As the experiences of Tanya and Henry illustrate, relying on public assistance was not an easy or stable way to support a household. When Tanya signed up for AFDC, neither she nor Henry appreciated the multiple ways in which that decision would affect their household finances. Henry did not anticipate being called in by the state's welfare agents, and he found himself unwilling to lie in order to protect the couple's income. Defying their own expectations, Tanya and Henry found that their economic situation deteriorated when they began to rely on aid. In Chávez, a much larger number of residents relied on aid as a primary source of income. Chávez households had a larger aid grant, on average, than Guadalupe households ($7,400 in Chávez vs. $5,900 in Guadalupe, according to 1990 census figures), but the everyday dynamics of aid reliance were quite similar in the two barrios. In both LA and San Jose, relying on aid meant opening oneself up to inspection and interference by state welfare agents. In both barrios, relying on public aid was much more complicated and intrusive than simply opening the mailbox and cashing a check.[10] In Guadalupe, Tanya and Henry discovered this painful reality through firsthand experience. In Chávez, residents benefited from the experiences of family and neighbors; many had enough experience as an indirect beneficiary of aid to appreciate the difficulties of making ends meet as a direct recipient of public assistance.

Despite the difficulties and despite knowing the difficulties, barrio residents ended up reliant on aid. Some women relied on AFDC because of problems with a male wage earner. For some, the problem was that their relationship to a wage earner was uncertain or ambivalent, so that the woman was unable to count on her partner's social and financial support. Commonly, women turned to AFDC when wage-earning partners were not just socially but also physically absent: they had been killed or disabled by violence in the streets or injuries on the job; they were incarcerated; or they had abandoned their family.[11] Other residents—men and women—came to rely on GA because of problems with substance abuse.

Many more residents in Chávez traveled these two pathways to AFDC and GA reliance than in Guadalupe.[12] But even in Chávez few residents *sought out* aid as a long-term source of income. Barrio residents usually fell into aid reliance despite their desires, not in pursuit of them.

## Pathways to AFDC Reliance

The finances in many single-head households in Chávez depended on income from AFDC. Few women in Chávez planned to rely on welfare, but a substantial number ended up doing so anyway. For some residents, AFDC use began with an uncertain or ambivalent relationship with a wage-earning father. In Chávez, I knew several couples, including Aurora and Eduardo, who used AFDC as a way to "cover bets" while involved in ambivalent relationships. Other residents in Chávez—such as Norma and Beatrice, friends and neighbors for more than a decade preceding my arrival in Chávez—turned to AFDC after their relationship with a wage earner ended. Of course, I did not see Norma and Beatrice become reliant on AFDC; by 1995, I could see only that they both *did* depend on aid to make ends meet. Similarly, in 1995 I could not predict which of the couples covering their bets with short-term use of AFDC would end up dependent on aid for decades. I use the experiences of Aurora, Norma, and Beatrice not to predict what causes aid reliance but to show the kinds of small steps and larger leaps that could propel some residents toward that outcome.

Aurora and Eduardo were committed to each other but ambivalent. In 1992, twenty-year-old Aurora was living with her parents, who came from the Mexican state of Oaxaca, and her two younger sisters in a small house about twenty minutes away from Chávez. A high school graduate working as a waitress, Aurora led a straight life. When I met her in 1995, Aurora still seemed remote from Chávez street life. Compared to the streetwise young people of the barrio, her clothes and appearance were conservative and she was shy and reserved in conversation. Thus, I was a bit surprised when I found out the identity of her common-law husband. Eduardo, who was known on the streets as Hutch after the 1970s TV show detective, was a member of Elm Street whose temper and illicit exploits had earned him a notorious reputation, a set of false teeth (the real ones lost to a baseball bat), and several bullet wounds. When Aurora first met Eduardo, she recalled, "I liked him because he was funny, and he treated me well. So I started going out with him." A few months after she started seeing Eduardo, Aurora found out she was pregnant. When I asked her about her thoughts at the time, she said, "I'm Catholic, so an abortion was out of the question. But I also didn't expect Eduardo to get married."

After her daughter Josefina was born, Aurora continued to live with her parents. By 1995, she had been receiving AFDC for several years, turning over most of her monthly check to her father. Eduardo retained his fierce reputation in Chávez, but he began spending most of his nights at the house. He paid Aurora's father $100 a month in rent, and he regularly brought groceries, baby clothes, and diapers to the house. These loose arrangements meant the couple had separate and independent lives, both of which were organized around their role as parents. They made mutual plans for the day and the week ahead, and they coordinated finances. For example, when a friend of Eduardo's offered to install a new stereo system in his car for only $185, Eduardo replied that he had to check with Aurora before he could go ahead. That night, he and Aurora went over the finances. "Well," conceded Aurora after they finished going over the numbers, "I guess we'll still have enough to pay the rent and other expenses, so I guess that's your money. You can spend it how you want."

One evening in the summer of 1995, Eduardo disappeared into a bedroom with a Chávez teenager. A few days later, he boasted of having sex with the girl, and I asked him what this meant about Aurora. Annoyed by the question, he told me it was a stupid thing to ask and then explained, "I don't want to get married yet. Maybe in five years I'll be ready, and then maybe we'll get married. But not yet. Right now, I would never leave Aurora for another woman—even if I do sleep with her." A few weeks later, Aurora discovered a receipt from a local motel in the pocket of Eduardo's jeans. She demanded to know what Eduardo had been doing in the motel and whom he had been with. Eduardo had been with the Chávez girl, but he refused to answer Aurora's questions and instead began sleeping on a friend's couch in Chávez. His financial contributions to Aurora's household—both rent and baby supplies—stopped. Two weeks later, Eduardo ended the affair with the teenager, saying, "It was time. She was starting to get too attached. And I didn't like being away from Josefina." Eduardo never told Aurora about the Chávez girlfriend, but shortly after the affair ended Aurora let him back into her parent's house and their financial relationship resumed. By the fall of 1995, after mediation by Eduardo's sisters, the couple's social life seemed no different than before the receipt discovery.

The experiences of Aurora and Eduardo illustrate the social and financial dynamics of AFDC use in two-parent households with multiple sources of income. For these families, economic status turned on the state of social relationships. Most residents in Chávez did not see AFDC as an enticement to breakup or single parenthood, but for parents in an ambivalent relationship AFDC was a way to cover bets. While Aurora had used AFDC for several years and was not planning to end her use in 1995, she also did not expect to remain on AFDC permanently. She, like many other Chávez residents, suspected that the government was preparing to cut off her welfare. Anticipating an end to her current residential and financial arrangements, she explained that "once Josefina is a little older and Eduardo is doing a little better at work, we'll probably find a place to move in together."

In other households of Chávez, single mothers turned to AFDC when they found themselves truly on their own. In these families, violence had disabled and killed fathers, fathers had been incarcerated for long periods of time, or fathers had abandoned their children. The lives of Norma and Beatrice, next-door neighbors in Chávez who had been close friends for more than ten years, illustrated how AFDC reliance arose among female household heads on their own.

Norma was in her late forties, an attractive *morena* whose public appearances were always accomplished with stylish flair even when the occasion was a solitary jog around the streets of Chávez in the early morning. She had four children. Her high school son remained at home, and the next oldest, a daughter, was enrolled in an LA college and regularly visited with the boyfriend she had met in the dorms. Norma's two older sons—one a college graduate who lived in Arizona and the other a telephone company employee in LA—did not visit as frequently. Chávez barrio had several official resident representatives to the Los Angeles Housing Agency, and Norma had recently become an official Chávez representative. Beatrice was a few years younger than Norma, and she could often be found chatting with family, friends, and neighbors while sitting on her front stoop. Beatrice had two girls and a boy a few years after Norma, and all of her children were still in school, including the oldest, who was attending high school with Norma's baby. Norma and Beatrice both began receiving AFDC in the 1980s, and both were reliant on aid in the mid-1990s. Their lives and families, similar in structure and intertwined in everyday life in 1995 Chávez, had followed a parallel path for years.

Norma was not eager to explain how she had ended up depending on AFDC, and I eventually stopped asking directly. More than once, she abruptly ended casual banter (she suddenly became "too busy to talk right now") and left the room when I asked her a question about her life history. But over the course of several months, Norma's history revealed itself during casual conversations. For example, when Norma and a friend reminisced about living in the same courtyard with a Chávez political rival—the two were howling in appalled laughter at the woman's filthy apartment—it led to a conversation about how Norma had moved to that particular apartment following the final departure of her ex-husband.

The final departure of her ex-husband came, after ten years and four children, in the late 1970s. One evening, Norma and I found ourselves standing across the street from her old apartment, and she started talking about the parties there, laughing as she flailed her arms in imitation of her ex-husband's drunken gait along the front path.

"He was a handsome man. A tall *güero* [light-skinned man] from Sonora. He treated me well, and he treated the kids well too. He drove a truck . . ."

"Long distance?" I interrupt her.

"No, just making deliveries around the city. He came home every night. And he brought home his paycheck. But he was like all the men from Sonora, he liked to drink. We would have parties, and he would drink too much sometimes, but it was okay. I was okay with that. But then he started to leave home to drink. He went to the bars a few times, and drank up his paycheck. Then a few times, he didn't come home after going to the bars. We had some fights. And finally, I told him not to come home any more."

Other longtime Chávez residents recalled a similar history but offered a different interpretation of events between Norma and her ex. In the fall of 1995, I accompanied Norma and several other residents on a late-night trip to the local police precinct to look into what residents saw as the unprovoked arrest of a Chávez fifteen-year-old. The precinct officers refused to discuss the incident, and after forty-five minutes tensions were thick. Five officers stood in front of the station house door and several members of the Chávez group looked ready for a physical confrontation. Then Norma stepped up to the lead officer, tilted her head back to look the man in the face, and demanded that she be allowed to see the boy. She spoke forcefully with the officer, and tensions subsided as the officers blocking the door parted to allow Norma and the boy's mother into the back of the station house. Albert, a forty-five-year-old whose head had been "cracked open by the bulls" a number of times in his life, was a friend of Norma's who had been ready to attack the police. As Norma disappeared into the back of the station house, we stood on the sidewalk outside and he said, "That is one strong woman. Look at how she stared that bull down. You know she's strong—raising those boys on her own like she did. After that man left her."

I encourage Al to say more, "What was up with that man?"
"It was easier after he left them, *de veras*. Because before she had to raise all the kids, and she had him to deal with. He would drink all the time, and he got himself into trouble—lots of fights, other women. He was a bad man. This isn't the first time she had to come down here."
"She's better off without him . . ."
"Everyone thought he was trouble and that she should never have been with him. Look at her; she could still get lots of men in Chávez. But she never listened to what everyone was saying. When he walked out on her, lots of people—her friends and family—they told her she was better off without him. But she didn't see it like that. It was hard at first. A couple of really hard years. *Pero* right now, I think she's better. You know, the last couple years she's doing okay, more involved with the community again."

Norma started on the pathway to AFDC reliance by having children with a man whose drinking made him an unreliable provider and father. After he left her, she turned to AFDC, and the next decade was consumed by the exigencies of daily living. By 1995, with three of her four children out of the house and supporting themselves, Norma was thriving socially, and she was optimistic about her prospects of advancing economically. TANF was still a year away, but Chávez residents were already being recruited into programs designed to encourage the transition from welfare to work. Norma enthusiastically talked up these programs among her friends, and toward the end of 1995, she and Beatrice submitted applications to a program that promised to teach them carpentry and get them started in construction jobs that could eventually lead to union employment.

By 1995, Beatrice had ended up in the same position as Norma—an enthusiastic applicant to job training after years of reliance on AFDC— but she had arrived at that position via a different path. In the 1970s, while Norma's marriage was breaking up, Beatrice and her husband were starting a family. They had two girls and a boy by the early 1980s, and Beatrice was at home taking care of them while her husband worked at the tire plant south of Chávez.[13]

I bumped into Beatrice one afternoon on the street outside the housing office in Chávez. She had just been inside filling out forms for the job-training program. She was excited about the prospect of getting back into the labor market and was eager to talk about the program and how she had ended up on aid. After work one day, she recalled, her husband had gotten into a fight that left his opponent badly injured.

"They arrested him for assault. That first time, he was in jail a couple months," recalls Beatrice. "I went back to work. I was used to working. Before we had kids, I worked as a secretary at a couple places. . . . When my husband got locked up, I found a job as an office manager at a rec center. One of the things I had to do was drive the kids on field trips, and they gave me a van and said I had to keep it clean. Then the van broke down, and I fixed it myself. I had older brothers who taught me how to work on cars. The head of the rec center was really surprised that I could use tools. I surprised a lot of mechanics and men who don't think a woman can use tools. They had three vans at the rec center—big ones that could carry ten or twelve kids each—and I fixed them all. And that was my job. My favorite job. I liked having my own van and driving it, and I liked fixing all the vans. I got to set my own hours, and if there weren't any vans to fix I could just hang out in the office or take a day off."

When Beatrice's husband got out of jail, the tire plant was beginning to shut down. He did not return there, but he did find work making enough money to support the family. Beatrice left the rec center job to return home and take care of the children. Her mother had been providing child care, but that was never meant to be a permanent arrangement. Unfortunately, Beatrice's husband was unable to stay out of jail. "They found some drugs on him," said Beatrice.

"And after that, they just kept picking him up. He'd go in for a couple months and then come out, but then he'd go back in again for something else.

I wanted to keep working, but my mother couldn't keep the kids. So I started getting aid. I didn't like it, but I wanted to raise my own children. I'm glad that they started this program up. Me and Norma are the only women applying, but I trust Arnold [the housing official running the jobs program]. He knows what he's doing, and he knows that I can use tools. I have a pretty good chance."

Chávez residents had a positive view of Beatrice's husband. One friend said that he wasn't a bad man but that he had a temper and he sometimes did stupid things—the kind of person who "stumbled into" illegal activities. He treated Beatrice and his children well, but he could not stay out of trouble consistently enough to support them. As a result, Beatrice had been receiving AFDC for more than a decade since her husband's second arrest in the mid-1980s. In the mid-1990s, this reliance appeared poised to end. Beatrice still felt connected to work and qualified to work. Her children were beginning to leave the house. Like other AFDC-dependent residents in Chávez, Beatrice was aware of the political forces that appeared poised to revamp public assistance.

Households in Chávez were often set down the pathway to AFDC reliance when a primary wage earner stopped supporting a mother and her children. Sometimes, as it was for Norma, a "bad man" got into trouble and left the family to its own devices. In other cases, such as for Beatrice, a "good man" appeared unable to stay out of trouble and his family spiraled into dependence. In hindsight, Chávez residents could blame one household's predicament on a "bad man" and pin the problems of another household on the police department's unwillingness to give a "good man" a break. In the uncertainty of everyday life in the barrio—that is, without the benefit of hindsight—it was hard to distinguish which households were headed for long-term AFDC reliance and which would avoid it. As Aurora and Eduardo's experiences highlight, in Chávez AFDC reliance rarely appeared inevitable. Rather, reliance arose as the eventual outcome of many small steps in a process that unfolded over a period of time. In the space of a few months, Aurora sent Eduardo out and then took him back—all the while consulting her family and his about whether he was a "good" man worth keeping or a "bad" man whom she would be better of without. Similarly, it required many transgressions before Norma finally told her "bad" husband to stop coming home, and to Beatrice it seemed that the police were simply determined to prevent her "good" husband from remaining at home.

From both ambivalent and committed relationships, well-traveled pathways led to AFDC reliance in Chávez. Residents proceeded along the pathway to reliance via small steps, such as the discovery of an affair, some bad luck job hunting, or a few too many drinks on a few too many occasions. These small steps toward reliance were often counterbalanced by movement in the other direction, as when residents forgave their partners' affairs, brought home a few hundred dollars when the financial pressure was on, or managed to stay away from street life for a few weeks. In some cases, these little steps delivered a mother and her children into AFDC reliance; Norma's experience exemplified this slow spiral. In other situations, however, these little steps were like the half-distances of Zeno's paradox. Every step brought a teetering household closer to AFDC, but no single step proved capable of providing the final push. In these situations, a sudden and substantial change in life circumstances—a change that occurred outside the everyday framework of the relationship—could prove crucial; that was Beatrice's experience. Aurora and Eduardo, a couple brought together by an unplanned pregnancy and unable and unwilling to publicly declare themselves a committed couple, also used AFDC. Compared to Norma and Beatrice, Aurora still teetered on the edge of long-term dependence. The next motel receipt in Eduardo's pocket could be the final small step on the path to dependence. Eduardo's participation in Chávez street life might put him in the wrong place at the wrong time; in that case, Aurora's final leap into aid reliance could come from the intervention of a bullet or an arresting officer. Or the couple might teeter along, combining Eduardo's wages and Aurora's aid and taking small steps to avoid falling into dependence. If they avoid bad breaks long enough, their hoped-for outcome—an independent household in private housing a comfortable distance away from welfare and Chávez—might become a reality.

The experiences of Aurora, Norma, and Beatrice juxtaposed illustrate the path dependence of reliance. Few women planned to use welfare, but, like Aurora, a substantial number put themselves at risk of long-term use of AFDC by using aid to cover bets in an ambivalent relationship. Few women planned to raise their children on welfare, but, like Norma and Beatrice, a substantial number were pushed into long-term dependence after external events ended their relationship with a wage earner.

### Pathways to GA Reliance

In Chávez, some single men and an even smaller number of single women relied on income from the county's GA program. The income from GA, which amounted to a few hundred dollars each month, was puny. Residents who relied on GA did not support themselves solely on the money provided by the county. But for many GA-reliant residents I knew, the monthly check provided the most money they had under their control at any given moment. The lump sum provided the foundation for the month's other income-generating activities, and in this sense residents in Chávez came to rely on the couple hundred dollars provided by aid.

Among the residents I knew in the barrios, GA reliance was invariably preceded by substance abuse, mostly of alcohol and heroin. As it did for single mothers and AFDC, the path to GA reliance involved small steps and large leaps. Gary, an active heroin user during 1995, was taking small steps, while Jaime and Manny, the former a heavy heroin user and the latter a former heavy drinker who still collected his check from the county, illustrate the dynamics of large leaps.

Gary was in his late twenties, a tall man with black hair, a near-handlebar mustache, and thick glasses that magnified his eyes. He had grown up in Chávez, and during 1995 he lived in his mother's apartment not far from the hot spot. He was a familiar figure on the streets, socializing with passersby from his mother's stoop, keeping an eye on who was coming and going to the *tienda,* and hanging out with Elm Street members at the hot spot. Gary was a member of Elm Street, but he had been inactive since he began using heroin heavily. One Elm Street member explained that Gary and other heroin users couldn't be trusted in the *varrio* because they would do anything to get the drug; they started fights by stealing from the other homeboys, and you couldn't trust them to do what they said they would.[14]

Gary left school when he was sixteen, as soon as he could work construction. When he couldn't find work in construction, Gary enrolled in LA County's GA plan. At some point, a doctor certified that Gary was disabled by his heroin addiction, and he began to receive a monthly disability check along with his GA. The disability went straight to his mother, but he cashed and spent the GA on his own. The corner *tienda* would cash government checks, but most people in Chávez took the time to walk the half-mile to one of the check-cashing outlets where the fees were lower. Gary usually made it to one of these storefronts the same day his check arrived. He put most of the check "up his arm," but he did not binge the moment his check arrived. Usually, GA cash lasted about two weeks after the check arrived. With GA gone, Gary could count only on the cash he earned as an unskilled worker at nearby construction sites; he dug trenches at one site and hauled scrap wood away at another. He enjoyed helping out around the community, and this earned him some in-kind support and, occasionally, a few dollars as well. As a food bank volunteer, he always ended up with a choice box of goodies to contribute to his mother's household, and sometimes parents would give him a couple dollars when he helped out at the local Head Start or supervised kids in the recreation programs at the Chávez gym. Gary also occasionally went from group to group and door to door with some merchandise to sell. One day, he sold an old nineteen-inch black and white television to one of the *señoras* in a building on the far side of the projects for $24. A few weeks later, he was offering, at half their usual price, packets of socks that he had stolen from a street vendor.

There were different ways to interpret Gary's heroin use and GA dependence. On the one hand, his heroin use and dependence on GA—which were nearly synonymous in his own mind—arose from day-to-day conditions in his life, as the following notes illustrate:

> On a pleasant late-summer night, Gary and I are sitting on the stoop of his mother's house. Early this morning, I accompanied Paul when he gave Gary a ride to the job-training center, and when I saw him sitting on the stoop I came over to ask him how the day went. Gary says that it went okay, boring actually because they didn't teach him much of anything. But, he explains, he had to go because that's what the county said in order to get his GA. "It's hard, though," he explains. "Because they said they were going to get me a job but so far nothing has come up. That's been really hard because I'm struggling with some personal problems right now."
>
> "What kind of personal problems?" I ask.
>
> "It's not the problems, really. It's hard to be home all day. I'm not employed right now and so I'm home taking care of house—I'm basically a homemaker. And now with the unemployment and everything, I've gone back and started taking drugs again. I know it doesn't help in the long run, but it helps today so I fell back into it."

Gary seemed hopelessly mired in heroin use and GA dependence on some days and more assuredly on the path away from reliance on other days. At the same time, his reliance on heroin and GA in 1995 formed one part of a long personal history of involvement with drugs and alcohol, and many features of his everyday life in Chávez in 1995 recapitulated this history. A few months after we spoke on his mother's stoop, Gary discussed his heroin use and GA dependence as one episode of his longer personal history.

> On a fall Saturday, I am sitting near the shooting gallery during the hottest part of the afternoon. Gary is in the gallery with a couple of other men. I watch him tie up his arm with a bandanna and shoot up with a syringe that one of the other men has prepared. The others shoot after him, and then he ties up the works into a small kit and emerges from the gallery. He lights a cigarette and sits down on the grass next to me.

"I was born in County Hospital and I grew up in Chávez my whole life," he says with a contented and relaxed voice as the drug starts to kick in. "I used to go up and down that hill right there going to Liberty School. We used to have so much fun going up the stairs and then riding the logs down. Those were fun days."

"Is that right?" I say, not quite sure where Gary is going with this. He keeps reminiscing.

"Then I started drinking when I was ten or eleven. I joined Elm Street about the same time, and I started going to their parties. I met the older guys there, and they gave me coke and crack, and I liked them, and they gave me cools [PCP], but they just made me crazy. I can't stand the cools. Then I was maybe fifteen, one of the older homeboys showed me how to shoot up. That was the best. I haven't stopped since then. . . . The thing is, it gets complicated to keep using. When you're younger, you can deal with it. But once you get older, it gets more complicated and more difficult to deal with this all the time."

Cash, in the hands of a GA recipient, was a deadly weapon. When checks arrived, many recipients went on drug or alcohol binges. GA checks—and other income-generating schemes—sustained disabling substance abuse, and in this sense cash fueled reliance. Recognizing this relationship between cash and self-destructive substance abuse, many Chávez residents were thankful that the GA grant was so small.

The danger of cash was illustrated by the interactions between Ramón and Jaime—the former a forty-five-year-old resident who had been a heroin user until he joined Narcotics Anonymous and the latter an intensive user of heroin in his early thirties. Ramón had grown up with Jaime, and he became concerned about his friend's deterioration as Jaime's heroin use increased in the winter of 1994–95. Jaime's family, tired of his partying and theft, had evicted him, and he now squatted in vacant apartments with other homeless Chávez drug users. He spent all his money, which came from GA and theft, on heroin. He was emaciated, and his clothes were filthy. By the spring of 1995, when I first began spending extended periods of time with the two men, Ramón thought that Jaime had finally sunk low enough that he might be interested in getting some treatment. After weeks of cajoling, Ramón convinced Jaime to enroll in a treatment program in early April—at a time, not coincidentally, when his GA check had run out and he was desperate for cash to buy heroin—and I accompanied the two men to the downtown treatment center. Jaime signed up for treatment, but the program was fully enrolled. The first open slot was three weeks away. Ramón got Jaime to promise to return to the treatment center for his intake appointment and then rewarded Jaime for taking this first step on the road to recovery by giving him $2, even though, as he said at the time, "I know he's just going to go put it in his arm."

On the day of the intake appointment, Ramón checked the squatters' apartment, but Jaime was nowhere to be found. A few hours later, Jaime appeared on the street and Ramón cornered him. Jaime refused to go downtown. His GA check had just come in, and Jaime was having no trouble keeping himself supplied with heroin. Ramón told him that he was killing himself with heroin, and was that what he really wanted to do? Jaime muttered that he guessed so, and after asking three times, "Are you sure?" Ramón left him in peace. The next time I saw Ramón and Jaime together was in the fall of 1995. Ramón and I were walking down the street when Jaime stepped in front of us and asked for a couple dollars. Ramón refused. Jaime turned to me, and I also refused. Then Ramón dug out of his pants pocket a scratch-it lottery ticket and handed it to Jaime. "Imagine if that ticket hits," I said, as Jaime walked away. Ramón laughed. "The worst luck an addict could have would be to win the lottery. He'd kill himself in a day."

Because substance abusers had a hard time getting their hands on large sums of money (the scratch-it did not hit), cash was a small step along the pathway to reliance. The leaps along that pathway came from treatment programs, churches, and incarceration. Many Chávez residents, including Ramón, saw their enrollment in a treatment program as a turning point in their lives—a moment when they took a giant leap away from dependence on drugs and reliance on GA. At the same time, treatment seeking also could result in Jaime's experience. Many Chávez residents who used GA enrolled in treatment programs as a condition of aid receipt, but it took a rare combination of circumstances—including, in the view of many residents, the proper depth of desperation—to make treatment work. GA users who had recovered from substance abuse cited the importance of spiritual awakening. For some, the spiritual awakening had come via twelve-step programs, while others had found spiritual support in local Christian, non-Catholic, churches. Finally, the experience of incarceration propelled residents along the pathway to GA reliance. For some residents, drug addiction began in jail. More commonly, however, incarceration provided a "wake-up call" that moved residents away from GA reliance. The experiences of Manny illustrate this latter experience.

Manny was thirty-five years old, but he looked and moved like a much older man—a condition he attributed to the heavy drinking he had started at thirteen and had quit, he hoped for good, in 1993. For most of his drinking years Manny partied with Leticia, a childhood friend from Chávez five years his senior who now was living in private housing and raising their six year-old daughter on her own. Manny had received GA on and off for the last five years. One June afternoon I sat with Manny and his friend, who had also recently become sober, on the curb of a Chávez parking lot. For about forty minutes, I listened to the two men talk about the daily challenges of sobriety. Manny pulled out his wallet and showed me some pictures of his daughter, one taken recently and another of her when she was about two years old. In the recent picture, the girl was wearing gold rings on her hands and a gold necklace around her neck. The friend had left us by this point, and Manny talked about how he had gone sober.

"Leti kicked me out a couple years ago," says Manny. "But now that I've been clean for about a year and a half now, I can go over any time I want and see them. I didn't use AA or the church or anything. It happened because of Leticia. The whole time we were together we used to party. I remember one time I cashed my GA check and we threw a huge party. Blew it all in one night. Busted up the apartment and the TV.

"When I was drinking, I used to hit Leti. She'd call the cops on me. . . . First I got jail for forty-five days, then ninety, then six months. What stopped me was going to jail a couple years ago and getting the DTs [hallucinations caused by alcohol withdrawal]. I saw my mom's face and I asked the guys there if they saw it and they said, no that I was having DTs and I should call the sheriff and they would take me out. And I saw the shoes—where they're all lined up on the shelf—I saw animals coming out of the shoes. And I was all fucked up and I called the sheriffs and they took me out and the doctor gave me a shot and they tied me up with straps."

"How long were you tied up like that?"

"I think three days. I remember the DTs in the beginning but then I just was out of it and I woke up and they said can you walk to the restroom and I said yes so they untied me and I walked over and used the restroom even though I didn't have to because I hadn't eaten for a couple days and I had lost ten pounds. And they said can you sign here and I said okay and they let me go for time served."

This last visit to jail changed Manny's life. He had been at rock bottom before this visit. Leti refused to see him or allow him to see their daughter. The DTs in jail convinced Manny to stop drinking, and after a few months of sobriety, Leti agreed to let him see their daughter again. As his sobriety continued, he said, Leti wanted to get back together and resume their relationship. "But I don't love her anymore," said Manny. "It was boring with her if we weren't partying."

The dramatic changes in his social life that came from that last visit to jail did not spill over into his economic life. In 1995, Leti worked for the phone company, and Manny was still on general relief. The county required him to work at a youth center downtown, but the day I sat on the curb with him, he said, "The cock-a-doodle-doo alarm clock went off at 5:00 a.m., as usual, and I just turned it off and went back to sleep. My mother came in and told me that the alarm had gone off, but I told her I was taking the day off." He made about $200 a month through GA, but he had few expenses because he lived with his infirm mother in a Chávez apartment. "Leti," he explained, "wants to get some more money out of me for the girl. But I tell her to look at all the jewels and gold and stuff she already has," and Manny waved the recent photo in front of me for emphasis. "That's what my wife wants the money for, but she's got enough of that already."

In the dynamics of GA, parties and binges could turn into small steps toward reliance, while church attendance and twelve-step programs at times moved residents in the other direction. The large leaps often involved drug rehabilitation or jail time. Rehab did not always work, of course, but it also seemed to rarely encourage reliance. Jail time, in contrast, could move residents both directions on the pathway of reliance. Sometimes jail proved a final insult that pushed residents into reliance, and at other times it represented the rock bottom that turned residents away from GA.

Guadalupe and Chávez housed a variety of welfare users. Residents turned to all kinds of agencies and programs during short periods of economic dislocation, and they consistently generated small amounts of income or in-kind resources by participating in local helping organizations. Sometimes they relied on the marginal economic boost from these local sources for long periods of time. A few residents in Guadalupe and a substantial number in Chávez relied on public aid for most of their income for an extended period.

Residents did not plan to rely on aid. Reliance was the end result, the default outcome, that followed from a series of unplanned and often tragic small steps and large leaps. In this sense, long-term aid reliance stood in contrast to short-term aid and aid on the margin. Residents turned to short-term aid after an unavoidable interruption in a broader income-generating strategy: for example, when an unexpected bill or unplanned absence from work wreaked havoc with the economic strategy of overwork in Guadalupe barrio. Residents used aid on the margin as a long-term supplement to other sources of aid, so it was commonplace among Chávez residents engaged in hustling. Long-term reliance on aid did not play a similar role in residents' economic strategies. Residents did not travel the various pathways into reliance on welfare as a result of taking advantage of socially available resources in the barrios. Rather, they ended up in the position of having to rely on long-term aid after a series of miscalculations, mishaps, or tragedies left them with no other means to make ends meet.

Whether by small steps or a large leap, it was not easy to end up reliant on aid. No single small misstep condemned a person to reliance. Substance abusers such as Gary and Jaime and former abusers such as Ramón and Manny knew that addiction and dependence were not inevitable results of injecting heroin at a party or drinking a case of beer with friends. Substance abusers often used drugs or alcohol as a way to deal with other problems, and substance abuse often exacerbated those problems. GA-reliant residents in Chávez were painfully aware that their lives were stalled in a vicious cycle. This painful reality was equally clear to the many residents who had struggled with addiction and dependence in their own lifetime. At the same time, large leaps that led to sudden aid reliance rarely came as a complete surprise. Many barrio residents knew that mothers, such as Norma, Beatrice, or Aurora, were vulnerable to dependence as long as their spouse could not stay away from trouble. But few residents could intervene to prevent the foreseeable tragedies that led to aid reliance. For residents managing the day-to-day exigencies of poverty, including its ambivalent relationships, the large leap into dependence might be anticipated, but it still came from circumstances beyond individual control.

This chapter has described the many faces of welfare in the low-income barrios. Many residents of the barrios used public aid in the short term and on the margin, and in Chávez a substantial number of residents also used welfare as a way to make ends meet over the long term. In the United States, receiving aid is generally considered shameful, and aid users are generally stigmatized. Shame and stigma are the symbolic tools that help keep the welfare rolls small. But policy makers have been concerned that shame and stigma may be losing their hold in low-income communities. When many residents in a community use welfare, isn't it inevitable that aid use comes to be seen as less shameful and more acceptable? Don't aid recipients start to serve as role models in poor communities? Can American policy makers really count on shame and stigma to discourage welfare use in a community where a resident's mother, aunt, and neighbor are all long-term aid recipients? In the next chapter, I address these questions by analyzing how barrio residents made sense of aid receipt. I compare the meaning of welfare in Guadalupe, where long-term use was rare, with its meaning in Chávez, where long-term aid was relatively common. This chapter has shown how public assistance affected the economy of the barrios; the next chapter shows how it shaped the culture of the barrios.

# CHAPTER 9

# Making Welfare Stigma

In the United States, public assistance is uncommon yet controversial, its economic impact joined by its symbolic significance.[1] Originally intended to support a narrowly defined group of "deserving" Americans, such as workers injured on the job and the children of widows, public aid has increasingly gone to people Americans think of as "undeserving," such as working-age men and never-married mothers.[2] This use of aid concerns Americans who fear that the availability of aid may act as a perverse incentive that encourages the able-bodied to shirk work or the morally sound to eschew marriage.[3]

What I have shown so far about public aid in the barrios addresses parts of this controversy. Aid in the barrios did not tempt residents away from their jobs or entice them to avoid marriage. Barrio residents came to rely on public aid as a result of bad luck and tragedy, as I showed in Chapter 8, not as a result of calculations of economic self-interest. Residents did not see aid reliance as a sensible way to make do or get ahead economically, and they did not see aid as a reasonable alternative to a steady job or stable marriage.

Even if aid did not constitute a perverse economic incentive, however, it could have negative social and cultural consequences of other kinds. Means testing can isolate and disempower aid recipients; recipients can constitute a negative role model to others; and public largesse to the "undeserving" appears to violate cardinal American norms and values of self-reliance and individual responsibility.[4] The concern, in short, is that even if aid does not constitute a perverse incentive to reject mainstream culture, it could nevertheless foster a troubling isolation between cultural orientations in low-income communities and those of mainstream America.

In this chapter, I focus on this concern by analyzing the role of public aid in everyday social and cultural life in the barrio. I address several questions. How did welfare requirements affect interpersonal relationships in the barrios? Did welfare use by some negatively affect everyone? If public aid, *prima facie,* violates cultural norms and values of self-reliance and personal responsibility, how did this affect barrio culture as a whole?

To address these questions, I describe the meanings of public aid among the residents I knew in the low-income barrios. I focus in particular on how these meanings organized themselves into subcultures that informed residents' behavior and outlook toward welfare. In my experience during fieldwork, barrio residents championed ideals of self-sufficiency and personal responsibility, but in everyday interactions and conversations residents constructed the meaning of "self-reliance" and "personal responsibility" in different ways. At times, they saw "self-reliance" and "personal responsibility" as strict standards of behavior to be applied to everyone all the time. According to this view, welfare was universally unacceptable, and residents who subscribed to this view expressed a Manichaean disapproval of aid and aid recipients. At other times, residents applied the norms of "self-reliance" and "personal responsibility" more flexibly. They recognized that some forms of public aid received by some people under certain circumstances were understandable and even acceptable; framed this way, welfare stigma was selectively applied and open to contestation.

In the particular structural circumstances of Guadalupe and Chávez barrios, the meanings of welfare organized themselves into subcultures with their own dynamics and their own influence on everyday life. In Guadalupe, where relatively few residents had suffered the bad luck and tragedy that led to welfare reliance, the universal and Manichaean view of welfare prevailed. In Chávez many residents had the misfortune to end up reliant on aid, and selective and contested meanings of self-reliance and personal responsibility commonly held sway. I see these differences in welfare cultures in the two barrios as an exemplar of how culture actually works in everyday life—of subcultures in action. In this chapter I lay to rest fears that receiving aid undermined the values of residents in the low-income barrios by carefully examining how residents in Guadalupe and Chávez used their culture to make sense of aid receipt in everyday life. I document a lot of variation in how residents made sense of aid receipt. This variation reminds us that culture is not a static set of values and norms but rather a dynamic set of behaviors, talk, habits, and orientations. Differences in how barrio residents used and made sense of public aid reveal culture operating in everyday life, not a troubling isolation from mainstream norms and values.

## UNIVERSAL STIGMA

Most of the residents I knew in the barrios viewed public aid the way Americans are supposed to view aid—as wrong under any circumstances. They expressed this view in confidential comments about family, friends and neighbors who received public aid as well as in direct confrontations with aid recipients. Even when recipients turned to aid during a time of temporary economic dislocation or following a major disruption in income generation, many barrio residents remained steadfast in their belief that welfare use remained unacceptable and unexplainable.

Confidential or behind-the-back comments often provided the opportunity to criticize welfare receipt and recipients. Without the recipient there to explain him- or herself, reasonable explanations of aid receipt could be quickly dismissed and discounted, as the following conversations in Guadalupe barrio illustrate. The conversations took place in July 1994, when I joined Rosa, Chela, Verónica, and Carmen—the heart of the *convive* group—at a children's play date they had arranged in a Guadalupe park.

José Mendoza is going to drop me off at the park on his way to work. In the car, he tells me that work has been slow recently. He's gone home at 6:00 every day this week, so he's losing two to three hours of wages a day. "A lot of people are on vacation right now. So that means that no one is putting in new orders." At the park, the *convive* ladies are gathered around a shady picnic table with a clear view of their children in the sandy play area. José greets them, and when Rosa asks why he isn't working he tells her how slow work has been. He leaves a few minutes later to resume his trip to work.

When José is out of earshot, Rosa turns to Chela and says that she saw José down at the food bank the other day. "They gave him some money to buy food at Lucky's [supermarket]," she says disapprovingly. "About $100 a month. It wasn't the first time. I don't know how long he's been getting it but it has been a while." Chela looks surprised, and shaking her head remarks, "*De veras?*" with a disapproving click of her tongue.

Rosa and Chela's comments illustrate a truism in both Guadalupe and Chávez: when recipients were not present to explain themselves, residents felt free to ignore the context of aid receipt. Rosa and Chela knew that José had turned to the food bank when forces beyond his control had reduced his wages. Moreover, Rosa knew José and his family well, and she knew the long hours his entire family worked in low-wage jobs. Experience could have told her that José's use of assistance would be brief—as it was—and that he would soon make ends meet through work—he did so by obtaining false papers. Had José remained at the park, he could have corrected the impression that Rosa created of his aid receipt. But by the time Rosa spoke her mind about his aid receipt, José was already on his way to work.

The barrio residents I knew expressed particular suspicion about recipients who relied on aid as a primary source of income or received aid for long periods of time. Later that same July afternoon, I walked with the women and their children from the park toward the apartment buildings where most of them lived, and the group passed by Señora Lupe's house. Someone asked where the *señora* was that day, and Rosa said that last night her son had been in an accident—maybe a broken arm—and she was at home taking care of him. Verónica looked annoyed. "What I don't understand," she said. "Is why can't her husband take care of him? He's home all day anyway." Nodding her head in agreement, Carmen said that when the group met at Señora Lupe's house a few weeks earlier, her husband seemed perfectly fit—remember how he had chased the kids all over the backyard that day? Raising her voice above the noise of the traffic, she said, "It is a disgrace for them to get welfare. He needs to leave the house and get back to work."

In Chávez barrio, where more residents relied on public aid, private gossip about aid recipients arose frequently and sometimes unexpectedly, as it did one Monday night in the back seat of my car. I was driving toward Chávez with Marco, a twenty-one-year-old father, and Ben, whose fiancée was at that moment six months pregnant. Marco missed his daughter, whom he had seen infrequently in recent weeks, and he blamed his girlfriend. "She's a real bitch," he said, referring to his daughter's mother. "She don't get along with her mom but she still won't call me up when she needs a baby-sitter. She'll just leave her with whoever." Ben replies that when his child is born, he's not going to have any problems like that because he will spend lots of time with his child. "That's what you say now," counters Marco.

"But just wait until the baby's here. You watch what happens. That's what happened to me. I was taking care of the baby. Then, she decides she wants to get on aid. So, now she just stays at home all day doing nothing. She says she can't go to school even because there's no one to look after the baby. But she won't even let me see her, and she won't let her mom. She's just lazy. She wants to stay home and do nothing all day. You'll see what happens. It's not so easy."

In both Guadalupe and Chávez, gossip about aid recipients ranged from the disapproving side comments that Chela and Rosa leveled against José to Verónica and Marco's personal attacks on recipients' motivations and behavior. Confidential comments reflected an atmosphere of Manichaean disapproval of aid in both barrios, and they provided ready opportunities for residents to express disapproval toward recipients. At the same time, the Guadalupe and Chávez residents I spent time with did not confine their criticism of aid receipt to behind-the-back gossip; they also confronted recipients publicly and personally.

Gary, the Chávez GA recipient I introduced in the last chapter, regularly found himself encountering criticism over his welfare use. Gary was personable and popular—someone who spent a lot of time in the public places of Chávez and seemed to know everyone in the projects. He usually went out of his way to exchange greetings and pass some time with groups hanging out on the street, but he also cultivated and maintained friendships with many residents who preferred to have nothing to do with street life or the gang. During fieldwork in Chávez, I spent time with Gary in the shooting galleries and in groups of beer-drinking Elm Street members as well as at meetings of activist community leaders and at church events sponsored by the Chávez *señoras*. People in each of these groups told me that Gary made positive contributions to the community by keeping an eye on neighborhood children in the Chávez gym, for example, or contributing to the food bank and other community-based projects.

Despite these wide-ranging friendships and positive evaluations, Gary did not escape stigma that stemmed from his receipt of aid and lack of a job, as I saw one spring afternoon at a church gathering we attended. The gathering had been called to organize an upcoming performance of Native American dances. The church and housing authority had donated a small amount of funds as well as some in-kind support for the performance, and I was curious to see how the organizing committee would allocate these scarce resources. Most of the people at the meeting that day were the Chávez women who organized and controlled the food bank. Gary sat quietly through discussions about the event date, publicity, whether to invite the local priest to open the dances with a prayer, and whether to try to raise a little money for the community center by setting up a barbeque and selling hamburgers and hot dogs. Finally, the co-organizers asked for volunteers to help out on the day of the event by asking residents to move their cars from the parking lot near the community center, setting out trash barrels, helping at the barbeque, and picking up detritus. Gary raised his hand to volunteer, and the co-organizers appeared ready to welcome his help. But one of the other members of the organizing committee objected. The people who volunteer for this event, she pointed out, represent the community. Do we want someone who is unemployed and receiving aid to do that? Isn't there someone else who can help out? Some others on the organizing committee agreed that it might be better if Gary were not involved and if the volunteers came from the planning committee. Gary did not object, and the organizers decided against his participation.

I left the church with Gary when the meeting ended and we chatted about how things had turned out. He said that he was not happy that the committee would not let him take part, but he also understood their perspective. They did not want someone like him out there representing the community, maybe representing the community before the priest. The organizers preferred to represent themselves. He could still go to the event—they couldn't stop that—and probably someone wouldn't show up and he would find something to do if he wanted to.

Public confrontations such as Gary experienced at the church meeting were also common at the Guadalupe job-training center, where nearly all enrollees received aid from federal, state and local programs. One March afternoon, for example, Henry was taken to task for participating in AFDC.

When ESL (English as a Second Language) class begins today, Vero asks to make an announcement. Max, the instructor, lets her take the floor on the condition that she speak English, but speaking in front of the class makes Vero nervous, and after a few halting English phrases she makes a frustrated gesture in Max's direction and switches to Spanish. She says that next week is the birthday of Judy [a job skills instructor], and she is taking a collection to buy a present.

Henry jokes that he'll contribute a whole book of food stamps, but Vero responds humorlessly. She tells Henry that she's not taking any food stamps. "We're not buying her a present at Lucky's, right? Why do you have food stamps anyway? You make your wife get welfare and then come in here with the stamps that are for her and the baby. That is disgraceful." Max breaks in, also in Spanish, to tell Vero that if she's done he will start class.

Vero did not hesitate to publicly confront Henry about what his use of food stamps and AFDC. In her eyes, it was inappropriate for Henry's wife to receive AFDC, and it was even more inappropriate for Henry to offer *her* food stamps as a gift contribution. His jovial demeanor also inspired Vero's public rebuke. Like other friends and acquaintances of Henry, Vero believed he used AFDC too instrumentally and cavalierly, that he could support his family through legitimate work but that he chose to hustle and rely on welfare instead. They did not know that Henry's participation in AFDC was only instrumental to a point, and Henry did not concede that he saw aid as an unattractive but necessary way to make ends meet given his family's financial circumstances. Rather, he acted as though receiving aid and hustling at the flea market were his preferred means of earning a living. In fact, during the months I spent time with Henry he had repeated bad luck finding a job—several times signing up with firms that could offer only a few months of work or did not pay an hourly wage sufficient to pay the rent for himself, Tanya, and the baby. In the summer of 1994, he finally found steady work and stopped receiving aid. But in March, his friends and acquaintances in Guadalupe knew little about his frustrating job search. As far as Vero and others were concerned, Henry had chosen aid, and this belief sustained the ire of their public criticism.

The appearance of choice tainted how residents viewed Henry's circumstances, but residents who clearly did not choose aid also faced public criticism. Tricia was in her late twenties and had two children, a seven-year-old boy and a four-year-old girl. She had come to Guadalupe from Michoacán to join her husband Luis in 1988. Tricia and Luis were settled migrants who were, according to Tricia, fairly happy with the life they were constructing in San Jose. The couple's daughter was born in the States, and they both received permanent residence, or green cards, in 1991. Luis found steady work for a construction firm, and Tricia cleaned houses part time. Everything changed in early 1993, however, when Luis was arrested. There were multiple stories about what had happened. Some of Tricia's acquaintances said Luis was involved in the drug trade, but Tricia insisted that the police had unfairly detained Luis following a minor altercation simply because he was Mexican. In any case, the courts treated Luis like a drug offender. He was sentenced to two years in jail, and Tricia had to turn to AFDC to support herself and the children. In December 1993, a social worker referred Tricia to the Guadalupe job-training center in hopes of getting her into the workforce.

Like many aid recipients in Guadalupe, Tricia was treated as though her use of welfare constituted fraud. During the time I spent with her, she appeared to be participating according to the spirit of the welfare rules. She attended job-training classes nearly without fail, and she made progress learning English and acquiring job skills. She seemed to want to work, and as it turned out she found a swing-shift position at $8 an hour with one of the Silicon Valley's largest employers in May 1994. While she received aid, however, Tricia's Guadalupe friends suspected that she used welfare inappropriately. Their suspicions came clear one Thursday morning in April. That day, Tricia arrived at the center wearing a black dress instead of her usual jeans and blouse. Paco reported that Luis was coming home on furlough and predicted that Tricia would miss class the next day. During lunch later that same day, Tricia, Paco, Ron and Virginia played dominos, and Virginia asked if it was true about Luis coming home. Tricia said that Luis was coming home for twenty-four hours and that she was going to skip class tomorrow. Her news sent Paco into a quiet celebration of his soothsaying ability, and it prompted Ron to ask for more details about Luis: What did he do? How long was he locked up? You're getting welfare that whole time? The last question touched a nerve.

"No. Why do you think I'm here? I want to get a job," says Tricia, obviously annoyed at Ron's last question. Ron replies, "But how come you just got welfare for a year after he got locked up? You didn't come here looking for a job." Virginia interjects to chastise Tricia: "You should have known Luis was involved with drug selling." Tricia denies to Virginia that Luis had anything to do with drugs, and Ron continues, "I just don't think it is right to give welfare to someone when they break the law. That's not right."

The imprisonment of Tricia's husband was common knowledge, but Ron and Virginia still questioned Tricia's motivation for using AFDC. They wanted assurances from her that she had tried her best to avoid using aid, and they wanted her to explain how she could have left herself vulnerable to aid dependence by starting a family with a criminal.

Ron and Virginia's comments to Tricia—like Guadalupe residents' comments about José, Señora Lupe, and Henry—illustrate the universal stigmatization of aid recipients and the Manichaean unacceptability of aid receipt. Guadalupe residents stigmatized all aid recipients, no matter what the particulars of their economic situation. They stigmatized residents whose participation in aid seemed an active choice, such as Señora Lupe and Henry, and they stigmatized residents whose participation seemed to stem from a misfortune over which they had limited control, as was the case for José and Tricia. Guadalupe residents also saw aid receipt as a moral failure and thus a legitimate object for criticism. They criticized aid in conversations when recipients were out of earshot, such as José and Señora Lupe, and they confronted recipients in public, as Henry and Tricia experienced. In Chávez, some residents experienced a similar stigmatization. Marco found a ready audience for his complaints about his girlfriend's indolence in the back seat of my car, and Gary experienced firsthand how receiving aid colored residents' views of a person's worth and value in the community. In these instances among the persistently poor of East LA, and more generally among the immigrants of San Jose, participation in any welfare program for any reason under whatever circumstances occasioned questioning and suspicion. Aid required explanation, but it was also inexcusable and unexplainable.

Guadalupe residents—some of them with only a few months or years of residence in the United States—embraced a view of welfare use and abuse that closely coincided with the views of U.S. policy makers in Washington, D.C. Like the policy makers, Guadalupe residents regarded aid use as a character flaw at best and a premeditated attempt at fraud at worst. This understanding of aid was nearly universal, and Guadalupe residents were as suspicious of aid use among family or friends as they were of aid use among acquaintances or rivals.

## SELECTIVE STIGMA

Residents in Guadalupe and Chávez mostly expressed disapproval of aid, and they regularly stigmatized recipients both confidentially and face to face. This disapproval was not unremitting, however; at times, residents I spent time with in both barrios selectively excused the aid use of family, friends, and neighbors.

Discussions and debates over the propriety of aid receipt reflected the particular aid program in question. Gary's experiences at the church meeting illustrate one truism in Chávez: residents rarely defended GA receipt. Even recipients declined to justify their GA receipt as a way to generate income or as a reasonable response to unavoidable economic dislocation.

On a hot afternoon in July 1995, I am standing near the corner *tienda* when Danny comes up and says hello. I usually spend time with Danny around the shooting gallery, as he is a regular heroin user. Seeing him near the *tienda*, I ask him what he's up to. He says that he's going to go down to the store on Broadway to cash his check. "I just got paid," he says showing me his GA check. "I want to get to Broadway and cash this. . . . You got a car, right? Give me a ride?" I agree to give him a ride if he's waiting on the corner for me in half an hour when I'm heading out of the projects. Danny says, "Okay, but don't take too long because they're going to close up there."

A half-hour later, Danny is waiting on the corner and gets in for the ten-minute ride from the projects up to the check-cashing store on Broadway. "I

woke up this morning, and I thought what am I gonna do today?" he says. "And
then I remembered that I had this check, so I could use it to get some beer and
stuff." Good thing you got that GA, I say to him. "No, I don't think so," he
replies. "I don't like it. It's not enough to live on. I get one eighty something
a month, and I can't live on that. I stay with my sister so I get by for a couple
weeks but the end of the month is tough. . . . I'd rather be working. Most
definitely. I get some work sometimes—little things for people when I need
the money at the end of the month. . . . But I have trouble keeping a job because
of the drinking and drugs and shit. So, I guess GA is better than nothing. But it's
not a good thing."

For Danny, as for many residents in Chávez, an awareness of the personal histories and daily rounds of GA recipients made it hard to conceive
of GA as "a good thing." In this sense, GA receipt had a relatively fixed
and simple meaning in the barrios. GA was part of the experience of substance abuse. The connection between GA and alcoholism or heroin left
little reason for residents to discuss whether one recipient "deserved" to
receive aid or whether another's aid receipt might somehow constitute
"cheating." It seemed painfully obvious why Chávez residents received
GA, and this self-evidence meant few residents would even discuss
whether a GA recipient should be exempted from welfare stigma.

In contrast to the apparently clear meaning of GA in the lives of people
with substance abuse problems, programs such as AFDC or food stamps
played a number of relatively varied roles in the complex lives of aid
recipients. These varied meanings gave residents more leeway to make
and justify selective exceptions to the general rule of universal stigma.

Sometimes, selective exception took place in a "confessional" atmosphere where recipients expressed shame because they used aid and others
excused their use. In Chapter 8, I described a gathering in June 1994
where a discussion about California's anti-immigrant Proposition 187
led to "confessions" of aid use by Rosa, Chela, and Doña Lupe. Rosa
was ashamed of the food stamps her family used for a year, and she
recalled with particular dread taking the stamps out of her purse in public to buy groceries at the local market. Chela recalled how she had been
forced to use public aid after her husband left her, and Doña Lupe had
recently turned to food stamps to help make ends meet while her husband recovered from an on-the-job back injury. In response to these
"confessions," their friends gathered around the table that day offered
supportive comments that in effect absolved the three recipients—and
Rosa in particular—of the shame they felt using public assistance.

In Guadalupe, I rarely heard residents excusing or explaining aid use outside the kind of confessional atmosphere such as that at the *convive* group. More typically, residents refused to excuse aid receipt—as the *convive* group itself steadfastly criticized aid recipients at their park play date several weeks after the confessional lunch. In Chávez, on the other hand, residents more frequently conceded that receipt sometimes reflected economic necessity rather than personal impropriety. Welfare receipt *could* arise from circumstances beyond the recipient's control. I listened in on many conversations during which Chávez residents discussed whether a particular family member, friend, or neighbor used public assistance deservedly.

Often, these conversations paralleled stories of how "bad" men could leave women reliant on AFDC and how "good" men could have the misfortune of being unable to provide for their wives and children. For example, their friends in Chávez held different opinions of the aid used by Norma and Beatrice, the two women I introduced in the last chapter. In many ways, both women followed similar pathways to AFDC reliance. For both women, the loss of a male provider—Norma to alcoholism and abandonment, Beatrice to violence and imprisonment—preceded long-term use of AFDC. Explaining how these single mothers ended up on aid, their Chávez friends told morality tales about the shortcomings of absent fathers and husbands. In the case of Norma, friends often depicted her reliance as one of the inevitable problems that stemmed from involvement with a "bad" man, while tales of Beatrice's situation focused on the fact that sometimes a "good" man could not get a break. Chávez residents told similar morality tales about the deservingness of AFDC use by the mothers and wives who remained in the community—tales I heard from the moment I arrived in the barrio.

During my first few weeks in Chávez, it became clear that Norma, Al, and Paul were not getting along with Blanca and Gladis. These residents made up distinct groups that, while polite in public, had few positive things to say in private. At first, I spent more time with Norma and her friends, and I heard from them about the selfish and immoral behavior of their rivals. According to Norma, Blanca had made fraudulent claims on AFDC. Al said that Gladis had included several family members who lived outside Chávez on her lease in order to get a larger apartment. The food bank provided further evidence of the rival group's fraudulent ways, according to Paul. He said that Blanca and Gladis gave food only to their friends inside and outside Chávez, and that this had led to the food bank's cutting off Chávez from the program. The paperwork he had to re-create, as well as the fact that non-Chávez residents expressed surprise when his team of volunteers tried to restrict their entrance to the food bank, appeared to substantiate Paul's version of events. The rivalry between these two groups appeared related to competition over who would serve as official resident representative to the Los Angeles Housing Agency. The story, as I understood it during my first months in the projects, was that Blanca and Gladis had lost their hold on these coveted positions because they had engaged in various kinds of welfare fraud.

But as I became more familiar with daily life in Chávez and began to develop an independent view of income-generating routines based on interactions with a variety of residents, Norma, Al, and Paul's accusations of fraud against Blanca and Gladis began to seem superficial and perhaps even hypocritical. Residents struggling to make ends meet regularly violated the letter of the rules governing AFDC receipt and eligibility.[5] Housing authority officials regularly ignored lease violations by pretending not to notice friends and family members sleeping on living room couches or doubling up in bedrooms. If the morality tale about Blanca and Gladis's disenfranchisement had a hypocritical facet, it involved the food bank. The misbehavior that Paul attributed to his rivals seemed hardly different from his own volunteer team's habit of stashing away choice food for themselves, their families, and their friends. And under Paul's supervision, the food bank continued to distribute food to people who did not live in Chávez—just different outsiders than had benefited from Blanca's largesse. Perhaps Blanca's method of allocating food bank resources had differed from Paul's in extent, but it could not have differed much in kind.

Accusations of fraud made by Norma, Al, and Paul against Blanca and Gladis were not simple hypocrisy, however. By accusing Blanca and Gladis of defrauding AFDC and the housing authority, Norma and Al established their own legitimacy to replace the former barrio leaders. By accusing Blanca of abusing the food bank program, Paul used stigma to consolidate his own control over food bank resources. These accusations showed residents of the barrios selectively deploying welfare stigma.

In the contest between Norma, Al, and Paul on one side and Blanca and Gladis on the other, deployed stigma flowed in both directions. One midsummer afternoon, at a time when my circle of relationships in Chávez had expanded to include her, Blanca told me how she and Gladis had been displaced as Chávez's official representatives.

I've retreated to a back room of the housing office, one of the inconspicuous spots I use to write notes, when Blanca comes into the room to ask if I have seen Paul. "I need to talk to him about the food bank," she says, watching me return pen and notebook to my jeans pocket. I say I think he went upstairs, but instead of going upstairs to look for him, Bianca seems inspired by the sight of my notebook to sit down and talk.

"I've been living in Chávez for forty-one years," she says. "I know that there are all kinds of rumors going around about me and my friends—that we don't like Norma or Paul—but there's nothing to that. It is just a vicious thing going around. People say I want to stop the food bank, but that's not true. It all started because I supported Norma and her friends to be representatives when me and Gladis stepped down. I didn't know her then, but I heard she was okay, so I said, okay I'll vote for her, and I told all my friends to vote for her, too. And that's how she got elected. But now that she is representative, all the power is going to her head. She and Al are messing everything up, and now people are coming to me and saying, 'My God, that lady is a witch!' And here I am just trying to make sure that some food goes to the community. She and Al—and now Paul, too, except Paul is too young and doesn't really know what they're doing—they're doing all these horrible things and stealing all the food for themselves. . . . Now, I go to Santa Margarita to try to get some food to the community, and I find out from people there that Norma has always been like this. I didn't know that before. But she has been cheating on welfare for years—did you know she has a man in that house?"

In our conversation that afternoon, Blanca deployed the stigma of aid against Norma, Al, and Paul in much the same way that Norma and her allies had used it against Blanca herself. Her narrative confirmed the rivalry and enmity between the two groups of residents, and it demonstrated how selective stigma could be invoked in different ways by various players in intrabarrio rivalries and friendships.

In the months following this conversation with Blanca, I heard from both sides of this rivalry, as well as from residents who did not identify with either group, of how different forms of stigma and gossip had provided potent tools for forging and defining lines of political alliance and enmity in Chávez. Several residents confirmed one version of events.

In 1994, when Norma first took over as Chávez representative, she asked Al to take charge of the food bank. A short time later, Blanca spoke with Buddy, a senior member of the Elm Street *varrio*. She told him that she was afraid that Al was ruining the food bank by disrupting relationships with suppliers, keeping food for himself, and distributing food to nonresidents. At the time, Blanca had good relations with Elm Street. During her time as housing authority representative, she had sponsored several community events that members attended and enjoyed, especially an annual Thanksgiving turkey dinner at a local church. At the next Elm Street meeting Buddy reported to other members of the *varrio* that the food bank was in danger and that something had to be done. One group of Elm Street members confronted Al with Blanca's accusations, and from other members Al heard a rumor that this *clika* planned to physically attack him. Fearing for his own safety, Al left Chávez for a few weeks and went to stay with relatives.

In his absence, Norma and Paul intervened on Al's behalf. Norma circulated the rumor that, following her success at getting gang members to confront Al, Blanca had taken to calling herself the "Queen of Elm Street." Blanca understood that this moniker hurt her standing with Elm Street. "It's disrespectful," she explained to me. "And the guys were upset about it. I have no control over Elm Street—they know that. But I had to go and get Buddy to explain it and straighten it out." Buddy successfully restored Blanca's good name in Elm Street, and in the process Paul worked to restore Al's reputation and secure a withdrawal of the threats against him. In the end, Paul garnered *varrio* support to head the food bank himself as part of a compromise that allowed Al to safely return to Chávez.

### SUBCULTURES IN ACTION

Few Americans generate income by participating in public assistance; even in low-income neighborhoods, the number of welfare users rarely approaches the number of residents who earn their income through other means. But because welfare receipt is seen to violate core societal values of personal responsibility and self-reliance, even small amounts of welfare use generate concern. Aid receipt may be seen as socially isolating poor people from the nation's mainstream institutions. Many believe that welfare recipients subscribe to cultural orientations that foster dependence, and it is troubling that this "culture of dependence" might undermine the work ethic of all residents in the low-income community. For policy makers, these concerns have proved a powerful lever to push welfare programs in new directions. The end of AFDC and the introduction of TANF represent a fundamental shift in the goals of the American welfare system: from supporting the economically vulnerable to making all Americans economically self-sufficient. Ethnography provides the means to examine the cultural consequences of welfare use and assess to what extent concerns about dependence reflect the cultural reality of welfare in low-income communities.

At first glance, attitudes toward welfare in Guadalupe and Chávez appeared to confirm policy makers' fears that aid receipt undermines core American values. In Guadalupe, where few received aid, residents appeared firm in their belief that no matter what the circumstances, welfare was an unacceptable way to generate income—an orientation I call here universal stigma. Their principled belief appeared to pay off in self-reliance, as few residents traveled down the pathway to aid reliance. In Chávez, on the other hand, residents appeared to waver in their cultural commitment to the ideals of personal responsibility and self-reliance. They roundly and consistently impugned GA receipt, but their resolve weakened when it came to AFDC and in-kind local aid programs. Moreover, when Chávez residents did condemn aid receipt, it appeared to occur in hypocritical expressions of intrabarrio *chisme* and in the service of local politics rather than as an expression of a genuine belief in its impropriety. Chávez residents regularly excused the aid use of friends and allies while invoking welfare stigma to discredit the character of rivals and enemies. Was this cultural capriciousness one reason that welfare receipt was more common in the housing projects of Los Angeles than in the immigrant barrios of San Jose?

Policy makers fear that poor people living in places like Chávez endorse self-reliance selectively because welfare has diluted this ideal in their community—a simple and direct model of the relationship between public aid and cultural orientations. A brief comparison of aid receipt and welfare cultures in Guadalupe and Chávez appears to offer support for this simple model. But closer examination of how residents used welfare and deployed welfare stigma day by day reveals several problems with this simple model and suggests a more subtle and complex understanding of the relationship between aid use and cultural ideals.

Day to day, barrio residents constructed the meaning of reliance through their talk about and behavior toward family, neighbors, and local institutions. They declared that some people had achieved self-reliance and that others had fallen short. They celebrated those they saw as overcoming barriers to achieve self-reliance, and they criticized others who appeared to have succumbed to the temptations of irresponsibility. Residents applauded or condemned local institutions such as churches, job centers, local aid programs, and community leaders depending on their assessment of whether they helped or hindered residents in their efforts to stand on their own two feet. These cultural construction projects contrast sharply with the policy maker model. In that model, poor people either embrace or reject ideals of self-reliance, and their attitudes toward welfare is a relatively stable part of their personal and community cultural orientations. In day-to-day reality, in contrast, barrio residents ruminated over the meaning of self-reliance and personal responsibility; they argued about the circumstances which justified their abandonment—such as in reaction to disrespectful treatment from a hostile boss; and they tirelessly debated who was living up to these ideals, who was falling short, and why. The first way in which the simple policy maker model falls short of day-to-day reality in the barrios, therefore, is in failing to recognize that barrio residents construct local welfare cultures. Fears of poor people simply abandoning mainstream ideals once and for all misrepresents how culture operates in everyday life.

The policy maker model misrepresents not only how culture operates but also how everyday conditions in the barrios shape local cultural orientations. Cultural construction projects in the barrios often began with the same notions of personal responsibility and self-reliance that, in the policy makers' simple cultural models, pervade other U.S. communities. These ideals make up the locally available cultural materials in the barrios too. Residents criticized each other as lazy or undeserving precisely because these ideals were pervasive. They alleged that political rivals failed to measure up to these behavioral benchmarks because these cultural ideals retained their power to tarnish reputations, sway opinion, and influence action. The policy maker model fails to recognize the enduring power of mainstream ideals in the low-income barrios.

Where ideals thrive matters. In the low-income barrios, these ideals thrived in a social environment of economic need. Welfare cultures of Guadalupe and Chávez reflected the concrete reality of urban poverty as much as they did the abstract American ideals of personal responsibility and self-reliance. Differences in the concrete reality of poverty in Guadalupe and Chávez produced markedly different cultural constructions around welfare. On the one hand, greater poverty in Chávez meant more welfare stigma because more residents used aid to generate income. On the other hand, welfare stigma in Chávez had a different quality than its counterpart in Guadalupe. Compared to Guadalupe residents, with their Manichaean views of welfare, Chávez residents more frequently excused aid or acknowledged the circumstances attending receipt. They paid closer attention to the shades of gray in welfare recipients' economic circumstances. Family, friends, and neighbors, it was understood, used welfare for different reasons. Welfare had multiple meanings, and the stigma associated with welfare could take myriad forms. Chávez residents skillfully deployed these meanings in everyday life. Like the residents of Guadalupe, Chávez residents knew what welfare in America was *supposed* to mean, and in some circumstances Chávez residents invoked these meanings of welfare. But Chávez residents also adeptly shaped and manipulated the meaning of welfare in light of local circumstances and personal desires and interests.

Regular interactions with aid and aid recipients shaped how Chávez residents thought about self-reliance through a process of cultural proliferation—not isolation, withdrawal, or rejection. Simply put, Chávez residents had *more* ways to make sense of aid receipt than residents in Guadalupe. Chávez residents were more skilled manipulators of welfare stigma and more adept users of the culture surrounding welfare than residents in Guadalupe. This is not surprising. Guadalupe residents had less experience with the dynamics of the U.S. welfare system and its peculiar significance in American society. As they become more familiar with these meanings, we might expect the immigrants of Guadalupe to become more comfortable using culture in ways that would match their local circumstances and further their personal interests. We might expect them to become more skilled at deploying cultural content as they acquired a nuanced sense of self-reliance and personal responsibility in the U.S. context and abandoned the simple rules that define these concepts. Comparing welfare stigma in Guadalupe and Chávez shows how stigma is not simply a cultural construction but an institutional means for managing the use of welfare in everyday life.

PART V

# Conclusion

## *Work, Crime, and Welfare*

It would be our business to show how through every instant
of every day of every year of his existence alive he is from all
sides streamed inward upon, bombarded, pierced, destroyed
by that enormous sleeting of all objects forms and ghosts how
great how small no matter, which surround and whom his
senses take: in as great and perfect and exact particularity as
we can name them . . . but it is beyond my human power to
do. The most I can do—the most I can hope to do—is to
make a number of physical entities as plain and vivid as possible, and to make a few guesses, a few conjectures; and to leave
to you much of the burden of realizing in each of them what
I have wanted to make clear of them as a whole: how each is
itself; and how each is a shapener.

James Agee and Walker Evans, *Let Us Now Praise Famous Men:
Three Tenant Families*

WORK, CRIME, AND WELFARE EVOKE powerful feelings in the United States. Work represents one of the central positive values in our society, while crime and welfare are seen as disruptive, shameful, even self-destructive lifestyle choices. I adopt these loaded terms to title the sections of the book purposely yet ironically. Connotations aside, work, crime, and welfare are in the first and last analysis neither values nor lifestyles but merely different ways to generate income. Setting aside and stepping outside the usual frames of reference for assessing the place of these activities in American society is particularly important when we examine the low-income barrios, in which the usual meanings of income-generating activities can be altered and transformed readily.

Work provides the most important example of this transformation of meaning. Jobs were the most important source of income in both Guadalupe and Chávez barrios, where residents worked in low-quality jobs that paid poor wages, provided unstable hours on a daily and long-term basis, involved unpleasant or dangerous workplace conditions, and had few paths for promotion. Jobs confronted the barrio with as many difficulties as opportunities and forced the community to explicitly address the meaning of work and the question of whether the labor market represented a glass half-full or one half-empty.

Barrio residents addressed these questions daily and individually, but on most days most residents arrived at answers that reflected the social situation of their community as much as their individual circumstances. The immigrants of Guadalupe often saw the glass as half-full. Five dollars an hour earned in San Jose could purchase property in Michoacán or provide the nest egg to start a business in Oaxaca. As importantly, Guadalupe residents could break up the brutal work routine of low-wage work with visits "home." Many planned to stop working in six or ten months; they had to return to Mexico City or Guadalajara to visit relatives, to show off the new baby, or to check up on household renovations. In contrast, residents in Chávez more often saw the opportunities in the LA labor market as a glass half-empty. They could not afford meaningful purchases such as market-rate rents or a new car on $5 an hour. They rarely expected to get a break from the daily grind of low-wage work in the immediate future because they generally did not plan big trips abroad to visit family. From their perspective, the grind of low-wage work had no natural stopping point.[1] In both barrios, work carried positive connotations, but the specific meaning of locally available jobs—a potential pathway to success versus an economic and social dead-end—varied with the social network of the worker as much as with the objective opportunities on local labor markets.[2]

Local job opportunities shaped daily work life as well as crime, welfare, and social life more generally as Guadalupe and Chávez lives unfolded in communities with different understandings of the prospects and problems of low-wage work.[3] For recent Mexican immigrants, the local culture of Guadalupe made pursuing available jobs, for all their shortcomings, sensible. They adopted the strategy of overwork as a way to manage the problems of the labor market. Crime in Guadalupe involved violations of immigration and labor law in the pursuit of jobs in the informal economy. Guadalupe residents used welfare as a temporary stopgap and had trouble understanding why anybody would use it in any other way. In Chávez, on the other hand, seeking alternative sources of income outside the labor market seemed a more reasonable way to manage the shortcomings of the low-wage work. Residents hustled. Hustling meant taking advantage of opportunities in the informal as well as in the illicit economy, and as a consequence few Chávez residents could avoid encountering law enforcement in the course of their daily rounds. Hustling meant a more flexible understanding of welfare. Many Chávez residents participated in aid programs, and many found themselves vulnerable to the sting of welfare stigma.

Comparing the two strategies, overwork may seem preferable. It entails fewer risks of personal harm and fewer extreme swings of financial fortune. Overworkers, like most Americans, earn their living at the job, try to avoid breaking the law, and abjure public assistance, behaviors that connect overworkers to the legitimate labor market and confer mainstream respectability and symbolic attractiveness on their economic strategy. Overwork allows low-income Americans to live the same lifestyle and play by the same rules as the wealthier Americans who dominate the country in the marketplace, in the polity, and in the imagination.

Hustlers expose themselves to interruptions of income via injury or incarceration and to the political vagaries and social stigma of the welfare system. From the perspective of economic rationality, these risks and drawbacks can make hustling appear a last-resort "survival strategy" rather than an actively chosen "economic strategy." Some poor people do end up reliant on risky criminal activities or dependent on public aid programs when they have no other choice for survival. But many others take advantage of opportunities to generate income through crime or welfare because these activities offer financial rewards beyond those available in legitimate labor markets. As importantly, even though crime and welfare attract stigma in the low-income community, poor people find symbolic support for hustling in American attitudes toward money and work. Hustling is consistent with the American emphasis on winning—and winning in the economic arena in particular—by any means necessary. Low-income people engaged in hustling see their own activities as consistent with those of high-income Americans who control vast resources. Moreover, poor people find validation of their perspective in the behavior of prominent institutions, from the criminal justice system that acquits the wealthy O. J. Simpson—whose trial transfixed Los Angeles during much of 1995—to the media that follow every movement of wealthy movie stars. In the barrios, residents can find plenty of evidence that hustling is consistent with the *actual* rules governing everyday life in the United States, where financial success trumps other considerations.

Income generation in Guadalupe and Chávez shows us that poor people actively decide whether to overwork or to hustle and why playing by the rules appears more sensible in some communities while striving to win at any cost makes more sense in others. Structural analyses of urban poverty tend to ignore individual decision making, while individual analyses of the urban poor often overlook local context. The previous chapters examined how structural circumstances and individual orientations overlapped, interacted, and reinforced each other in social institutions that supported and sustained income generation in the barrios. The next chapter examines the nature and implications of overwork and hustling: the price they exact on poor people; how they shape local cultures in low-income communities; how they are related to the so-called urban "underclass"; and how we should make sense of and react to these economic strategies.

# CHAPTER 10

# The Price of Poverty

Poverty exacts its price quietly in Guadalupe. The small houses and tree-lined streets, even the concrete-slab apartment buildings, do not advertise deprivation. But if you wait until late in the afternoon, you can see the signs of poverty appear. When school lets out, the sidewalks fill with children, mothers, and grandmothers, a hint of the large families in the neighborhood's small houses and apartments. Over the next few hours, driveways and streets, sidewalks and front lawns become choked with cars—another signal of overcrowding and an indicator of how many jobs it requires to sustain each of these Silicon Valley households. My landlady Gloria cobbled together the rent for her three-bedroom house from me and another full-time boarder by providing in-home care to the aged, from her sons' busboy and prep cook jobs in San Jose and San Francisco, and from the occasional odd-job earnings and constant in-kind services of the young *Salvadoreña* who stayed with us for a few months. "You don't need a key," Gloria told me the day after I moved into the house. "Just ring the bell. There's always someone around to let you in."

Travel to Chávez barrio, where the price of poverty announces itself. From the moment you top the hill above the projects and drive down into the complex of identical low-rise buildings, you know you have entered a poor neighborhood. The identical buildings need repair, men hang out on the sidewalk, storefront walls are tagged "Gato," "Stinger," and the ubiquitous Elm Street "ES." I first met Stinger (given name Tomas) and his family, including most of his seven brothers, in the spring of 1995. One of his older brothers told me that of eight boys in the family, four had been shot and one, his youngest brother, had been killed. "He was sitting in the back seat of a car, and someone came up and said, 'Where you from?' and they said, 'Elm Street,' and he started shooting and he hit my brother right in the head." Most of the sons in the family had retired from active gang life. Only Stinger and one other brother remained active, and Stinger was the only one not yet shot. One Sunday morning, I bumped into Tomas's mother as she climbed into a car driven by her husband. She carried flowers, and she told me that they were heading to the cemetery to visit her youngest son. She asked if I had seen Tomas; he had said he wanted to go with her that day. I had not seen him, but could I give him a message? "No message," she said. "Just tell him I love him."

The quiet toils of Guadalupe and the spectacular struggles of Chávez evoke profound and profoundly different reactions for Americans. Poverty in Guadalupe evokes immigrant hopes for socioeconomic mobility and thus represents an understanding of poverty and struggle that resonates in the experiences of early-twentieth-century European Americans and in the imaginations of their descendants. Deprivation in Chávez exemplifies an experience of intergenerational poverty and socioeconomic stagnation that seems to have no parallel outside the deteriorating African American ghettos of the late-twentieth-century Rust Belt. Yet we find reminders of both kinds of poverty in the Mexican American barrios of contemporary California, sometimes even in contiguous neighborhoods. Comparing poverty in Guadalupe and Chávez allows us to better understand what distinguishes the pedestrian price of poverty paid by recent immigrants from the more spectacular price exacted in neighborhoods of persistent poverty. Comparing Guadalupe and Chávez encourages us to speculate about the future of Mexican American poverty and incorporation in the United States, especially in comparison with socioeconomically disadvantaged groups such as African Americans. Examining poverty in Chávez and Guadalupe leads us to consider how citizens and policy makers should view barrio poverty and what public policy might do to reduce its price.

## SOCIAL INSTITUTIONS AND THE EXPERIENCE OF POVERTY

Poverty unfolds differently in Guadalupe and Chávez—severe overcrowding, relentless work hours, and migration-initiated family separation versus public drug markets, deadly violence, and family breakup. In popular and scholarly thought, these dislocations and hardships reflect not just different daily experiences of poverty but different kinds of poverty altogether. Popular accounts contrast the mobility and industry of recent immigrants with stagnation and dysfunction in persistently poor communities.[1] Contrasts persist in scholarly work, even though ethnographers have increasingly highlighted the internal divisions among seemingly united recent immigrants as well as the forms of community solidarity in even the most impoverished areas of persistent poverty.[2] My experiences in Guadalupe and Chávez add to an ethnographic record that emphasizes the continuities of experience in diverse low-income communities. Guadalupe and Chávez faced similar deprivation but developed quite different ways of managing it. Examining why similar structural circumstances and individual orientations energized different social institutions helps explain how these different kinds of poverty can exist side by side in the barrios.

## Structures of Poverty

Analyzing institutions of poverty in Guadalupe and Chávez highlights important ideas about the relationship between social structure and poverty. Generally, we think of social structure, as William H. Sewell, Jr., notes, "as primary, hard, immutable, like the girders of a building."[3] In analyses of poverty, this immutable structure often appears to directly determine income-generating possibilities and behaviors in poor communities. Structure exists outside the control of poor people and thus appears to "force" them to adopt certain behaviors. In the most influential statement of this direct relationship between structure and poverty, William Julius Wilson has analyzed deindustrialization's structural relationship to poverty. Deindustrialization, in this view, causes poverty along with social problems such as joblessness, crime, and welfare reliance by making it impossible for residents of low-income communities to find work.[4] My analysis of institutions of poverty in Guadalupe and Chávez suggests that deindustrialization shapes the experience of urban poverty in myriad ways.[5] The relationship between social structure and social dislocations is complex and hard to predict.

Structural circumstances affect poverty not just by causing economic dislocations but also by their effects on the institutions that poor people use to manage those dislocations. The barrio institutions of poverty that help residents find jobs (social networks), generate illegal income (indigenous organizations), and make sense of welfare reliance (subcultures) reflect a variety of structural factors.[6] Social networks that helped residents find jobs reflected the concentration of particular ethnoracial groups in particular kinds of jobs. Illegal organizations that helped residents participate in economic crime recognized the residential differentiation that meant that police crackdowns targeted some neighborhoods more than others. And local subcultures that made sense of welfare reliance took account of the family structure in households that received aid. Race, neighborhood, and family structure thus affected the experience of poverty in the barrios through their influence on social institutions.

Structural circumstances affect poverty in ways that are difficult to predict, owing to the complex relationship between structure and institutions of poverty. Even structural dislocations that have large and seemingly self-evident effects on the poor actually play out in a wide variety of ways in everyday life. Deindustrialization, for example, had quite different effects in Guadalupe and Chávez because residents of the two barrios mobilized social institutions in different ways to manage the problems of disappearing industrial employment. Comparisons between the barrios in general and other kinds of low-income communities also illustrate this point. Industrial plant closings in the Los Angeles Basin affected job opportunities in both the Mexican American barrios of East LA and the African American ghettos of South LA, but the effects of these plant closings worked themselves out quite differently in the two urban areas. Examining the role of institutions of poverty can help explain these different outcomes.

An institutional perspective encourages us to empirically examine how structural change and dislocation shape the experience of poverty. It reminds us that structural circumstances are rarely dire enough to "force" poor people to take particular actions. In a multitude of ways, social structures affect the resources and constraints that affect how poor people actively manage everyday life in conditions of material deprivation. But much of what shapes the daily experience of poverty and much of what makes life different in different kinds of low-income communities hinges on the operations of social institutions of the middle range. To predict and understand how structural change and dislocation shape the world of the urban poor, we must focus on the complex and contingent effects of social institutions.

## Individual Orientations

The role of individual orientation, initiative, and volition is one of the most controversial topics in studies of urban poverty. Oscar Lewis's culture-of-poverty theory introduces a recurring theme: that individual orientations of the poor are a proper object for social scientific research and that some poor people embrace self-destructive orientations and behaviors. Lewis argued that these orientations and behaviors are rooted in family relations and that they can constitute a self-perpetuating culture.[7] In this reading, culture consists of values and norms that people carry about in their heads as mental abstractions and images. In this sense, the culture of poverty resident in individual mental orientations can "tell" poor people what to do; observable behaviors arise fairly directly from individual orientations, initiatives, and volitions. In the wake of Lewis's influential statement of the theory, researchers asked poor people about their desires and aspirations and found that their answers suggested that the culture-of-poverty theory had serious empirical weaknesses.[8] Nevertheless, the theory continues to represent the dominant model for how culture operates in poor communities. For example, researchers who observe differing styles of dress and language in poor communities still worry that these areas are culturally "isolated" from higher-income America—and thus unwittingly invoke a model of culture in which what people do reflects precisely what they think or want.[9]

Outside the domain of urban poverty, scholars commonly speak of culture as a publicly available "web of meanings" or set of habits that people draw upon in the course of everyday life. From this perspective, cultural systems lend order and meaning to people's lives rather than acting as a set of rules telling them what to do.[10] In analyses of urban poverty, the older view of culture—a view still embraced in policy circles—remains influential.[11] Focusing on institutions of poverty encourages cultural analyses that do not invoke the culture-of-poverty theory's problematic view of the relationship between individual volition and observed behavior. Institutional analysis emphasizes that the relationship between culture and poverty is important not because culture tells poor people what to do but because it shapes when and how income generation takes place and poverty is reproduced in low-income communities.[12]

Cultural differences marked everyday economic life in Guadalupe and Chávez with respect to the meaning of money, the operational logic of locally controlled economic organizations, and the interpretation of material deprivation and welfare receipt. In short, culture matters for poverty when institutional arrangements allow it to touch on the relationship between poor people and material resources. Culture matters because social networks shape the meaning of money; because indigenous organizations structure participation in the illegal economy; and when material deprivation means residents cannot avoid public aid and its stigma. In each of these cases, culture shapes poverty not through a quiet "telling" of poor people what to do but in public forums where members of the community—the poor people who live there as well as outsiders ranging from relatives in a different country to police who patrol the streets to ethnographers conducting research—broadcast, discuss, and debate the honor, elegance, and effectiveness of various income-generating activities. Differences in income-generating activities do not stem from the cultural isolation of poor communities, nor does cultural distinctiveness in low-income communities usually create poverty. The institutional perspective emphasizes that the currency and legitimacy of cultural perspectives on income generation reflect real conditions in the low-income community. In particular, income-generating cultures reflect connections between particular poor communities and family, employers, and politicians who may live and work in distant neighborhoods, states, or nations.

## IS THERE A MEXICAN AMERICAN "UNDERCLASS"?

Questions about how culture and structure matter in poverty came to a head in debates over the so-called urban "underclass"—a debate that generated as much heat as light. In the early 1980s, journalists and conservative scholars depicted the "underclass" as a group with a self-destructive culture, as evidenced by their embrace of welfare, drugs and alcohol, crime, and single parenthood.[13] By the mid-1980s a more liberal alternative perspective, championed by Wilson, maintained that social problems in "underclass" neighborhoods reflected the disappearance of work, not a dysfunctional lifestyle choice.[14] Examining the "underclass" question focused a substantial amount of scholarly and policy maker attention on the contemporary experience of urban poverty but produced few new insights into the condition.[15] The term *underclass* was imprecise, pejorative, and distracting;[16] the debate's "culture versus structure" framework failed to generate theoretical epiphanies;[17] and the debate focused narrowly on the African American experience in Rust Belt ghettos rather than examining the diverse experiences of poverty among all ethnoracial groups, including Mexican Americans.[18] Chávez appears to be home to an "underclass"—which is to say that some residents struggled with severe or intergenerational deprivation and with problems including unemployment, welfare reliance, crime and violence, and family breakup. Guadalupe appears free of these troubles. Can we speak of a Mexican

American "underclass"? What are we saying when we call a neighborhood "underclass"? Over time, might the quiet immigrant poverty of
Guadalupe become the spectacular "underclass" poverty of Chávez?

*Underclass* is a pejorative and imprecise code word for poverty in
neighborhoods dominated by hustling. Hustling thrives in some Mexican
American barrios, including Chávez, as it does in certain African American ghettos, such as Chicago's Robert Taylor Homes.[19] Hustling does not
arise mechanically from a dysfunctional culture, nor does it surface spon-
taneously from the constraints of social structure. It represents one sensible economic strategy for people struggling to satisfy high expectations
for success in an environment of poor opportunities. Chávez residents'
cultural worlds emphasized palpable material success, including conspicuous consumption; labor markets in East LA provided opportunities to
work, but workers usually understood that these opportunities offered
few prospects for success. The situation in Guadalupe differed because
transnational networks allowed residents to deemphasize local consumption in their definitions of economic accomplishment. In Guadalupe, as in
other immigrant communities, overwork represented a reasonable pathway toward economic goals that were objectively more modest.

Hustlers use crime and welfare to generate income. The label *underclass* highlights the stigma we attach to these activities while it minimizes
the income they generate. The label implies that hustling is an isolated
and unneeded economic strategy, while the debate focuses on whether it
arises from the dysfunctional preferences of individuals or from a breakdown of the economy. Hustling and what some might label an "underclass" existed in Chávez but not in Guadalupe, but not because of simple
differences in residents' economic preferences or because of differences in
economic possibilities in the barrios of East LA compared to San Jose.
Chávez residents did not *want* to generate income through crime and
welfare, nor did a breakdown in the economy *force* them to do so. A
variety of local institutions made crime a reasonable way to generate
income in both communities, but we would never apply the label *underclass* to crime in Guadalupe because of the particular laws that residents
violated. Neither Guadalupe nor Chávez residents condoned welfare
receipt, but the ubiquity of deprivation in Chávez encouraged residents
there to be more flexible in their condemnation.

Calling people who engage in hustling and the communities where
they live "underclass" implies that they stand apart from and beneath
U.S. mainstream society. Examining how Chávez residents use crime and
welfare to generate income reveals hustling's foundations in mainstream

institutions—in residents' embrace of mainstream culture's measures of economic success and their position in the least desirable sectors of the mainstream job structure. Like most Americans, Chávez residents valued financial independence and conspicuous consumption. They could demonstrate financial independence by living on one's own in private housing—thus demonstrating independence from parents and the state. Conspicuous consumption meant having one's own car, at least occasionally dressing up in fashionable clothing, and having cash on hand to treat friends and relatives to a meal at the local *taquería* or McDonald's. Attaining success was a challenge, however, because of structural characteristics of the mainstream job market. Few local jobs provided decent wages and security—a benefit for mainstream employers and a reflection of local and national political arrangements. In these circumstances, hustling and the local institutions that supported hustlers allowed residents to continue to strive toward the goals of mainstream culture despite the constraints of mainstream structure.

Guadalupe residents also faced slim opportunities on the job market, and they sought local institutional support to manage the problems that resulted. In contrast to the Chicanos of Chávez, however, Guadalupe's immigrants did not embrace mainstream American expectations of economic success. As a result, the kinds of institutional solutions they adopted to manage job market problems led them to overwork rather than to hustle. Though Guadalupe could never be mistaken for an "underclass" neighborhood, the job market created problems there as it did in Chávez. Household routines had to accommodate long hours of work at low wages, undocumented workers had to find secure methods of meeting employers or obtaining *chuecos,* and mainstream cultural expectations were held in check only as long as residents could sustain vibrant connections with communities in Mexico. Guadalupe residents forged ties with existing San Jose institutions such as job markets, local schools, and barrio neighborhoods. They maintained their distance from others, including the peculiar materialism of American consumer society. These institutional arrangements changed slowly and incrementally, for example, when settlement snuck up on long-staying residents, and they changed quickly and dramatically, as when the passage of California's anti-immigrant Proposition 187 galvanized *Mexicano* interest in citizenship and other political institutions. In Guadalupe, a different—and less destructive—set of institutions provided solutions to the problems associated with work.

Hustling and overwork both used local institutions to solve dilemmas rooted in low-wage labor markets. Both economic strategies helped residents address problems related to lousy jobs, and neither erased the problems those jobs created. Lousy jobs—and the resource deprivation that accompanies them—inevitably exacted a price in both low-income communities. In many ways Chávez residents paid a higher price, but neither institutional solution was perfect or painless. Applying the pejorative term *underclass* to the institutional solution that dominated in Chávez—as well as in other low-income urban areas such as Rust Belt ghettos—reflects the cultural orientations of scholars and policy makers. Residents in Chávez and in Rust Belt ghettos similarly applied pejorative terms to overworkers, seeing them as slaves, suckers, or sellouts.

Focusing on institutions leads us to examine how different low-income communities are culturally and structurally integrated into the United States rather than to examine whether the "underclass" is culturally deviant or structurally disenfranchised. Low-income areas are not places separate or apart from mainstream America. Loïc Wacquant argues that these communities are properly understood as a particular social institution within U.S. society.[20] Is there a Mexican American "underclass"? Of course not. There are, however, many Mexican American communities caught between the rock of cultural expectations and the hard place of low-wage jobs. Poor people try to solve this problem, and their solution is to devise and energize local institutions that allow them to make do with resources that are available. Rather than label and condemn some of these institutional solutions as typifying an "underclass," we would do better to examine what sorts of institutions can do a better job at resolving problems generated by low-wage jobs and considering how to encourage and sustain those institutions.

PUBLIC POLICY AND THE PRICE OF POVERTY

Even as they argue over whether structure or culture is more important, policy makers subscribe to a fundamentally similar model of poverty. In day-to-day politics, disagreements about structure versus culture—with liberals supporting structural arguments and conservatives sympathetic to cultural ones—obscure this fundamental consensus. The consensus is that poverty reflects a lack of social mobility, that social mobility is the antidote to poverty, that mobility should occur in the space of a generation or so, and that mobility is facilitated by a good job in the legitimate economy. Disagreements about why poor people are immobile do not threaten this fundamental consensus.[21]

My analysis of barrio life suggests that institutions of poverty facilitate income generation even as they impede mobility. In some situations, small changes in institutions of poverty can substantially increase their potential to support income generation as well as upward mobility. In other situations, institutions of poverty can be a more significant barrier to mobility than structural dislocations or cultural deficits.

The fundamental dilemma confronting residents of both Guadalupe and Chávez was neither a structural disappearance of work nor a cultural disinclination to seek mobility through work. It was, rather, that available jobs paid so poorly that participating in work could not be counted on to produce upward mobility. Everyday economic life in Guadalupe and Chávez revolved around the institutional solutions that residents embraced to resolve this dilemma. In Guadalupe, they resolved it by using local institutions to redefine the rewards of low-wage jobs. In Chávez, residents turned to alternative income-generating institutions ranging from the illicit economy to the public aid system. Neither of these institutional solutions, however, provided a sure path out of poverty for barrio residents.

In Guadalupe, the institutional solution supported overwork, the key to which was maintaining the migrant's inflated view of the dollar. Those who subscribed most fully to overwork lived in abysmal conditions in San Jose so that they could send as many dollars as possible home to Mexico, and they crossed and recrossed the border to get relief from the difficult conditions of daily living in the States and to maintain connections and keep abreast of investments at home. These practices maintained ties to Mexico and sustained the cultural orientation that low-wage jobs in the States were valuable. But these practices also precluded socioeconomic advancement in the United States. Even if employers were happy to hire a hard-working immigrant who really believed $5 an hour was a good wage, they were unlikely to promote an employee who regularly left the job for weeks at a time or whose living situation did not promote the acquisition of English. Thus, overwork could serve as a barrier to mobility.

Not surprisingly, overwork broke down for many residents of Guadalupe. Many migrants left Guadalupe barrio permanently—exhausted, frustrated, and disgusted by life in the States. Others embarked on the path to U.S. settlement. They began to raise families and to devote less time, money, and attention toward practices that renewed links with Mexico. They sent smaller remittances less frequently, they took fewer and shorter trips to visit family, and they began to spend more time in social situations where people did not speak fluent Spanish. Something in the life circumstances of these residents disturbed the institutional solution of overwork. Landing a steady job could encourage a circular migrant to move family from Mexico to the States, or a fight with relatives in Mexico could interrupt remittance sending. Frequently, overwork broke down slowly and incompletely—for example, when family members in Mexico joined an already overcrowded household in Guadalupe. New arrivals meant new ties to people in Mexico. At the same time, new arrivals meant greater demands on U.S. household resources and a reduction in migrants' ability to sustain ties through remittance sending.

In even the best of circumstances, therefore, Guadalupe residents found that overwork could perpetuate poverty rather than facilitate upward mobility. This happened in different ways for recent migrants and for more settled migrants. Recent migrants inspired by the value of their dollars in Mexico threw themselves into low-wage work. But lousy jobs were worthwhile only as long as migrants maintained their ties to Mexico, and maintaining ties to Mexico could disrupt work routines in the States enough to preclude upward mobility out of lousy jobs. This was the price of poverty exacted by overwork among recent migrants in Guadalupe. More settled migrants frequently found themselves economically immobilized by a precarious social balancing act. Migrant success attracted family and neighbors to move north, and isolated migrants often welcomed their company. But new arrivals also strained resources. Earnings that might have supported upward mobility—moving to a larger house or a better neighborhood, for example—might instead be devoted to sponsoring more migration. Some settlers withdrew support from migration chains and devoted resources to their own mobility, but this meant paying a price in social isolation. Thus, institutions of poverty exacted a price from settlers who were forced to chose between mobility and isolation.

In Chávez, residents resolved the dilemma of low-wage work through hustling, an institutional solution that exacted a heavy price. Residents who embraced hustling risked arrest, incarceration, and violence in the illicit economy, and they endured stigmatization and a constant scramble for economic survival in the welfare economy. Nevertheless, residents embraced hustling because they believed it provided a better chance of economic success than low-wage work. The evidence for this belief came from three sources. First, there was the reality of life on the low-wage labor market. Chávez residents, unable to take advantage of a transnational perspective on the dollar's value, felt sure that devoting oneself to a low-wage job was a definite and certain economic dead-end. Second, there were some people who earned decent money through participation in the illicit economy and by taking advantage of welfare. Stories of long-term success through crime or welfare were often apocryphal and rarely well documented. But there was plenty of evidence—in the clothes, cars, and furniture of barrio residents—that drug sales or AFDC could bring short-term success. The final piece of evidence was that many residents who participated in crime or welfare seemed to find a way to garner eventual success, even if that success did not take place within the confines of the illicit or welfare economy. Elm Street affiliation, for example, seemed to open doors to some highly coveted jobs that paid decently, and some welfare participants could find good jobs through programs targeted to move them into the labor force. Thus, although participating in the institutions that supported hustling carried grave risks, it also seemed to increase participants' chances of enjoying long-lasting success.

Public policy may be able to affect the extent to which institutions of poverty impede and facilitate upward mobility among the poor. Policy makers might recognize that low-wage jobs do not necessarily represent the first step on the ladder of upward mobility, nor does migrants' willingness to take these jobs and natives' rejection of them indicate a difference in devotion to the work ethic or a difference in job availability. The dynamics of low-wage working among immigrants and natives reflect the operations of different institutions of poverty. Too often, however, the effects of these institutions are interpreted as evidence that immigrants and natives have different and immutable cultural orientations or that they live in different and incompatible structural circumstances. Policy makers would do better to seek out ways to strengthen the operations of institutions of poverty that encourage upward mobility.

Public policy can also shape the extent to which institutions of poverty exact a price from the poor in everyday life. That is, aside from whether an institution of poverty encourages upward mobility, these institutions play an enormous role in everyday life in low-income communities. Policy makers may sometimes find themselves in a position where they have little leverage to alter how institutions of poverty shape mobility. For example, the dilemmas surrounding migration and low-wage work in Guadalupe barrio are driven by international social dynamics that may lie beyond policy makers' ability to control. Relationships between the Elm Street gang and local police in Chávez bring into play legal issues that tend to tie policy makers' hands. However, even in these cases, policy makers may have a substantial ability to alter the price that these institutions exact from the poor in everyday life. Public policies that support a safe and decent workplace, that encourage a focus on rehabilitation rather than punishment in law enforcement, and that emphasize income support rather than fraud prevention in public assistance will all serve to lower the price of poverty in everyday life.

Policy makers worry that policies that reduce the price of poverty will affect the poor in untoward ways. They are concerned that increasing the minimum wage, for example, may have an adverse effect on structural circumstances by increasing unemployment. They are concerned that less punitive criminal justice or more generous welfare will harm poor people's cultural orientations. My sense is that this focus on structural and cultural factors is misplaced. Institutions of poverty are complex combinations of structure and culture. The only certainty is that lowering the price of poverty, if done properly, will improve the everyday quality of life among the poor and reduce the amount of social suffering that they endure.

If we as a society decide to change our institutions of poverty, the task will not be easy. It will require enormous energy, skillful politicking, and good luck. Institutions are, after all, durable arrangements of structure and culture, and they resist change. But if we take our goal to ameliorate poverty, it is essential that we moderate those institutions that exact its price.

# Methods of This Study

We undertake not much yet some, to say: what is his house:
for whom does he work: who is he and where from, that he
is now here; what is it his life has been and has done to him:
what of his wife and of their children, each, for of all these
each is a life, a full universe: what are their clothes: what food
is theirs to eat: what is it which is in their senses and their
minds: what is the living and manner of their day, of a season,
of a year: what, inward and outward, is their manner of
living; of their spending and usage of these few years' open-
ness out of the black vast and senseless death; what is their
manner of life.

> James Agee and Walker Evans, *Let Us Now Praise Famous Men:
> Three Tenant Families*

Ethnographers write methodological appendices to confess. They confess
that during the fieldwork they were confused or overwhelmed, that their
data gathering was driven by passion as well as science, and that until the
very end they were unsure even what to write. In this appendix, I hope
not to confess—not because I am innocent of the usual ethnographic sins
but because I am not sure that ethnographers have any special reason to
confess. All social scientists—whether they gather data from historical-
archival sources, through surveys or other kinds of structured interviews,
by mining administrative data gathered for nonresearch purposes, or
through ethnography—routinely commit the venial methodological sins
of confusion, passion, and uncertainty.[1] Confusion, passion, and uncertainty are part of social scientific research—perhaps of any kind of scientific research. So it does not seem proper for ethnographers and
ethnographies to confess to research sins that could be borne by most
scholars in most publications. I include this appendix to provide an
opportunity for readers to assess the material that has appeared in the

previous chapters by detailing how I conducted the study, to discuss some ethical dilemmas that arose during the fieldwork, and to explain how I chose the presentation of results that appear here.

SELECTING SITES

Ideally, I would have liked to study multiple communities in both San Jose and Los Angeles and perhaps in another city such as New York or Chicago to address the questions of this study. But practically, a community-based participant-observation study is demanding enough that even two study sites turned out to be quite a challenge. Conducting research with a community is disorienting, time consuming, and energy draining. The disorientation stems from the need to make sense of preexisting and constantly changing relationships among study participants in the field. In terms of establishing working relationships with study participants, often there is simply no substitute for time—time for all of the people in the study, researcher and subject, to see each other in different situations and get to know each other. The energy drain comes from the constant work that both researcher and subjects do to maintain relationships with each other.

With practical boundaries on how many communities I could study, I sought to maximize the utility of the comparison I could make by selecting study sites in a fairly systematic fashion. I spoke with individuals whose personal or professional experience in San Jose or Los Angeles included extensive dealings with the Mexican American community and gathered their impression about which areas of the city were most likely to have neighborhoods appropriate for this study. I then inspected many of these neighborhoods personally by driving or walking through them. I looked for indications that the area was populated by Latinos (commercial establishments catering to Latino tastes, the language of conversation, the appearance of pedestrians) and that the area was low income (as indicated by apparent overcrowding of residential units, distinctive commercial establishments catering to a low-income population, number and quality of automobiles, and signs of physical dilapidation of housing or commercial structures). I then gathered data from the 1990 census on the census tracts in those areas that I had identified as well as on a number of other areas of the city in order to provide comparison.

In San Jose, I used these data to focus on neighborhoods that met four criteria. First, I identified neighborhoods dominated by individuals of Mexican descent. The 1990 census reported detailed information regarding the national identification of those of Hispanic descent, and I identified those census tracts where 40 percent or more of residents identified themselves as being of Mexican heritage. Second, I ascertained the level of officially measured poverty in each of the census tracts (using 1990 census figures) and identified those tracts that were near the median level of poverty for all the targeted study areas. Third, I inspected data from the 1990 census on nativity (U.S. vs. foreign born) and the length of residence in the United States for those born abroad (five years or less vs. more than five years). For each of the target census tracts I calculated two ratios: the ratio of native born to foreign born and the ratio of those recently arrived to the total foreign born. I identified census tracts that were near the median of all target areas on these measures. Finally, I used data gathered through personal inspection to identify the kinds of housing stock in each neighborhood. Typically, the low-income barrios in San Jose had a mixture of single-family homes and some apartment buildings; neighborhoods that deviated greatly from this pattern (e.g., neighborhoods where all housing stock consisted of large apartment buildings) were identified.

In Los Angeles, I used data gathered in a similar fashion to focus on a slightly different set of neighborhoods. As in San Jose, I focused on neighborhoods in census tracts where more than 40 percent of individuals identified themselves as being of Mexican descent. But whereas in San Jose I focused on census tracts that did not deviate far from the mean in their poverty levels, in Los Angeles I identified neighborhoods in census tracts where poverty levels and unemployment were at the high end of targeted tracts. In San Jose, I focused on tracts with a typical ratio of native born to foreign born and a typical ratio of recent arrivals to foreign born; in Los Angeles, I focused on those areas with relatively large numbers of native-born residents and with relatively few recent arrivals. Finally, in Los Angeles, I used the data gathered through personal inspection to identify neighborhoods that displayed evidence of dilapidation, neglect, or other signs of residence by the persistently poor.[2]

In each city, more than one neighborhood met all of the above selection criteria, and I began to spend time in several of the neighborhoods that had qualified. I patronized local stores and hung out on the streets, observing how residents and passersby spent their time in the neighborhood. I simultaneously sought an opening to gain an introduction to the residents of several areas. In San Jose, I made progress in securing housing and gaining introductions in three separate neighborhoods (of which Guadalupe was the second); in Los Angeles, Chávez was the second of four neighborhoods where I made similar inroads.

As time passed, I focused increasingly on Guadalupe and Chávez because I made relatively quick progress gaining introductions and inserting myself into the daily routines of residents. In both cases, the church played an important role. In Guadalupe, as I mentioned in the book's introduction, a local activist introduced me to Gloria, my land-lady in San Jose. This activist had kindly agreed to speak with me about the various Mexican American neighborhoods in San Jose, and we were sitting in his donated office space in the local Catholic parish the after-noon that Gloria happened to stop by to mention she had a room avail-able in her house. The activist, who had met me only twenty minutes before Gloria's arrival, did not hesitate to recommend me to Gloria. For most of my stay in Guadalupe this activist remained based at the church, and although he did not live in Guadalupe, he seemed to know everyone in the parish. His office was an early hangout during my stay in Guadalupe, he introduced me to many of his friends and co-workers, and he even managed to get me involved in the church's Christmas activities.

In Chávez, the church was also important. Shortly after arriving in LA, I arranged to meet with an East LA priest to get his impressions about the different neighborhoods I was focusing on as possible field sites. He was familiar with all of the neighborhoods I was considering, and as we spoke in his office we began to think more and more seriously about Chávez. He offered to contact a woman he knew in Chávez and ask her if she would meet with me, and she agreed. A few days later, I met her at the Chávez community center, and we had been speaking for only a few minutes when she excused herself, saying that she had another appointment, and suggested that I continue my conversation with Ana-Berta. I spoke with Ana-Berta in the community center office for some time, and then we walked across the projects—incidents I relate in Chapter 7. At the end of that walk across the projects, Ana-Berta intro-duced me to Paul, and soon I had spent the afternoon and much of the evening in Chávez. A few days later, as I discuss below, the LA police helped further my entrance into the community.

GUADALUPE AND CHÁVEZ BY THE NUMBERS

How do Guadalupe and Chávez compare to San Jose and Los Angeles as a whole and to other low-income Mexican American barrios in those cities? This is an important question, and it is one that the ethnographic data I have presented in the book to this point cannot address directly. The U.S. census provides data at the census tract level, and these data are a valuable tool for comparing Guadalupe and Chávez to each other and to the metropolitan areas of which they are a part. However, census tract–level data must be interpreted with care for several reasons. Neither Guadalupe and Chávez is wholly contained within a single census tract, and lower-level geographic entities such as block groups did not report variables of interest. In San Jose, the census tract that best approximated the Guadalupe barrio included streets in the adjacent higher-income neighborhood, while some streets of Guadalupe barrio fell into a different census tract altogether. The Los Angeles census tract that included the Chávez housing project also included all the people who lived in the private homes adjacent to the housing project.

The lack of fit between census tract and Guadalupe and Chávez communities is the most important reason to interpret the quantitative data I present in this appendix with care, but there are several other reasons as well. These data are from the 1990 census and therefore might not reflect the actual situation in the barrios in 1993–95. In Guadalupe barrio, active immigration means rapid population change, and the economy in southern California was much more robust by 1995 than it was during the economic recession of 1990. Aside from changes over time, the figures I present here may not reflect the situation in the census tracts that most closely correspond to Guadalupe and Chávez. The census undercounted residents in low-income and immigrant neighborhoods, so it is possible that the enumeration of both Guadalupe and Chávez residents was not as accurate as possible in 1990. Finally, I have introduced some distortions in the figures because I have rounded the numbers that report results from the Guadalupe and Chávez tracts in order to ensure confidentiality.

In spite of all of these limitations, I believe it is worthwhile to use census data to compare Guadalupe and Chávez to each other, to San Jose, and to Los Angeles. These data give us some, far from perfect, ability to consider the context within which the barrio residents lived out the daily experience of poverty. Many of the census figures I discuss below do not convey the actual everyday experience of poverty in these two communities. The poverty rates seem lower than they should be in Guadalupe, and there seem to be more immigrants in Chávez than we would expect. This lack of correspondence is instructive. It highlights that census figures— even figures based on tracts, which is the smallest measure routinely seen in analyses of census data—always represent a heterogeneous experience. Census figures are always averages, so none really capture the everyday experience of people's lives.

Table 2 shows how the two communities compare to each other and

TABLE 2. AN OVERVIEW OF GUADALUPE,
CHÁVEZ, AND THEIR CITIES

| Measure | San Jose | | Los Angeles | |
|---|---|---|---|---|
| | City | Guadalupe | City | Chávez |
| *Sociodemographic Characteristics* | | | | |
| Individuals | 782,225 | 4,900 | 3,485,398 | 5,800 |
| Mexican origin | 22% | 80% | 27% | 90% |
| Immigrants | 26% | 45% | 38% | 50% |
| 1980s immigrants | 15% | 25% | 22% | 25% |
| Female-head families (% households) | 15% | 25% | 21% | 35% |
| *Socioeconomic Characteristics* | | | | |
| Per capita income | $16,905 | $7,700 | $ 16,188 | $6,100 |
| Below poverty line | 9% | 20% | 19% | 55% |
| In labor force (% 16+) | 73% | 65% | 67% | 60% |
| Unemployed (% labor force) | 6% | 10% | 8% | 20% |
| Employed (% 16+) | 68% | 55% | 62% | 45% |
| Receive public assistance (% households) | 9% | 15% | 11% | 25% |
| Mean assistance grant (per household) | $6,621 | $5,900 | $5,895 | $7,400 |

SOURCE: Tabulations by the author from U.S. Bureau of the Census (1990). Figures for Guadalupe and Chávez are rounded to maintain confidentiality.

to San Jose and Los Angeles as a whole according to several different social and economic measures available in the U.S. census.

While quite different in overall size, San Jose and Los Angeles were similar in some ways. They had similar proportions of Mexican Americans, and both cities had many immigrants, although Los Angeles had proportionally more immigrants and more recent arrivals than San Jose. The most striking difference between the cities was their prosperity. Compared to the United States as a whole, where per capita income in 1990 was $14,420, San Jose ($16,905) and Los Angeles ($16,188) were prosperous. Per capita income in California ($16,409) was also much higher than in the country as a whole. More significantly for purposes here, an extra $700 in per capita income in San Jose compared to Los Angeles was accompanied by large differences in poverty. The poverty rate of Los Angeles was more than twice that of San Jose. Los Angeles trailed San Jose in labor force participation and employment and had a higher unemployment rate. More families were headed by women in Los Angeles, but nearly equal numbers of households received public assistance in the two cities, even if San Jose aid recipients received larger grants.

Both barrios were dominated by Mexican-origin residents. Approximately half of residents in each barrio were foreign born, and a quarter of residents in both barrios arrived during the 1980s. Notably, the Guadalupe and Chávez figures for Mexican origin, immigrants, and 1980s arrivals were all substantially higher than the corresponding figures for San Jose and Los Angeles as a whole.

Further differences between Guadalupe and Chávez emerge when we look at socioeconomic standing. While poverty was more than twice as common in Guadalupe than in San Jose as a whole, the poverty rate in Guadalupe was still less than half the poverty rate of Chávez. Labor force participation was higher and unemployment was lower in Guadalupe than in Chávez. Taken together, the employment rate in Guadalupe was 10 percentage points higher than in Chávez. In both barrios, female headship was more common than in the surrounding city, as women headed one-quarter of families in Guadalupe and more than a third of families in Chávez. One in seven Guadalupe households received public assistance (about two-thirds higher than in San Jose as a whole), and in Chávez the rate was one in four (more than twice the rate of the city of Los Angeles). Chávez households received substantially larger public assistance grants than Guadalupe households.

Whether viewed side by side or within the metropolitan context in which they were a part, economic deprivation was a more pressing problem in Chávez than in Guadalupe. Both neighborhoods were areas of concentrated Mexican American settlement. There were many Mexican immigrants in the areas in and around Guadalupe and Chávez, and many of these immigrants had recently arrived from Mexico.

In poor center-city areas, a primary question concerns residents' access to the economic mainstream. Are jobs available for community residents? Data from the 1990 U.S. census help address this question. Table 3 shows data on labor force participation, unemployment, and employment in Guadalupe and Chávez compared to the surrounding "barrio complex" of which they were a part.[3] For easy reference, the figures for the cities of San Jose and Los Angeles and for Guadalupe and Chávez barrios (shown in Table 2) are reproduced.

The barrio complex of San Jose was approximately half as large as the

TABLE 3. LABOR FORCE PARTICIPATION
IN THE BARRIOS OF SAN JOSE AND LOS ANGELES

|  | San Jose | | | Los Angeles | | |
|---|---|---|---|---|---|---|
|  | City | Barrios | Guadalupe | City | Barrios | Chávez |
| Individuals | 782,225 | 129,076 | 4,900 | 3,485,398 | 244,469 | 5,800 |
| In labor force (% 16+) | 73% | 69% | 65% | 67% | 59% | 60% |
| Unemployed (% labor force) | 6% | 8% | 10% | 8% | 12% | 20% |
| Employed (% 16+) | 68% | 63% | 55% | 62% | 52% | 45% |

SOURCE: Tabulations by the author from U.S. Bureau of the Census (1990). Figures for Guadalupe and Chávez are rounded to maintain confidentiality.

barrio complex of East Los Angeles. In San Jose, labor force participation in the barrio complex was 10 percentage points higher than in East Los Angeles, and unemployment was a third higher in Los Angeles. Overall, this translated into an 11 percentage point difference in overall employment in the barrio complexes of the two cities (63 percent in San Jose compared to 52 percent in Los Angeles).

What do these differences tell us about the relative availability of jobs in Guadalupe and Chávez? Comparing job availability in Guadalupe and Chávez means distinguishing differences in the labor markets of the barrio complexes of San Jose and Los Angeles (a between-city explanation) from differences that arise from the distinct place of Guadalupe and Chávez within their respective barrio complex (a between-barrio explanation).

Comparing employment rates suggests that much of the difference between Guadalupe and Chávez was due to between-city differences. The 10 percent advantage in employment rates in Guadalupe compared to Chávez was mirrored by an 11 percent advantage at the barrio complex level. The geographic, demographic, and sociocultural similarity of the study neighborhoods and their surrounding barrio complexes lends further support to this between-city explanation.[4] The between-city explanation emphasizes that residents of Guadalupe and Chávez were exposed to labor markets similar to those faced by other residents of the barrio complex. According to this view, the differences between the experiences of residents in the barrios were due to differences between San Jose and Los Angeles.

When we break down employment within each city, we also find support for the between-barrios explanation. In San Jose, as we move from

TABLE 4. PUBLIC ASSISTANCE
IN GUADALUPE AND CHÁVEZ

|  | Guadalupe | Chávez |
| --- | --- | --- |
| Households | 1,300 | 1,200 |
| Households with aid | 15% | 25% |
| Mean grant size | $5,900 | $7,400 |
| Female-headed families | 25% | 35% |

SOURCE: Tabulations by the author from U.S. Bureau of the Census (1990).
Figures for Guadalupe and Chávez are rounded to maintain confidentiality.

city to barrio complex to Guadalupe barrio, labor force participation
decreases stepwise (from 73 percent to 69 percent to 65 percent), and
unemployment increases stepwise (from 6 percent to 8 percent to 10 percent). These stepwise changes in participation and unemployment suggest that Guadalupe is different from San Jose and its barrio complex in
degree but not in kind. In Los Angeles, labor force participation drops as
we move from city to barrio complex (from 67 percent to 59 percent),
but participation is almost the same in Chávez as in the barrio complex
as a whole. Unemployment is higher in the barrio complex than in Los
Angeles as a whole (12 percent vs. 8 percent). Lower employment in
Chávez is caused by a sharp increase in unemployment as we move from
the barrio complex to Chávez (from 12 percent to 20 percent). This pattern of changes in participation and unemployment suggest that the difference between Chávez, the barrio complex, and Los Angeles is one of
kind and not simply of degree. This between-barrio pattern might exist if
Chávez residents had a higher reservation wage than people living in surrounding communities.[5] It could also result if employers preferred not to
hire Chávez residents.[6]

Many residents of Guadalupe and Chávez had income from public
assistance. Far from being a monolithic entity, public assistance comprises
a variety of programs, including Aid to Families with Dependent Children
(AFDC), General Assistance (GA), and Supplemental Security Income
(SSI). Residents in Guadalupe and Chávez took advantage of public aid to
different degrees and in different ways. The data in Table 4 summarize the
different patterns of welfare use in the two communities.

These census data show that of the 1,300 households in Guadalupe,
one in seven had some income from public assistance; for the 1,200
households in Chávez, the figure was one in four. As is the case for public assistance in low-income neighborhoods more generally, these figures

suggest that public assistance played a limited role in income streams in both communities.[7] In addition, there were more public aid households in Chávez than in Guadalupe, and the amount of aid received by the average household in Chávez was larger. Average households that received public assistance income in Chávez received about $1,500 more than households in Guadalupe.[8] Compared to the average for all households receiving public assistance in San Jose (mean amount received was $6,621), the households of Guadalupe barrio had small grants. In contrast, the grant size in Chávez was higher than the mean grant in both the city of Los Angeles as a whole ($5,895) and the barrio complex of East Los Angeles in particular ($5,612).[9] More households receiving public assistance and larger public assistance grants suggest that Chávez barrio relied more heavily on public aid than Guadalupe.

## THE COURSE OF FIELDWORK

Social scientists often "wade" into community-based fieldwork by first working at a local social service agency, participating in a community survey, or interviewing residents. In contrast, I "jumped" into the deep end of fieldwork in Guadalupe. Only a few days after Julian showed me *Miami,* I rented a room, drove down from Berkeley with my futon and laptop computer, and began circulating throughout the Guadalupe community in my best attempt at full-time fieldwork.

After jumping into fieldwork, I found that a variety of factors helped facilitate my acceptance into the Guadalupe community, and later the Chávez barrio. First of all, although I am not of Mexican descent, my appearance did not cause me to stand out in either Guadalupe or Chávez barrios; I am short and have dark skin, eyes, and hair. I feel perfectly at home in the informal wardrobe common in the barrios. When I was speaking Spanish, my accent immediately placed me as having grown up in the United States. But many residents spoke Spanish with an American accent. In addition, the Spanish of the low-income barrios frequently included English words or elements from the Los Angeles barrio-based slang. Many barrio residents had learned their Spanish outside Mexico, so my own U.S.-tinged Spanish did not seem too out of place in either community.

My appearance and my facility with Spanish meant that ignorant outsiders often treated me like a resident. Time and again, this assumption helped ease my acceptance into both communities. In Guadalupe, it was easy to join pickup soccer games; at *Miami,* the young men outside the laundromat offered me offered forged social security cards when I passed by; and along with three participants in the program, I was recruited by an administrator at a local job-training center to move furniture from one office to another when he assumed that I too was a job seeker. In Chávez, when I was only a few days into the fieldwork, the Los Angeles police inadvertently aided my entrance into the community by stopping me, along with four other young men, as we stood talking on the side-walk near the hot spot. As the police had us kneel on the sidewalk, searched us, and questioned each of us in turn, it became clear that they were treating me as a member of the community, with all the unpleasant rights and privileges that such membership entailed. After about forty-five minutes, the five of us were released, all but one of the group unharmed. By this time, a group of residents had gathered to watch the spectacle, including four or five residents whom I had already met; knowledge of my presence in the community quickly became widely known throughout the area. In the months ahead, I occasionally referred to the incident as a way of establishing my bona fides with residents who did not yet know me.[10]

Most important, spending lots of time in the community helped me carve out a role in it. Many outsiders came to visit the community or spent a few hours a week with one group or another of residents. But it was rare that someone came into the community and spent extended periods of time. In some ways, of course, my tenure in both field sites was fairly brief. It is not uncommon for anthropologists or sociologists to spent three or four years studying a single community. But during the months that I was studying Guadalupe and Chávez, I was intensely involved in everyday life. I was fortunate to have the financial support that allowed me to conduct as much fieldwork as I could endure, seven days a week, twenty-four hours a day. Guadalupe and Chávez residents saw me day after day for weeks or months at a time. I was usually avail-able to accompany them on errands, to help out with tasks around the house, or to merely sit around and chat. I was a resource for some resi-dents and a friend for others. More than anything, this "face time" in both communities helped fostered my acceptance into them.

The acceptance I enjoyed gave me a great advantage: the ability to circulate freely around the barrios during the course of participant-observation. My strategy was to observe as fair a cross section as possi-ble of the everyday income-generating activities in Guadalupe and Chávez barrios. This purposeful data-gathering strategy is an impor-tant component of analytic ethnography, and it formed the heart of my participant-observation.[11] Anthropologists and sociologists often take advantage of informants in conducting ethnographic research. Informants may serve to orient the researcher to important aspects of a community's organization, history, norms, and practices. Researcher and informant may enter into a formal relationship, sometimes involving payment to the latter and frequently involving extended interviewing. At other times, the informant may serve as a guide in the fieldwork setting. This model is more common in sociology, beginning with William Foote Whyte's famous relationship with Doc, the young man who guided Whyte in his study of Cornerville.[12] During my time in Guadalupe and Chávez, I moved on a monthly, weekly, or even daily basis from spending time with one group to another. My relationships with people in the community changed as I shifted from group to group, and this tended to restrict my ability to take advantage of informants. Some individuals played key roles early on in helping ease my entrance into the neighborhood, and others emerged as regular contacts throughout the fieldwork. Day to day, however, I made my way in the community from one group to another, seeking to situate myself in such a way that I could observe as much as possible of the economic life of each community.

I conducted fieldwork with a self-conscious awareness of issues related to sampling, representativeness, and generalizability. In Guadalupe and Chávez, I never conducted the kind of individual or household survey that could have told me whether I had overlooked one group of residents or another during the course of fieldwork. Obviously some residents found it easier to integrate me into their everyday lives than others. I felt fairly comfortable hanging out with groups of young men my own age, but I had some awkward moments among groups of women—such as when I attended a series of living room cosmetics demonstrations in Guadalupe. Obviously, people engaged in illicit activities, such as the drug sellers at the hot spot, had good reason to avoid my prying observer eyes. For all of these reasons, I make no claim that the material in this book represents all of everyday economic life in Guadalupe and Chávez.

On the other hand, I can assure the reader that I conducted the fieldwork with an understanding of the need to seek representativeness. Although it was awkward, I did attend the living room cosmetics demonstrations, and I made sure to spend enough time at the hot spot so that the drug sellers could see I did not threaten their safety. I collected data in a way designed to maximize my ability to spend time with various groups in the community. I never took photographs in Guadalupe or Chávez because I saw that, as one advisor put it, in many low-income communities photos are called "evidence" and they make people nervous. For the same reason, I did not tape-record barrio residents but rather took longhand notes in a small pad that inconspicuously fit in my back pocket. My days in the field were filled with casual conversation rather than spent in formal interviews. Often these conversations had nothing whatsoever to do with my research concerns, but when possible I steered them to topics of particular interest to me. In both Guadalupe and Chávez income earning was a common topic of casual conversation, and this eased the task of getting people to speak with me about my research interests. Of course, none of this means that I gathered a representative cross section of data in Guadalupe and Chávez, and conducting the research the way I did raised other kinds of practical and ethical problems. I do believe, however, that *not* interviewing residents and *not* using a camera or tape recorder encouraged a broad cross section of Guadalupe and Chávez residents to speak freely about their income-earning activities. I believe that the informality of all my interactions helped me gain access to a wide variety of individuals in each community. And I believe that striving to reach a broad cross section of these communities has helped me address the central puzzles of this study.

DATA COLLECTION AND ETHICAL CONCERNS

While I was living and working in Guadalupe and Chávez, residents, friends, and colleagues commonly asked me, "What do you do every day?" My answer, which was truthful but also somewhat unsatisfying, was, "I hang out." The answer was unsatisfying for them because it did not really convey what went on while hanging out. The answer was also unsatisfying for me because it seemed that I should have a more concrete explanation of what I was doing with my time. After I left the field, I had the chance to reflect a bit more on what was happening while I hung out and to explain how hanging out produced the data that have filled this book.

Hanging out mostly meant watching, listening, talking, and participating in whatever was going on wherever I happened to be. In terms of the data in this book, "whatever was going on wherever I happened to be" is actually more important than "watching, listening, talking and participating."[13] Some days, I hung out with mothers at the playground in the morning, young men on the streets in the afternoons, and a family at home in the evening. At other times, I participated in activities ranging from teaching English to drinking beer to playing soccer to minding children. I was interested in capturing a broad cross section of experiences in these communities, and this meant spending time with a large variety of different residents in a wide variety of different settings. This interest in a cross section was consistent with the overall comparative design of this study. Hanging out provided a way to "sample" what was going on at different places and among different people in the barrios. Hanging out also reflected a decision on my part to focus on a wide variety of public behaviors and publicly expressed opinions rather than to explore in greater detail a more limited set of events (through participation) or orientations (through interviews). This reflects my approach to culture, whose importance, I believe, rests in publicly available symbols rather than in privately held ideas.

Hanging out raised ethical issues both in the field and in the academy. Researchers in the field assume the ethical burden of obtaining informed consent from the people who participate in their research project—a burden I believe all researchers should gladly shoulder, for reasons I discuss below. But this burden repeatedly placed me in a quandary while hanging out. Hanging out often did not announce itself as research. This was not a problem as long as the people with whom I was hanging out knew me and knew I was a researcher. But it was easy for people who did not know me to end up participating in my research project without ever knowing they were doing so. They did this simply by hanging out with me. I could have avoided this problem simply by repeatedly announcing, to perfect strangers, that I was conducting research. But this violated all the social norms governing hanging out, and it would have made the research impossible to conduct. I also found, when I tried this a few times, that it could have a negative effect—from an ethical point of view—on individuals who already knew me and were hanging out with me with full knowledge of my research. By keeping company with me, they were implicitly endorsing my presence wherever we happened to be hanging out, and they became guilty of vouching for a social imbecile as soon as I broke the rules of hanging out by making my announcement.

The resolution of this quandary emerged from recognizing the implicit endorsement of my hanging-out sponsors. A sponsor's endorsement of me, I decided, could serve as a temporary grant of informed consent from strangers with whom we were hanging out. When social norms permitted, I properly introduced myself to strangers and informed them of my research project. Often this happened quickly. My hanging-out sponsor often introduced me to strangers by introducing my work, or one of the first exchanges between a stranger and me might concern what brought us both to hang out wherever we happened to be. On several occasions, however, I acted the social imbecile out of a feeling of ethical obligation. On each occasion, I was hanging out with a stranger who was committing an illegal act. On each occasion, I was concerned that my sponsor was not doing an adequate job protecting the interests of the law-breaking and hence vulnerable stranger, and I made sure to inform the stranger that I was not, perhaps, exactly who I appeared to be. On most occasions this revelation did not appreciably change social interactions at the time, but one time the stranger stopped committing the illegal act and abruptly departed. Following that incident, I noticed that this person avoided me around the barrio, but after several weeks I no longer noticed any lingering effect of our awkward interaction.

Hanging out also raised certain ethical issues in the academy. Relative to my concern about informed consent and protection of human subjects in the field, however, I find the ethical issues raised by the academy to be irrelevant, at best, and perhaps even misguided. The Institutional Review Board (IRB) that ultimately approved my research plans had originally asked that I obtain written documentation of informed consent from anybody who participated in this study. Ultimately, the IRB granted a waiver of this requirement, but it is worth examining the issues underlying their original request.

The model of research underlying the IRB request is a medical model in which a human subject is recruited to participate in an experiment conducted by the researcher. As a hypothetical example, a psychologist interested in human visual perception might post a flyer offering $20 to anyone who will spend thirty minutes in the laboratory examining various objects through a device that tracks eye movement. What happened in my study is obviously different from this study of vision in some obvious ways: there is no experiment, no recruitment poster, no money, no fixed time frame, and no lab. But the most important difference regards the social rules under which the two studies are conducted. Ethnographers seek to alter the usual social rules of their research subjects as little as possible, while in the vision experiment research subjects' usual social rules are entirely suspended for the duration of the experiment. The psychologists in this hypothetical experiment construct not only a machine to track the movement of the pupil but also a social environment—which they also control—in which that tracking takes place. The well-known Tuskegee, Milgram, and Zimbardo experiments established that it is possible for a researcher to construct a dangerous social environment in a research setting.[14] At Tuskegee, medical researchers purposefully created a dangerous physical environment in order to conduct experiments on syphilis, while Milgram and Zimbardo inadvertently created a psychologically dangerous environment in their studies of authority. But is it reasonable to think that a lone ethnographer entering a community setting represents a danger to research subjects in that real social setting in the same way that the Tuskegee doctors or the Milgram and Zimbardo psychologists were a threat to their research subjects? Should the ethical guidelines developed in the wake of Tuskegee be applied to ethnographers in the same way they are applied to medical researchers?

I believe the answer to these questions is no. Different guidelines should be developed and applied to naturalistic research methods such as ethnography than to any kind of experimental research (including quasi-experiments such as a social survey) that involves researchers' construction of a social environment in which the research subject participates. In the latter case, informed consent must be applied in a different fashion than in the former case. Whether a study is naturalistic or experimental is easy to determine from the way research subjects are recruited. When the researcher *must* take the initiative to recruit a subject—whether for an experimental medical procedure or an open-ended interview—it indicates that the researcher is also constructing a social environment for the research and proper caution must be taken. When the researcher does not need to recruit the subject to conduct the research, a naturalistic investigation is underway, and different sorts of procedures to protect human subjects may be safely invoked.

PRESENTING RESULTS

One objection to what I have just said regarding protection of human subjects is that even when the researcher does not construct a new social environment, there may be a power differential between researcher and subject that requires careful scrutiny. This issue has come up, in particular, in discussions surrounding how research subjects are depicted in researchers' reports. Even if researchers have relatively little control over the social environment that they investigate, it is argued, they retain complete control over how they represent that environment in their research reports. There are three ways of managing this problem, two of which are in widespread use in ethnography and one of which is widely used in nonethnographic research.

One way that researchers have managed the problem of representation is to present their results in a fashion that makes clear to the reader that the research report is social construction of the researcher and not an objective report of conditions among research subjects. This technique has been popular among anthropologists, and it has led to the proliferation of literary techniques in anthropological writing. This is an effective way to manage the problem of researcher-subject power differential. The researcher, in this model, takes it upon him- or herself to shatter any illusion of objective representation for the reader. However, this technique is flawed from the perspective of social science. A central goal of social scientific research is to accumulate knowledge about a certain topic. Without certain standards for the presentation of research results, it is difficult for social scientists to assess what kinds of questions appear to have relatively stable answers and which questions remain relatively unexplored. Adopting stable standards for reporting research results inevitably creates the illusion—from the reader's perspective—that an objective reality is being described and analyzed. For this reason, disciplines that consider themselves scientific—including sociology—have generally not adopted the anthropological solution to the problem of representation.

The second way of managing the problem of representation has been to seek out research subjects' opinion of results before publication. This technique has been widely adopted by many social scientists, including many sociologists. The logic of this technique is that research subjects' views of the topic being researched form a valuable counterweight to the view of the researcher. Researchers ask subjects whether the research findings correspond to their own view of truthful reality. On the basis of this feedback, researchers may revisit or revise their conclusions, report subjects' opinion without altering their own findings or conclusions, or conduct more research based on the feedback offered by subjects. The advantages of presenting results in this way is that readers have the opportunity to compare at least two informed opinions about the research. When researchers' and subjects' opinions correspond, this provides confirmation of the research findings. When a disagreement is reported, readers can appreciate that a difference of opinion exists, and this addresses concerns about the power differential between researchers and subjects. However, there are also drawbacks to this approach. Researchers' and subjects' interpretation of research findings may be systematically biased in different directions. Researchers may be biased toward findings that will appear interesting or novel to their research colleagues, especially journal editors, book publishers and reviewers, and funding agencies. Subjects may be biased toward findings that appear to cast them in a "positive" light either in the view of other research subjects or according to their perception of public opinion. Of course, bias is inevitable in social science research, but systematic and different biases between researchers and subjects may lead to a systematic bias in reported research results—favoring results that are novel and interesting but also complementary and sympathetic. The drawback of this solution, therefore, is that subjects' endorsement of research results can lend them the appearance of a highly stable reality, which lends the researcher, in turn, a great deal of power over how the research is presented or interpreted. In essence, soliciting subjects' response to the research attempts to address the problem of research-subject power differential directly, but in doing so it risks simply endorsing the researcher's power to create the research reality without, however, offering a genuine space for a differing opinion.

The third way of managing the problem of representation is to rely on multiple research reports to develop an accurate representation of issues in a particular research area. This technique has not been widely adopted by ethnographers, but it is common in other kinds of social science research. This technique recognizes that every research endeavor is unique, that every researcher will choose to emphasize some findings rather than others, and that every researcher is subject to biases he or she cannot control. Multiple research reports on similar social locations and similar social questions allow readers to adjudicate between competing visions of social reality. Multiple research reports allow the research community to replicate results that appear important, controversial, or innovative. This technique does not address the power differential between researchers and subjects directly. Rather, it counts on the involvement of multiple researchers to ensure that subjects' concerns enter the research agenda.

I have relied on this third technique of managing the problem of representation in ethnographic research. At first glance, in its reliance on the research community to grapple with the problem of representation through a marketplace of competing ideas, this technique appears conservative and scientistic. On closer inspection, however, this approach advocates a radical revamping of the ethnographic research enterprise in three fundamental ways. First, it calls for *more ethnography* to ensure that a vigorous ethnographic marketplace of ideas exists in the research community. Under this technique, a single study is never enough; every ethnographic finding must be considered provisional until other ethnographers have replicated its findings. Second, it calls for *replicative ethnography* to consolidate and test theoretical propositions. This contrasts with current ethnography, which is often one-shot case studies that challenge extant theory. Finally, it calls for *diverse ethnographers* to ensure that the research instruments used to collect ethnographic data, the ethnographers themselves, are as accurate as possible. If a finding is robust, it should be recognizable by different ethnographers—that is, by different but comparable instruments—working in different but comparable research settings.

In selecting sites, collecting data, and presenting results in this study, I have sought to follow a series of methodological prescriptions that are relatively unusual in ethnography but quite common in other kinds of social scientific research. I have selected multiple field sites, collected data according to a research plan that follows an underlying logic of sampling, and presented data as solely the conclusions of the researcher. My reason for following these unusual methodological prescriptions was the belief that ethnography could benefit from conducting itself in the same fashion as other kinds of social science. I believe that ethnographers can offer a valuable corrective to research findings assembled via other methods but that to do so they must begin to form a coherent research community oriented toward producing replicable research results and developing and testing social theory. Ethnography is too important—its insights too valuable and universal—not to engage with the wider social scientific research community. By using comparison and replication, ethnographers can address the serious problem of representation in a way that allows them to inform and improve the social scientific community and, perhaps, their research communities as well.

# Notes

PREFACE

1. Other recent works include Anderson (1999), Duneier (1999), Patillo-McCoy (1998a), and Venkatesh (2000).

1: INSTITUTIONS OF POVERTY

1. Joan Moore (1991) discusses the *Mexicanization* of the East Los Angeles barrios that she has studied for decades. In a twist on this concept, Rafael Alarcón (1992) discusses how small villages in Mexico have been *Nortenized* by the migra-dollars of residents who have migrated to California.

2. In this sense, Guadalupe residents lived within a transnational community characterized by regular and frequent migration between Mexico and California. The work of Douglas Massey and his colleagues constitutes an exhaustive study of the social process of migration that links California and western Mexico (Massey et al. 1987; Massey and Espinosa 1997; Massey, Goldring, and Durand 1994). For an ethnographic examination of these processes in the San Francisco Bay Area, see Rouse (1989).

3. For discussions of changes in patterns of work and family as Santa Clara County's agricultural Valley of Heart's Delight was transformed into the high-tech Silicon Valley, see Zavella (1987). Subcontracting in the Silicon Valley workplace is discussed in Hondagneu-Sotelo (1994b), Mines and Avina (1992), Zlolniski (1994), and Zlolniski and Palerm (1996).

4. For theoretical overviews of contemporary immigrant assimilation and socioeconomic mobility, see Gans (1992) and Zhou (1997).

5. For more on the notion of a defended neighborhood, see Suttles (1972).

6. While a 40 percent poverty rate has been taken as a standard measure of

an "underclass" area (Peterson 1991), it has proven quite difficult to develop a reliable and valid measure of who actually makes up the "underclass" or how many people belong to the group. The size of the group depends on whether one conceives of the "underclass" as particularly impoverished, unemployed, black, marginalized, fatherless, welfare dependent, or culturally or socially deviant in some other way (Jencks 1992a).

7. As Katz (1997) points out, this is but one of ethnography's warrants.

8. For an overview of the relationship between immigration and the economic restructuring that has transformed the labor markets of large cities, see Sassen (1988, 1995).

9. The immigrant work ethic underlies many studies of immigration and immigrant labor markets. Piore (1979) presents a classic statement of this question that has been criticized by recent studies of immigration in two important ways. First, studies have highlighted the complex social dynamics of immigrant settlement that create the immigrant workforce (Schiller, Basch, and Szanton Blanc 1995; Schiller, Basch, and Szanton-Blanc 1992). Hondagneu-Sotelo's (1994a) ethnography of settlement in a northern California Mexican American barrio highlights the dual role of gender relations in this process as women act as agents of settlement but also find that gender roles are transformed in the process. Rouse's (1989, 1995) transnational study of Mexican migration focuses on the intrafamilial and intrapersonal dynamics of migration. A second set of critiques of the classic immigrant-assimilation model focuses on the process of migrant economic incorporation inside the United States. Gans (1992), Portes, Rumbaut (Portes and Rumbaut 1990; Rumbaut 1996), and Zhou (1997) are among the scholars who have argued that immigrants by no means form an undifferentiated labor force or social group and that a segmented process of incorporation plays an important role in the life chances and social position of immigrants and their children. Focusing on the demand for immigrant labor, Waldinger (1996a) shows how ethnic solidarity as well as employer behavior places immigrants and U.S.-born minorities in distinct niches in the urban labor market.

10. For social dislocations in Chicago, see Puntenney (1997); for Philadelphia, see the work of Anderson (1991, 1999); for South Central Los Angeles, see Glasgow (1981); and for the Puerto Rican barrios of New York's Spanish Harlem and Lower East Side, see, respectively, Bourgois (1995b) and Sharff (1998). For an empirical and theoretical comparison of urban poverty and social dislocations in Mexican American and other Latino barrios, see Moore and Pinderhughes (1993b).

11. Anderson discusses the decline of "old head" role models in the African American ghettos (Anderson 1990) as well as the difficulties that residents of impoverished communities experience trying to control crime and the street (Anderson 1999).

12. This explanation has been developed by Sampson and colleagues (Sampson and Groves 1989; Sampson, Raudenbush, and Earls 1997; Sampson and Wilson 1995). Puntenney (1997) describes how structural-economic disruption can lead to a breakdown of trust. Portes (1998) provides an excellent overview of the concept of social capital. Fernández-Kelly (1995) has shown how economic

dislocation affects the formation and deployment of social capital in low-income communities.

13. For exponents of this theory, see Mead (1986) and Murray (1984).

14. For an in-depth study of these small-scale interactions and narratives in one Chicano community, see Horowitz (1983).

15. For gender, see Hondagneu-Sotelo (1994a); for jealousy, see Mahler (1995); for loyalty, see Smith (1998). For a discussion of the kinds of contributions that ethnography can make to studies of stratification and inequality, see Horowitz (1997).

16. MacLeod (1995) argues that perceptions of opportunity do shape the expectations, aspirations, and ultimate school and job performance of residents in low-income communities.

17. For street life and crime, see Anderson (1999) and Pattillo-McCoy (1998a); for public housing, see Venkatesh (2000).

18. Social institutions are where structural circumstances and individual orientations meet in everyday life. They are smaller and less complex than nations, economies, or cultures. They are more readily and more predictably swayed by individual or collective action than these historically entrenched social formations. On the other hand, social institutions are larger and more socially interconnected than single families, business enterprises, or peer groups. They more often shape individuals' worldviews and life chances than reflect their will or initiative. In short, social institutions stand between the macro and micro; they make up a societal and sociological middle level. There are a number of different ways of defining a social institution. Nee and Ingram (1998) conceive of a social institution as a *"web of interrelated norms*—formal and informal—governing social relationships" (p. 19). This is a more general and larger use of the term than mine here. Granovetter (1974), whose study of the importance of social ties for job searchers sparked much of the interest in social institutions, conceives of social networks as the institutions that "embed" economic behavior in historically specific relationships of mutual understanding, trust, rivalry, or contention. Granovetter (1985) has used the notion of embeddedness to further our understanding of the organization and behavior of firms and economies, and in this sense the notion of embeddedness that he proposes is not directly applicable here. Coleman's (1990) work on social capital also focuses on the ability of social networks to create relationships of mutual understanding and trust, but his notion is closer to the one I use here. He develops a notion of social capital that operates within society more generally and not just within firms, and he illustrates the importance of social capital for economic standing by focusing on high school dropout, an outcome of importance for low-income communities (Coleman 1988). Still closer to the way I use the concept of social institutions is the notion of social capital and embeddedness developed by Portes and Sensenbrenner (Portes 1998; Portes and Sensenbrenner 1993). Portes and Sensenbrenner recovered an essential part of Granovetter's original notion of embeddedness lost by Coleman—that embeddedness could both facilitate and constrain economic action—and illustrated the range of empirical application of the concept using studies of immigration and immigrant communities. Still, while their usage is broader than Granovetter's or Coleman's, Portes and Sensenbrenner remain pri-

marily interested in social networks. Social networks are crucial forms of social institution, but they are not the only form. This is clear in the work of Bourdieu, whose notion of "fields" captures another facet of the notion of social institution I develop here (see Bourdieu and Wacquant 1992). Society consists of different fields that differ according to the rules of action, taste, or distinction within them. Fields are stabilized over time by governments, cultures, and organizations, with different fields competing, contending, or cooperating in complex ways within the life course of individuals and the history of societies. I use *social institution* to signal a midlevel social formation that may be found generally throughout society (*pace* Bourdieu's fields) but that must be identified within specific interactions of everyday life (something more akin to Portes and Sensenbrenner's notion of embeddedness).

19. Informal social networks (including transnational networks) are structural features of urban communities that shape residents' cultural orientations. Social networks have attracted poverty researchers' interest for decades, especially since Stack and other anthropologists argued that these networks play a central role in poor people's survival strategies (Boissevain 1974; Lomnitz 1977; Stack 1974). Sociologists interested in poverty, following Granovetter's (1973) influential argument about the importance of "weak" social network ties in job finding, have generally focused on the instrumental importance of social networks (Edin and Lein 1997b; Hagan 1998; Hao and Brinton 1997; Hondagneu-Sotelo 1994b; Uehara 1990). In focusing on the instrumental importance of networks, however, sociologists have paid less attention to the cultural importance of social networks, a theme that anthropologists have continued to develop in studies of transnational migration and identity (Rouse 1995; Schiller et al. 1995). The concept of social network that I use here includes both the sociological emphasis on structural position and the anthropological appreciation of networks as cultural environments.

20. The concept of social network that I use here includes both the sociological emphasis on structural position (and the resources that accrue to an individual by dint of their position within a social network) and the anthropological emphasis on culture and identity (the view that whom one spends time with and interacts with affects one's view of the world and one's own place in it). Thus, I argue that both the availability of jobs, which has generally been conceived of as a structural feature of poverty (Wilson 1987, 1996), and the work ethic, which has generally been conceived of as a cultural feature of poverty (Mead 1992), must be understood as a function of poor people's social networks.

21. Social networks have been a particular focus of interest among researchers studying transnational migration (Boyd 1989); for social networks and Mexico-U.S. migration, see Massey et al. (1987), Massey and Espinosa (1997), and Massey et al. (1994).

22. These local organizations arise and thrive within the constraints and opportunities of the low-income social environment; their goals, structure, and cultures reflect and create social conditions in low-income communities. These organizations make up larger fields, social spaces that encourage the adoption of particular forms of organizations that are directed toward a commonly understood set of problems or opportunities (Dimaggio and Powell 1983; Scott 1995).

My focus on how indigenous organizations reflect and shape everyday life in low-income communities is a generalization of Sánchez-Jankowski's (1991) analysis of the relationship between street gangs and their social environment. Others have shown how individual residents of low-income areas see street gangs as a response to local opportunities and constraints (Hagedorn 1988; Moore 1978; Padilla 1992; Vigil 1988) and how the street gang and its community respond interactively to changes in the social environment over time (Moore 1991; Venkatesh 1997a). Venkatesh (2000) has argued for the importance of understanding indigenous organizations in low-income communities in two further ways. He documents the importance of indigenous organizations in his analysis of everyday life in the Robert Taylor Homes public housing development in Chicago, where residents relied on indigenous groups for law enforcement and security as Chicago police became less and less responsive to their requests for assistance. In addition, in an analysis of helping organizations in impoverished communities, he differentiates among organizations according to their social distance from the community to which they are providing assistance (Venkatesh 1997b).

23. This view contrasts with an influential perspective on urban crime that sees criminal activity as reflecting a lack of individual or social control (see discussion above as well as Sampson and Morenoff 1997). I argue that criminals and criminal justice officers are part of one organizational field. Their organizations, including gangs, crime syndicates, police forces, and prisons, and their cultural orientations toward law-breaking and law enforcement reflect a shared understanding of crime and criminal justice. In this view, criminals and criminal justice officers have something in common with each other that neither shares with residents of the low-income community who are not involved in crime or criminal justice.

24. Situational subcultures arise from the scarcity-induced compromises, such as participating in public assistance programs, experienced by many residents of low-income areas; subcultures are cultural systems that are meaningless outside the structural circumstances within which they arise. This develops the notion of a "shadow culture" introduced by Liebow (1967). Subcultures (shadow or otherwise) may be understood—along with population size, density, and heterogeneity (Park, Burgess, and McKenzie 1967)—as part of the urban experience per se (Fischer 1975, 1995). When one is analyzing the low-income community, however, it is theoretically difficult to show how subcultures and economic constraints shape the behavior of the poor (Hannerz 1969). Past research on the cultural antecedents of poverty—most notably Lewis's (1966, 1968) culture-of-poverty theory and Moynihan's "Report" (Rainwater and Yancey 1967)—teaches that cultural explanations of poverty must be precisely articulated and carefully applied to avoid being divisive and unproductive (Wilson 1987, chap. 1). The notion of subculture that I use here recognizes Lewis's insight that economic need shapes the symbol system and social relations of the poor. At the same time, it questions the ability of these symbolic forms and social relationships to take on a life of their own and socially reproduce themselves absent some external source of economic dislocation. It is in this sense that these are *sub*cultures. I use the concept of a subculture because other concepts, such as Bourdieu's (1977) *habitus* and Swidler's (1986) tool kit, are difficult to opera-

tionalize in community-based research. To use the concepts of *habitus* and tool kit in practice requires the researcher to distinguish when symbolic beliefs or behaviors are habitual or tool-like means and when they are desires, goals, or other ends in themselves. The measurement tools of participant-observation are generally unable to distinguish between these kinds of subtle differences on a consistent basis, although there are important exceptions, such as Patillo-McCoy's (1998b) discussion of how church-based interactions form a portable cultural "tool" that is then exported to other community settings.

25. My argument here contrasts with two influential explanations for welfare use among the poor. First, an influential cultural argument states that poor people end up using welfare after making a series of rational calculations (Murray 1984). Against this cultural view, an influential structural argument denies that welfare has a significant cultural component because poor people turn to welfare only in the absence of other income-generating opportunities (Edin and Lein 1997b; Wilson and Neckerman 1986). I argue that welfare use stems from institutional circumstances that are beyond individual control, such as the workings of criminal justice institutions, and that welfare use affects the culture of the low-income community.

26. See Moore (1991), Moore and Vigil (1993), and Whyte ([1943] 1981). There are many other exemplars. Herbert Gans (1962) catalogued the social and community institutions in the working-class community of Boston's West End. Elijah Anderson has examined the institutional dynamics behind interpersonal relationships at a Chicago bar and takeout (Anderson 1978) as well as how deindustrialization has reshaped family and commercial life in the ghettos of Philadelphia (Anderson 1990). In recent studies of Chicago, Mary Pattillo-McCoy (1998a) focuses on the institutional connections that make it difficult for a middle-class African American community to insulate itself from the social problems of nearby impoverished ghettos; Sudhir Venkatesh (2000) has used participant-observation and in-depth interviews to examine institutional change in the Robert Taylor Homes, a massive public housing development on Chicago's South Side; and Loïc Wacquant (1998) provides a close-textured examination of practices associated with hustling.

## 2: INCOME GENERATION IN THE BARRIOS

1. See Riis and Sante ([1890] 1997).

2. The juxtaposition of barrio and campus has not escaped notice. Guadalupe barrio represents the emergence of a new face of poverty with origins in renewed immigration and the rise of the information-based "hourglass" economy. For more on this economy, see Lamphere (1992), Mahler (1995), Sassen (1990, 1993), and Zlolniski and Palerm (1996). For an interesting contrast, see Patricia Zavella's (1987) account of life in the low-income barrios of San Jose among workers in the declining agricultural industry.

3. Every income-earning resident of Guadalupe and Chávez had between one and three distinct kinds of income-generating activity. People with *only* legal earnings *or* illegal earnings *or* public assistance are counted once in Figure 2. People who combined legal with illegal earnings, illegal earnings with aid, or

legal earnings with aid are counted twice. Residents who received income from legal sources, illegal sources, *and* public aid are counted three times. The percentages shown in Figure 2 are based on 178 distinct kinds of income-generating activity among Guadalupe residents and 219 activities in Chávez.

4. See Patterson (1994).

## 3: THE JOB MARKET

1. Wage labor is the most important source of income in low-income neighborhoods more generally (Jargowsky 1997).

2. See Mines and Avina (1992) and Waldinger et al. (1997).

3. This is an example of how barrio residents exerted local control over charitable and public aid resources. I discuss this in greater detail in Chapter 8.

4. Slack labor markets disproportionately affect the employment chances of young men in general and of young men of color in particular (Freeman and Holzer 1986; Glasgow 1981).

## 4: THE EXPERIENCE OF LOW-WAGE WORK

1. For more on the demands that low-wage jobs make on the job, see Newman (1999). Newman points out that low-wage jobs in the "Burger Barn" fast-food establishments she studied were more demanding than nonworkers might think. Several of her graduate student research assistants quickly found themselves overwhelmed by the demanding work routines when they took jobs at Burger Barn as participant-observers. Nevertheless, it is clear even in her account that significant resources were needed simply to get and keep a job at one of the Burger Barns she studied, where only one in fourteen applicants was accepted.

2. In an oft-cited study, Kirschenman and Neckerman (1991) document how employers in Chicago searched for workers using race and ghetto residence to screen out those who did not have the "proper" work comportment regardless of their job-specific qualifications for the position. A similar dynamic was evident in the Burger Barn restaurant that Newman (1999) studied, where employers used education, nativity status, and personal recommendation to search for employees they thought likely to have the proper disposition on the job. Fernandez, Castilla, and Moore (2000) have shown that employers may have economically rational reasons for recruiting new workers through employees' personal networks, including lower training costs and greater chances of hiring a worker who remains in the job over the long term.

3. See Edin and Lein's (1997a) study of single mothers' economic lives.

4. Neither of these mechanisms is particular to the low-income barrios; see Danziger et al. (2000) and Glazer (1986).

5. Strategic use of information also benefited Manuel and his nuclear family in more concrete ways. Each summer, a limited number of jobs were available for teenage Chávez residents to work with the city department of recreation. These positions were reserved for residents of the public housing development, but for several years in a row, Manuel's sixteen-year-old son, who lived with Manuel outside of the housing development, managed to obtain one of the coveted slots.

Family members who lived in the housing development and had a close relationship with the head of the local housing authority office sponsored Manuel's son. They filed his paperwork with the housing authority and assured the head of the office that Manuel's son really was supposed to be working in the recreation department office.

6. The experiences of Ted, the young Chávez resident who angrily quit his job after being screamed at for a late arrival, is another example of how unreliable public transport affected low-wage workers' ability to keep a job.

7. See Katz (1986, 1989).

8. See Kelso (1994).

9. See Valentine (1968).

10. See Mead (1986) and Murray (1984).

11. See Jencks (1992b) and Massey, Gross, and Eggers (1991). Social scientists working in the Netherlands used a survey of cultural orientations among the poor to directly address the nature of the work ethic in that country (Engbersen 1993). Their results are instructive in that they demonstrate cultural diversity among the poor, with notable variations in people's attachment to the ideal of working. In this sense, their results suggest the possibility of variance in the cultural values toward work, but it is unwise to generalize their results to the U.S. situation directly, as both the cultural meaning of work in the American context and the practical alternatives to work offered by the American welfare state differ substantially from the Dutch situation.

12. See Wilson (1991).

13. See Wacquant (1996).

14. See Petterson (1997, p. 612).

15. See Bourdieu (1977, 1990).

16. See Swidler (1986).

17. Chicanos in San Jose also expressed objections to work conditions in the poorest quality jobs. These objections to working in low-pay jobs were thus a feature of the Chicano experience rather than something particular to Los Angeles.

18. Research on immigrant-native differences among Mexican Americans has documented the existence of an oppositional culture among U.S.-born Chicanos in two ways. In school, anthropologists have documented an oppositional culture among U.S.-born "involuntary minorities" (including Mexican Americans) that is not present among "voluntary immigrants" (such as Mexican immigrants) of the same ethnic group (but also see Ainsworth-Darnell and Downey 1998; Gibson and Ogbu 1991; Ogbu 1987). Historically, researchers have documented the development of oppositional cultures as part of the process of settlement and political incorporation that allows settled Mexican immigrants and U.S.-born Mexican Americans to distinguish themselves from more recent Mexican immigrants (Gutierrez 1995; Sánchez 1993). The anthropological and historical literatures emphasize that oppositional culture emerges from dynamics of majority-minority power relations in certain societies at specific historical moments. Structures of discrimination that limit the opportunities and attainment of lower-caste groups (in the educational context) and politically disenfranchised groups (in the historical literature) encourage the development and elaboration of an oppositional culture. The conditions that accompanied an

oppositional culture among Chávez residents were similar to those described in the anthropological and historical literatures.

## 5: NETWORKS AND WORK

1. Differences in the meaning of work arose in interactions that outsiders could observe and whose meaning residents could articulate. This represents a sharp contrast with Lewis's culture of poverty, which has its roots in the thick layers of family-based cultural systems (see Archer 1990 for more on the cultural system). Differences in the meaning of low-wage work in Chávez and Guadalupe were actively constructed, publicly available, and often self-consciously expressed.

2. The importance of social isolation in areas of persistent poverty was highlighted by Wilson's (1987) work in Chicago. Case studies have shown its importance in other areas of the country as well (see, e.g., Anderson 1989, 1999; Glasgow 1981; Hagedorn 1988). Some theoretical questions concerning social isolation remain: whether it denotes a social experience distinct from earlier notions of a subculture (Newman 1992); whether the native poor experience social isolation or simply differential social integration (Fernández-Kelly 1995); and how social isolation among the persistently poor is related to the kind of social integration experienced by urban and rural residents of different socioeconomic status (see, e.g., Fischer 1982).

3. As an alternative to a low-wage job, illicit work has both economic (see Sánchez-Jankowski 1991) and social (see Bourgois 1995a) advantages. Public assistance provides a reliable income with included medical benefits that allows recipients to continue to care full time for dependents (see Edin and Lein 1997a). Of course, compared to working in the legal economy, there are substantial drawbacks to illicit work (high risk of violence or incarceration) and public aid (social stigma) (see Newman 1999).

4. The geosocial space connecting the United States and Mexico has arisen historically from the regular migrations of people between the areas that generally send immigrants (such as the states of western Mexico) and those that generally receive them (such as the cities of California); for overviews, see Castles and Miller (1998) and Durand and Massey (1992) in addition to works cited below; for Mexican-U.S. migration, see Massey et al. (1987) and Sassen (1988). Migration between Mexico and the United States began as an explicit work migration, and labor has remained central to the experiences of Mexican migrants (see, e.g., Chávez 1992). In recent years, scholars have also noted the ways in which nonwork factors such as family and gender relations influence the process of Latin American migration (Hagan 1998; Hondagneu-Sotelo 1994a).

5. See Hannerz (1969, chap. 9).

6. An economic strategy is a pattern of meaningful and creative economic behavior that occurs within a specific context of constraints and opportunities. Ann Swidler (1986) points out that a strategy is not "a plan consciously devised to attain a goal. It is, rather, a general way of organizing action (depending upon a network of kin and friends, for example, or relying on selling one's skills in a market) that might allow one to reach several different life goals" (p. 277). Pierre Bourdieu (1977) emphasizes that strategic action is inherently improvisational

and creative. Effective strategies are grounded in the cultural rules of one's social setting—a grounding that he designates the *habitus*. The boundaries of *habitus* determine the social circles within which strategic action may take place and within which it is understood and appreciated. The economic strategies of residents in Chávez and Guadalupe combine elements of these views of strategy. Economic strategies are distinctive and consistent ways of organizing economic behavior, and they develop through creative engagement with local understandings of the economic and social world.

7. For more on hustling, see Valentine (1978), Venkatesh (2000, chap. 2), and Wacquant (1998).

8. Anderson (1990, 1999) develops and describes the opposition between "decent" and "street" in his studies of Philadelphia ghetto communities. Pattillo-McCoy (1998a) argues that while residents of the Chicago neighborhood she studied recognized the distinction between "decent" and "street," Anderson's two-category distinction failed to capture the multiple shades of meanings that surround illegal and legal income generation.

9. These images are a staple of policy and lay-oriented discussions of urban poverty (see Auletta 1982; Murray 1984), and they inform policy decisions such as the implementation of welfare reform, the Personal Responsibility and Work Opportunity Act. In a more subtle guise, they also inform sociological theories of crime in low-income communities that depict criminals as preying upon residents of low-income areas (see Sampson and Groves 1989), a topic I take up in much greater detail in Chapter 7.

10. The language Frankie uses ("unloading a truck") is typical of how residents of Chávez referred to illicit activities that are part of a hustling. This language is transparent to Chávez residents (see description of Pablo's reaction later in this field note) but obscure to outsiders (see my own reaction here).

11. As a strategy of income generation, hustling required the cooperation of Chávez residents. We see this here in the use of phone calls and young Marielena to check out the situation near where the young men were unloading the truck. The youngsters of Chávez are again involved—this time they have been recruited by police officers to help retrieve the stolen furniture. Later, I am recruited to help out Frankie and Guillermo by trading shirts. The dynamics of this community cooperation are shown in the discussion about snitches. Frankie and Guillermo are sure that the activities of Elm Street guarantees that the security guards will not snitch, but children are unpredictable; they may have snitched inadvertently. Children and adolescents had real advantages when it came to illicit income generation; if apprehended, the consequences were less severe than for adults. But the discussion about snitching illustrates the inevitable trade-offs of involving young people in illicit activities.

12. Here, Frankie and Guillermo describe how they decided to "unload the truck." Up to this point, their involvement in the theft seemed haphazard; they appeared to have stumbled into it. But this exchange shows that observation, calculation, and planning preceded the decision to take the furniture. This was a typical pattern for illicit activities in Chávez. Residents often presented hustling as opportunities that they "stumbled into."

13. Tina's admonition here and Pablo's more extended criticism show how

Chávez residents critiqued illicit activities in their community. Young women predictably spoke out to criticize the unorganized illicit activities of young men, and younger Chávez residents were consistently criticized by older residents. Open criticism was less likely when the group of residents involved in the activity was larger or more organized. In these cases, residents were fearful that criticism might provoke retaliation, and they were sure to be out of earshot when they had critical remarks to share.

14. Criticism was specific. Pablo reminded Frankie and Guillermo of exactly which laws they were breaking and of the exact consequences of their action should they be caught.

15. For Chávez residents, the unearned income of hustling were intimately tied to activities on the job. At times, these connections were direct and causal. Residents long detached from the labor market, such as single mothers economically pinched by child-rearing responsibilities and disabled working-age men whose labor had little value for employers, were forced into hustling. More frequently, the connections between illicit or welfare activities and jobs were intimate but nonspecific. Guillermo's experience was typical. Many Chávez residents left jobs when it became clear that their long-term prospects were poor, when employers appeared to renege on promised advancements, or when job demands or responsibilities increased without a similar increase in rewards. Repeatedly, young people in Chávez explained that they would not participate in public assistance or illicit activities except that there were "no jobs" to be had in Chávez. At times and for some residents, this statement was literally true. In a greater number of instances, however, this statement arose from frustration not with the *absolute* lack of jobs but with the fact that tenure in available jobs extracted such a high price from Chávez residents. There was thus an intimate but nonspecific connection between jobs and hustling. In the view of most Chávez residents, both low-wage jobs and illicit or welfare activities demanded trade-offs, and these trade-offs were comparable. In this sense, labor market dislocations did not directly force residents into hustling; rather, the existence of illicit and welfare opportunities made it possible for residents to respond in an active and strategic way to misfortunes on the labor market. Each day at work, they could assess how the compromises demanded by wage labor compared to those demanded by illicit and welfare activities.

16. For more on the daily lives of transnational migrants, see Hagan (1994) and Smith (1998). For more on the notion of transnationalism, see Basch, Schiller, and Szanton Blanc (1994), Rouse (1995), Schiller, Basch, and Szanton Blanc (1995), and Schiller et al. (1992). For the cultural effects of transnationalism on sending communities in Mexico, see Alarcón (1992).

17. See, e.g., Castles and Miller (1998) and Piore (1979) on the importance of remittances in immigrants' labor processes. Scholars have also noted the importance of remittances for economic development in countries that send migrants and for the global economy as a whole (see Sassen 1991).

18. For more on the dual nature of social network obligations and other forms of social capital, see Portes and Sensenbrenner (1993). For a study that highlights the ambiguity of relationships within immigrant communities, see Mahler (1995).

19. Fernando explained, "I was one of the first Mexicans he [the owner]

hired, but then he started hiring more and more immigrants. But he couldn't speak Spanish, and I knew a little English. So more and more he used me to talk to the workers. . . . When he moved [the business] out of San Jose [a year earlier], none of the Americans stayed on the job, so I was the only one who had been there a long time and knew how all the machinery worked, and he made me the supervisor."

20. See, e.g., Massey et al. (1987).

21. I am following Bourdieu (1977, 1990) in my focus on how local sensibilities shape the process of income generation in the low-income barrios.

22. Carol Stack's (1974) argument that low-income African Americans in "the Flats" relied on kin support as a survival strategy was an important challenge to the culture-of-poverty theory. Other studies of low-income people's survival strategies include González de la Rocha (1994), Lomnitz (1977), and Valentine (1978). Edin and Lein (1997a) note systematic variation in the survival strategies of the single mothers they studied. They attribute this variation to differences in economic resources in the immediate economic environment such as whether mothers had access to a supportive kin network, the number of jobs available in the local economy, and the presence of opportunities in the underground economy (Edin and Lein 1997b).

23. Compared to the situation in contemporary urban areas of the United States, survival was clearly a more daunting hurdle during other historical periods in the United States (see, e.g., Agee and Evans [1941] 1988 and Riis and Sante [1890] 1997), and survival remains a pressing problem in modern less-developed countries (e.g., Lomnitz 1977; Scheper-Hughes 1992).

24. See Jargowsky (1997).

25. We need look no further than the island of Manhattan—a Puerto Rican barrio on the Lower East Side (Sharff 1998, 1987), sidewalk vendors in Greenwich Village (Duneier 1999), and drug sellers in El Barrio of East Harlem (Bourgois 1995b)—to appreciate the degree of variation in the salience of survival for different members of particular low-income communities. Sharff shows this variance by highlighting the different roles of residents in the underground economy as well as the contingencies that shape exposure to violence in childhood. Duneier shows that survival is more problematic among the men who hold places, transport books, or "lay out shit" than for the men who run sidewalk bookselling businesses. Most of Bourgois's informants experienced extreme forms of deprivation, but their particular struggles for economic survival depended on the context within which that deprivation occurred; women "churned" off the welfare rolls (deliberately removed from the welfare rolls by administrative action to save the welfare system money, since recipients have to reapply and many don't) faced quite different survival challenges than young men who deliberately moved into the crack business.

## 6: ILLEGAL ROUTINES

1. Informal activities are those that are "unregulated by the institutions of society, in a legal and social environment in which similar activities are regulated" (Castells and Portes 1989, p. 14). For a more detailed discussion of the

relationships between different kinds of "underground" economic activity, see Portes (1994).

2. Scholars have documented how these networks organize the work experience among women who work in the informal economy as housecleaners and as providers of child care and elder care (Hondagneu-Sotelo 1994b; Salzinger 1991).

3. Sudhir Venkatesh (2000) describes a variety of indigenous organizations in the Robert Taylor Homes housing development in Chicago, with a specific focus on organizations that provide law enforcement services (p. 92).

4. Jagna Sharff (1987) describes the intrahousehold distribution of risk in her ethnography of the illicit economy in New York.

5. Researchers have examined the negative consequences of social support networks in a variety of ways. Roger Waldinger (1995, 1996b) focuses on untoward consequences at a macro level, where ethnic solidarity can lead to extreme disadvantage for excluded ethnoracial groups. Mary Pattillo-McCoy (1998a) argues that social networks make it difficult for middle-class blacks to insulate themselves from the untoward consequences of poverty in her ethnography of Chicago's "Groveland" neighborhood. Pattillo-McCoy's findings suggest the possibility that supportive social networks can foster "crabs in the bucket" conditions in which network obligations consume resources that might be used to sustain individual mobility. John Ogbu's (1974, 1987) research on oppositional cultures in schools suggests that network-based cultures can discourage academic achievement among involuntary ethnoracial minorities.

6. Day labor markets are found in many American cities (see Sassen-Koob 1989). For a thorough examination of the demographics and economics of street corner day labor markets in Los Angeles, see Valenzuela (1999).

7. Their activities thus resembled what Mitchell Duneier's (1999) Greenwich Village informants referred to as "laying shit out."

8. As was the case for Duneier in New York, I found it hard to determine precisely where flea market vendors acquired the goods they sold. Vendors routinely claimed to have purchased goods at low prices at yard sales, but it is possible that goods may have been retrieved from the trash, stolen, or bought after being stolen.

9. The activities of María and Rosa were similar to those of popsicle vendors in San Jose and orange sellers in Los Angeles, who are the most common face of street vending in many low-income barrios. For more on the activities of San Jose's popsicle vendors, see Zlolniski (1994).

10. There is a long history of tension and hostility between East LA residents and police. Notable outbreaks of tensions occurred in the 1940s and late 1960s (Gutierrez 1995; Moore 1978; Sánchez 1993).

11. For the dimensions of gang-community relationships more generally, see Sánchez-Jankowski (1991, chap. 6). For another example of how gang-community relationships worked themselves out over time, see Venkatesh (1997a).

12. According to recent and past members, several large East LA *varrios*, including Elm Street, had expanded beyond the geographical territory they had historically controlled. Organizationally, these *varrios* accomplished expansion by setting up affiliate gangs in both contiguous and distant neighborhoods. Elm

Street and other expanding *varrios* did not abandon the traditional age-graded structure of Chicano gangs (Moore 1991). Despite organizational expansion, these gangs did not fully "corporatize" and remained primarily territory- and culture-based gangs rather than business organizations (Padilla 1992; Venkatesh 1997a).

13. Elm Street thus "defended" Chávez. For the concept of the defended neighborhood, see Suttles (1972).

14. For the relationship between staging areas and violence among residents of low-income communities, see Anderson (1999). Individual identification with the gang may be particularly strong for young people experiencing multiple forms of marginality due to a breakdown of the natal family, pressures of immigration, or other factors (see Vigil 1988). The identification of Chávez with Elm Street was more usually created and maintained in everyday interactions with individuals and institutions outside the barrio. Young residents in the low-income barrios of East LA would be asked, "Where are you from?" The gang affiliate would reply with the name of his or her gang: "I'm from Elm Street." Individuals not affiliated with a gang were required to say, "I'm not from anywhere." Gang affiliates looking to avoid a confrontation at times said they were from "nowhere," while nonaffiliates eager to affiliate with the gang might "claim" a particular gang. Thus, when one street worker asked a young Chávez resident, "Where are you from?" and the young man reluctantly replied, "I'm not from nowhere," the street worker considered this a victory against gang involvement and gave the man a joyful hug.

15. Social capital is the resources and obligations that accrue to an individual by dint of membership in a group. For an overview of the concept and its recent applications, see Portes (1998).

16. For more on the nature and significance of "street wisdom," see Anderson (1990).

7: THE CONSEQUENCES OF ILLEGAL WORK

1. For an overview of studies of violent crime, see Short (1997). For a study that rejects the view that violent crime may be depicted as a plague, see Pinderhughes (1997).

2. In his ethnographic study of youth crime in New York City, Mercer Sullivan (1989) found little support for explanations that likened economic crime to an infectious inevitability in low-income areas; rather, structural-economic conditions and ecological opportunities affected youth crime in the three neighborhoods he studied ( chaps. 9–10). Jagna Sharff (1987) found that patterns of economic crime on the Lower East Side of New York City had a familial logic, with some members acting as protectors in the underground economy while others focused on achievement in school. In separate studies of street gangs, Felix Padilla (1992), Martín Sánchez-Jankowski (1991), and Sudhir Venkatesh (1997a) all found that at least some of the crime committed by gangs and gang members reflected their rational pursuit of economic advancement as well as other community-specific or historically contingent factors. Sarah Mahler (1995) has documented how economic marginality and illegal work among recent Cen-

tral American immigrants to suburban Long Island, New York, foster individual anger and undermine community solidarity. In all of these studies, residents of low-income communities at times quell, at times accept, and at times facilitate the illegal economic activities of family, neighbors, and organizations in their community. For an overview of the relationship between deindustrialization and economic crime at a more macro scale, see Wilson (1996). For a broader perspective on the relationship between lack of power in the legal labor market and economic crime, see Edin and Lein (1997a).

3. See, e.g., Furstenberg (1993, 1999), Kotlowitz (1991), and Puntenney (1997).

4. For some examples focusing on New York City, see Duneier (1999), Mahler (1995), and Sassen-Koob (1989).

5. Emphasizing residents' *lack* of choice in undertaking economic crime inevitably suggests that the people of Guadalupe and Chávez were overwhelmed by structural circumstances. In some cases, as Scheper-Hughes (1992) has documented in certain communities in northeast Brazil, structural circumstances *are* overwhelming. In Guadalupe and Chávez, the amount of structural dislocation is not empirically comparable to Scheper-Hughes's Brazil. Clearly, residents of the Mexican American barrios do not face anything empirically comparable to the physical coercion experienced by residents of the Brazilian *favelas*. Thus, to depict economic crime in the low-income barrios of California as forced upon residents by the exigencies of structural circumstances is to make a theoretical statement about the nature of "force." At the least, the use of the concept "force" implies that the residents of the Mexican American barrios are subjectively overwhelmed or defeated by the structural circumstances in which they find themselves. My experiences in the barrios are inconsistent with that depiction. The residents of Guadalupe and Chávez were active, strategic, and resourceful in the face of difficult structural-economic circumstances. To analyze economic crime as actively chosen rather than forcefully undertaken thus makes both a theoretical and an empirical point about the nature of social dislocations in the United States. In later chapters, I revisit these issues. There, I argue that despite the common association of structural dislocation with "forced" responses that govern everyday life, there is little evidence that structural dislocation rises to the empirical level at which it might elicit a forced response in any low-income area in the United States.

6. Fernandez-Kelly and Garcia (1989) remind us of the heterogeneity of the experiences among workers in the informal realm and especially of the fact that workers do not turn to informal work out of destitution or desperation (pp. 248–49). An analysis of the dynamics of Mexico-U.S. migration show that migrants are usually *not* the most disadvantaged members of their communities of origin (Massey and Espinosa 1997). This is not necessarily the case for other migration streams (see, e.g., Portes and Bach 1985; Portes and Rumbaut 1990). In Guadalupe, different relationships between migration and survival were thrown into sharp relief by the experiences of my landlady Gloria and her family. Their flight from El Salvador was motivated by political violence—her son recalled a close call with the Salvadoran army as a particularly important event precipitating their departure—that did threaten their survival.

7. Sullivan (1989) reports similar patterns in his New York study. For youths from the two more impoverished neighborhoods he studied, "the income that they did derive was used to satisfy those personal needs beyond basic subsistence for which their parents could not provide. In fact, most of their early income, from whatever source, was spent on clothing and recreation" (p. 117).

8. Elijah Anderson's (1990, 1999) description of the battle between infectious "street" elements and a resistant "decent" community in the impoverished ghettos in Philadelphia provides an elegant analysis of this opposition. On the other hand, Mary Pattillo-McCoy (1998a) describes a more nuanced line of demarcation between "street" and "decent" in her ethnography of a Chicago community (chap. 4).

9. For neighborhoods, see Anderson (1990) and Williams (1992); for single mothers, see Edin and Lein (1997a); for young people, see Glasgow (1981), Hagedorn (1988), and Williams (1989). Except for single mothers, all of these studies concern the importance of economic crime for survival among African Americans. This is not a coincidence. African Americans have been more severely affected by structural-economic dislocations than Mexican Americans and other American ethnoracial groups (Massey and Denton 1993). Compared to its role in the African American experience, economic crime has played a more limited role in survival strategies among Latinos in general (Moore and Pinderhughes 1993a) and in Mexican American East Los Angeles in particular (Moore 1991; Moore and Vigil 1993). Among Latinos, economic crime plays a more significant role in the survival strategies of Mexican American border communities (Valdez 1993) and urban Puerto Rican barrios (Sharff 1987; Sullivan 1993).

10. Normalizing illicit activities through simplistic stories of good and/or bad occurred generally in the barrios of East LA. However, the details of the story depended on community-gang-police relationships. In Lawndale homes, where intergang violence was common, many residents told "gang bad, cops bad" stories, as described in Chapter 6. Chávez residents often told "gang bad" stories when describing past years when intergang violence between Elm Street and the VPs threatened civilian safety.

11. Martín Sánchez-Jankowski (personal communication, 2000) suggested this distinction between schooling in the streets and education in the classroom.

12. Elijah Anderson's ethnographic work in Philadelphia has vividly described and analyzed the importance of street culture for everyday life in the low-income community (Anderson 1999), as well as the nature of the wisdom that is important for successfully managing the streets in everyday life (Anderson 1990). What Anderson described in Philadelphia was true of Chávez. The public spaces of the barrio had distinct cultural norms and interaction rules. Learning those rules and integrating those norms into one's everyday public persona meant an easier time during daily rounds and a greater sense of physical and emotional security.

13. This is a common practice that has been described in other low-income communities as well (Anderson 1990).

14. Pierre Bourdieu (1977) discusses the difference between following the rules of social norms and having a sense of social norms.

15. See Bennett, DiIulio, and Walters (1996).

16. See Crane (1991).

17. Elijah Anderson (1990, 1999) documents the logic of the culture of violence, how it reproduces itself and its relationship to structural-economic change in the impoverished urban ghettos of Philadelphia.

18. See Cummings and Monti (1993), Decker and Winkle (1996), and Klein (1995).

19. See Sampson and Groves (1989).

20. This way of conceptualizing the relationship between crime and community has enjoyed both a long history and a contemporary revival in urban sociology (Sampson and Morenoff 1997; Sampson et al. 1997).

21. See Furstenberg (1993), Merry (1981), and Puntenney (1997).

22. See, e.g., Edin and Lein (1997a).

23. See, e.g., Anderson (1990), Bourgois (1995b), Liebow (1967), Moore (1978), Sharff (1987, 1998), and Venkatesh (2000).

24. Gerald Suttles (1968) documents similar means of communication.

PART IV: WELFARE

1. See Jencks (1992b, 1992c), Mead (1986), and Murray (1984).

2. For some exemplars, see Merton's (1968) discussion of anomie, as well as Liebow's (1967) discussion of a "shadow culture."

8: MAKING ENDS MEET

1. Quadagno (1994) argues that identification of welfare with African Americans is not simply a coincidence that has arisen since the 1960s but rather part of a larger pattern of the racial organization of American social welfare programs. Gilens shows that antiblack attitudes among white Americans, particularly the belief that blacks lack commitment to the work ethic, continues to motivate their opposition to welfare programs for the poor (Gilens 1995) and that these beliefs are the most potent source of political opposition to these programs (Gilens 1996).

2. While politicians depicted long-term dependence on AFDC as a problem urgently in need of fixing, data tell a different story. The best data to address the question come from the Panel Study of Income Dynamics (PSID). PSID data show that only a very small number of AFDC recipients rely on aid for long periods of time. The vast majority of recipients use AFDC either temporarily or for a short period of time (Corcoran 1995; Gottschalk, McClanahan, and Sandefur 1994).

3. For an early assessment of the progress of welfare reform, see Danziger (2000). For a discussion of the barriers faced by poor women moving from welfare to work, see Danziger et al. (2000).

4. See, e.g., Flanders (2001), Lewin (2001), Peterson (2001), and Rivera (2001).

5. I adopt this definition of public aid not only because it is the working definition of aid in the contemporary barrios but also because it is an accurate reflection of the place of public aid in the United States. American institutions that provide public assistance have changed during the history of the Republic,

but even as the specific institutions that provide aid change, the dynamics and meanings of aid provision in America have remained relatively stable (Katz 1986). A broad definition of public assistance captures the practical meaning of public assistance in everyday life. It also reflects the fact that public aid has a stable meaning in the United States, even if aid is provided and administered by a diverse array of institutions, including private charities and public bureaucracies. This broad definition is doubly appropriate given contemporary changes in the public system of aid provision—changes that will certainly alter the how private institutions provide assistance in low-income communities. I discuss in somewhat greater detail recent changes in American understandings of welfare recipients and the recent history of welfare institutions in Chapter 9.

6. Doña Lupe *expected* to be off aid in a few weeks or months, but whether she *actually* would leave the aid roles when her husband recovered—or whether the couple would continue to claim an injury in order to collect disability—was a subject of intense gossip among her Guadalupe friends. I analyze this gossip in Chapter 9.

7. Rotating and informal credit associations have been described in a variety of immigrant and ethnic communities. They are particularly important for accessing capital for entrepreneurship (Light and Bhachu 1993; Light and Karageorgis 1994) and may also help cushion unexpected economic shocks

8. Cannery work was still important for a number of women workers in Guadalupe, but it clearly was much less important in the Guadalupe of 1993–94 than it had been in the past. Only a few canneries remained open, and many women who had made their income according to the yearly cycle of cannery work–unemployment insurance had been forced to turn to other jobs. For a fuller discussion of the cannery industry in the Santa Clara Valley and Mexican American women's participation in it, see Zavella (1987).

9. The work of Edin (1991) shows a similar pattern among AFDC recipients in Chicago and, as her work with Lein shows, more generally among low-income single mothers (Edin and Lein 1997a).

10. Ethnographers have long documented the difficulties and instability of relying on public aid to make ends meet (Bourgois 1995b; Susser and Kreniske 1987).

11. This dynamic resembles what Wilson (1987) referred to as a lack of marriageable men. Wilson argued that female headship and AFDC reliance were high in underclass neighborhoods due to a low "marriageable men index." In his view, a low index was primarily due to a lack of employment opportunity. Women did not consider a man "marriageable" unless he held a steady job. He also noted that violence and incarceration played a role in lowering the marriageable men index (pp. 95–100). In Chávez, AFDC reliance arose from death, injury, incarceration, and abandonment rather than through lack of employment alone. In many cases, it appeared that these problems were related to lack of employment opportunity, but there were multiple and complicated paths to AFDC reliance. Variance in more proximate causes—in the chance circumstances that led to death and injury, in criminal justice practices that facilitated incarceration, and in individual choices that led to abandonment—played a prominent role in shaping the everyday dynamics of aid reliance.

12. A few women in Guadalupe ended up relying on AFDC following the death, injury, incarceration, or abandonment of a male wage earner, but I did not meet any residents who ended up on GA due to problems with substance abuse. In contiguous San Jose neighborhoods, substance users played a prominent role in street life. It is possible that residents who had problems with substance abuse and turned to GA quickly moved from Guadalupe to these nearby areas. Some Guadalupe residents who were incapacitated by alcohol use never turned to GA; rather, they left San Jose with plans to return to Mexico.

13. The tire plant had employed a substantial number of Chávez residents. Along with several other large industrial plants in central and east LA and in nearby Commerce, California, the plant closed in the late 1980s (Moore and Vigil 1993, pp. 32–35). During one of the runs to the food bank in Mike Gonzales's flatbed, we passed by the old plant. There were four of us squeezed onto the bench seat of the truck. I was the youngest by a decade and a half and the only one who had never spent time at the plant. Tommy, sitting next to me, recalled seeing his co-worker's crushed leg after an enormous truck tire rolled over it and how he used to come home from the plant so covered in grease that it took an hour to clean up. Jim, sitting next to the window, made deliveries to the plant, and he recalled workers sneaking outside to use speed or booze to get through their shifts. "I used a lot of speed when I was there," said Mike, who was behind the wheel. "I was on piece rate when I started. I hated that place so much, I would go in there and do my quota in a day or two. I'd be working like a madman, tossing tires everywhere, burning my hands, saying, 'Let's go let's go.' Then they said I had to come in forty hours—four tens. I couldn't take it. I quit a couple weeks later."

14. Researchers have found similar rules among Chicano gangs in East LA (Moore 1991; Padilla 1992), as well as among other gangs (Pattillo-McCoy 1998a; Sánchez-Jankowski 1991; Venkatesh 1997a).

## 9: MAKING WELFARE STIGMA

1. Welfare plays no significant economic role in most American communities, and even in low-income areas the number of welfare users rarely approaches the number of residents who support themselves without turning to public assistance (Jargowsky 1997). As a drain on the federal coffers, moreover, the economic impact of welfare is also small: it accounted for approximately $22 billion in fiscal year 1995, an amount larger than NASA ($14 billion), smaller than Veterans Affairs ($38 billion), and not in the same league with defense ($260 billion) or social security ($314 billion) (U.S. House, Committee on Ways and Means 1996).

2. Katz (1989) and Gans (1995) both track and analyze this recent transformation in the provision of public aid in the United States. Quadagno (1994) argues that these recent changes may be understood as part of a larger transformation in both who received public assistance and whom the American public and American policy makers perceived as receiving public assistance.

3. In Murray's (1984) model of perverse incentives, a hypothetical couple would rationally calculate the economic costs and benefits of cohabitation and aid receipt versus marriage and wage labor. On the basis of this rational calculus,

they would choose to remain unmarried and unemployed rather than establish a stable household with connections to the labor market.

4. The Personal Responsibility and Work Opportunity Reconciliation Act of 1996 (PRWOA, Public Law 104–193) sought to address all of these issues by ending "welfare as we know it"—in particular the Aid to Families with Dependent Children (AFDC) program—and instituting Temporary Assistance to Needy Families (TANF).

5. This pattern holds not only in Chávez but among low-income single mothers nationwide (Edin and Lein 1997a).

PART V: CONCLUSION: WORK, CRIME, AND WELFARE

1. In fact, in both barrios expectations often differed from reality. In Guadalupe, planned visits home were often delayed again and again as residents settled in San Jose without ever making an explicit decision to stay. In Chávez, few residents stayed long in any particular low-wage job because conflicts at work, a new job, or the opportunity to pursue income outside the wage labor market motivated their departure.

2. In studies of work, networks' practical importance has overshadowed their cultural effects. Practically, social networks were crucial for finding and keeping a job in the low-income Mexican American barrios. In Guadalupe and Chávez, as in higher-income American communities (Granovetter 1974), residents often found out about available jobs from family and neighbors. As in other low-income communities (Hagan 1998), networks in Guadalupe and Chávez tended to be information poor. Most of the news of job openings that circulated through Guadalupe and Chávez was about poor-quality jobs. When residents learned of a better-quality job opening, they tended not to circulate this news as readily or as widely. Rather, they used the information strategically by, for example, sharing it only with a family member or powerful friend who was in a position to return the help in the future. In both Guadalupe and Chávez, social networks were also logistically important for keeping a job—a finding that has been widely documented in other studies of low-income people and communities (see Hao and Brinton 1997; Harris 1993, 1996; Stack 1974). Working low-wage jobs meant long and hectic workweeks arranging child care, commuting, and household upkeep. Residents of the barrios turned again and again to their family, friends, and neighbors to help manage these logistics. Without monetary resources to buy child care, transportation, or domestic help, residents needed support from their social network to continue working in low-wage jobs.

3. Studies of work have tended to deemphasize these cultural effects and focus on the practical support provided by social networks. But the cultural significance of social networks has been discussed in the case of school-based peer groups (e.g., Ogbu 1974; Willis 1977).

10: THE PRICE OF POVERTY

1. Compare, e.g., the bleak world of persistent poverty in Auletta (1982) and Kotlowitz (1991) with the vision of positive transformation of Davis (2000).

2. Douglas Massey (1993) discusses important reasons for analyzing persistent and immigrant poverty separately in his discussion of the differences between African American and Latino poverty. For community organization in Chicago's Robert Taylor Homes, see Venkatesh (2000); for internal divisions in Long Island's Salvadorean community, see Mahler (1995); for an ethnography that neatly highlights the lack of distinction between persistent and immigrant poverty, see Jagna Sharff's (1998) discussion of violence on New York's Lower East Side.

3. See Sewell (1992, p. 2).

4. See Wilson (1987). Wilson's explanation was extremely influential, but structural explanations of poverty are not new (see Patterson 1994), and Wilson was not the first to focus on the effects of structural-economic factors in contemporary American poverty (see Glasgow 1981).

5. It is nearly inconceivable that an ethnographic study could convincingly refute a structural theory such as Wilson's. This is because that social structure's very immutability makes it difficult to examine through participant-observation. In everyday life in Guadalupe and Chávez, for example, it was always difficult for me to know when and whether I was seeing social structure. How could I be sure, for example, that a particular interaction or decision was part of some immutable structure—of capitalism, say, a structure that organizes behavior around the globe and has a centuries-long history—rather than a relatively ephemeral and changeable pattern of behavior? Large comparative research designs give some researchers confidence that they are observing and analyzing structure, but it is often more difficult to be sure what is structure and what is not in the course of ethnography.

6. Exemplary analyses of poverty that focus on noneconomic structural factors include studies of race and social networks (Blauner 1972; Bonacich 1976; Massey and Denton 1993; Waldinger 1996b), nativity and immigration (Borjas 1990), geography and neighborhood (Duncan and Brooks-Gunn 1997), and family structure (Furstenberg 1999).

7. See Lewis (1968).

8. The specific predictions of the culture-of-poverty theory were long ago refuted (Irelan, Moles, and O'Shea 1969; Valentine 1968).

9. See Maxwell (1993).

10. Clifford Geertz (1973) speaks of webs of meaning, and Sherry Ortner (1984) discusses changes in theories of culture. Criticism of the culture-of-poverty theory thus has taken both an empirical form—in the finding that the poor share mainstream values and norms—and a theoretical form—in the assertion that culture is not really carried around in people's heads. New ideas about culture and poverty have emerged from both the empirical and the theoretical critique. Empiricists, noting that the values and norms of the poor are the same as those of other people in society, have argued that poverty and culture are related because poor people are unable to live their lives according to their chosen values and norms—an argument that can be traced back to Robert Merton's (1968) statements about anomie and value stretch. Lawrence Mead (1997), for example, argues that "most poor people accept conventional values" but that values still matter because many poor people lack the "personal competence" to adhere to

the mainstream values toward which they pledge allegiance (p. 24). This inability to follow mainstream values is the root cause of poverty. Theorists who follow Geertz in thinking of culture as something more than the ideas carried around in people's heads have argued that publicly available symbols are different in low-income communities than in higher-income communities. Ann Swidler (1986), for example, has argued that culture is "a 'tool kit' of symbols, stories, rituals, and world-views, which people may use in varying configurations to solve different kinds of problems" (p. 273). Like Mead, she acknowledges that poor people have the same values and aspirations of others, but she points out that

> class similarities in aspirations in no way resolve the question of whether there are class differences in culture. People may share common aspirations, while remaining profoundly different in the way their culture organizes their overall pattern of behavior. Culture in this sense is more like a style or a set of skills and habits than a set of preferences or wants. . . . One can hardly pursue success in a world where the accepted skills, style, and informal know-how are unfamiliar. (p. 275)

Lacking a cultural "sense" for middle-class life can impede poor people's ability to enjoy upward mobility. Pierre Bourdieu (1977) argues that culture is a "sense" for how to behave, contrasting this to the value-norms paradigm in which culture is a set of rules for behavior. Swidler's cultural tool kit might be thought of as the elements that make up a cultural sense.

Some residents of the low-income barrios, such as those whose daily lives were consumed by heroin or alcohol use, at times seemed to lack the personal competence to follow mainstream values and norms, as Mead might predict. Other residents, such as some active gang members, appeared to have embraced a distinct public culture that made it difficult for them to pursue mainstream economic success, as Swidler might predict. James Vigil (1988), for example, has discussed the process by which Chicano gang members draw on a distinct set of publicly available symbols to construct gang-centered identities. In Guadalupe and Chávez, however, these residents were the exception. Most people in Guadalupe and Chávez did not want to live in poverty, understood what was required to get out of poverty, and had an "intuitive" sense of behavioral norms among the nonpoor in the United States. The fact was, however, that the everyday behaviors that mattered most for economic standing were not directly determined by widely shared cultural ideals about the value of upward mobility, about what was required to enjoy upward mobility, or about how to behave like someone who is upwardly mobile.

11. For an example of the difficulty of integrating a more sophisticated version of cultural theory into analyses of urban poverty, see Pattillo-McCoy (1998b).

12. It leads us, as the anthropologist Sherry Ortner (1999) notes, to "emphasize the issue of meaning-*making* . . . as against the notion of cultural 'systems' " (p. 8).

13. The accounts of the journalist Ken Auletta (1982) first attracted attention to this "underclass" and defined the group behaviorally. Initial scholarly assessments endorsed Auletta's lifestyle perspective, as analysts including Lawrence Mead (1986, 1989) and Charles Murray (1984) argued that the "underclass"

had its roots in cultural conditions such as a generalized devaluation of work among the poor or a predictable outcome of misguided social welfare policies. While Auletta's articles and book attracted policy maker and scholarly attention in the 1980s, he was by no means the first to apply the term *underclass* to the urban poor of America (Jones 1992). In fact, he was not even the first to apply this term to the American urban poor in the 1980s (see Glasgow 1981).

14. See Wilson (1987, 1996).

15. For a critical discussion of the productivity of "underclass" research, see Massey (1997).

16. On an empirical level, scholars could not agree on how to define the "underclass," nor could they develop reliable estimates of its size or distribution (Jencks 1991). Some viewed this lack of applicability as suggestive that the "underclass" debate arose from threatening changes in urban society rather than from any new form of poverty (Katz 1993). Researchers who recognized new forms of urban marginality among the poor criticized the term's negative connotations harshly. They began to speak of a "so-called urban 'underclass'" and argued for the term's abandonment (Gans 1995; Wacquant 1996, 1997). Herbert Gans (1990) argued, "The term has taken on so many connotations of undeservingness and blameworthiness that it has become hopelessly polluted in meaning, ideological overtone and implications, and should be dropped" (p. 272). Wilson (1991) acknowledged these criticisms of the term and stopped using it. For the theoretical and practical difficulties of applying the "underclass" concept, see Haitsma (1989), Heisler (1991), and Maxwell (1993).

17. For an overview of the cultural and structural terms of the debate, see Kelso (1994).

18. Except when applied to Puerto Rican barrios—especially those located in the same Rust Belt cities where the ghetto "underclass" was concentrated (see Sullivan 1993)—"underclass" analysis seemed misapplied outside the African American ghettos of the U.S. Rust Belt. The essays in Joan Moore and Rachel Pinderhughes's (1993a) edited volume show a loose connection between the concerns of the "underclass" debate and the experiences of poverty in most Latino communities. Some of the factors identified by "underclass" researchers, ranging from economic restructuring to a maturation of drug markets, affect poor Latino communities in many areas of the country. But the effects of these factors in Latino communities vary substantially from their effects in the African American ghettos that "underclass" research focused upon (Moore 1989; Moore and Pinderhughes 1993b). Douglas Massey (1993) encouraged researchers "to decouple Latinos from the larger underclass debate and to forge a new research agenda on Hispanic poverty governed by its own theoretical models and analytical methods." This "conceptual divorce," he noted, does not deny the existence of poverty, social problems, or "patterns of behavior that are often associated with the underclass" in the barrios; it merely grounds the study of Latino poverty in the experiences of Latinos rather than in the experiences of African Americans (p. 452).

19. See Venkatesh (2000), especially chap. 2.

20. See Wacquant (1997).

21. I am purposely ignoring a third argument that attributes lack of mobility to biological factors (Herrnstein and Murray 1994). For a thorough refutation of this argument, see Fischer (1996).

APPENDIX: METHODS OF THIS STUDY

1. Michael Burawoy (1998) categorizes the "sins" of ethnography as general problems confronting social science researchers, such as reflexivity and reactivity, and reviews various methodological solutions—none perfect—to the challenges they present.

2. For more on the methodological logic that guided selection of the Chávez barrio, see Katz's (1983) discussion of the significance of contrary cases. See Jargowsky and Bane's (1990) discussion of the utility of dilapidated housing and commercial stock as a measure of persistent poverty.

3. I define a barrio complex as the set of census tracts that are (a) dominated by Mexican-origin individuals, (b) geographically contiguous, and (c) consistent with field observations about commercial establishments and daily habits of residents. The San Jose barrio complex consisted of twenty-two contiguous census tracts. The population of thirteen of the twenty-two tracts was more than 50 percent Mexican origin, and the population of seven of the remaining nine tracts was more than one-third Mexican origin. The Chávez barrio was part of a barrio complex in Los Angeles that consisted of nineteen census tracts plus the entire population of unincorporated East Los Angeles. The Mexican-origin population of each tract was over 65 percent. San José had only one barrio complex (of which Guadalupe was a part), while Los Angeles had several discrete barrio complexes. It is possible that the different barrio complexes in Los Angeles had access to different local labor markets.

4. Demographically in San Jose half (51 percent) of barrio complex residents were of Mexican origin, two-fifths (43 percent) were immigrants, and one-quarter (23 percent) were recent (1980s) immigrants; socioeconomically, one-fifth (19 percent) of San Jose barrio complex residents had incomes below the poverty line. In Los Angeles, nearly nine-tenths (87 percent) of residents of the barrio complex that included Chávez were of Mexican origin, half (52 percent) were immigrants, and one-quarter (27 percent) had arrived during the 1980s; one quarter (26 percent) of residents had incomes below the poverty line.

5. The reservation wage is the wage at which an individual will sacrifice his or her leisure and go to work. All things equal, we expect people with nonwage sources of income—such as investment income, income from illicit activities, or income from public assistance—to have a higher reservation wage than people entirely dependent on the labor market. Residents of Chávez might have a higher reservation wage than residents of the surrounding barrio complex because Chávez residents lived in subsidized housing, which effectively gave them an alternative source of income.

6. Employers in Chicago reported that they excluded job applicants on the basis of perceived commitment to ghetto culture (Kirschenman and Neckerman 1991; Wilson 1996). A similar mechanism could lead to exclusion of Chávez residents due to their residence in public housing.

7. Jargowsky (1997) shows that public assistance provides only a small portion of income in poverty neighborhoods. The rates of public assistance receipt in Guadalupe and Chávez were typical for census tracts of comparable poverty (pp. 100–03).

8. Both of these figures are substantially higher than mean public assistance grants in low-income communities in the United States in general (Jargowsky 1997, p. 101). This may be due to the fact that, compared to other states, California provides relatively generous public assistance benefits.

9. All things equal, larger households should receive larger public assistance grants. Guadalupe households averaged 3.9 persons (compared to 3.1 in San Jose as a whole), and Chávez households averaged 4.7 persons (compared to 2.9 in the city of Los Angeles as a whole and 4.3 in East Los Angeles). The larger amount of public assistance income in Chávez may be due to larger households there. Aggregate data do not allow us to rigorously test for this possibility.

10. Police also inadvertently facilitated Liebow's (1967) entrance into the community where he conducted fieldwork.

11. The many varieties of ethnography differ according to research practices, epistemological orientations and theoretical goals. Analytic ethnography is, as John Lofland (1995) notes, "one variety of mainstream or even positivistic strategies of social research, sharing much with the strategies of experiments, surveys and historical comparisons. Among these shared features is the framing of one's task as the asking of basic questions about the domain of human social life and organization" (p. 37).

12. Another way of establishing relationships with informants when conducting participant-observation research is through the buddy role (see, e.g., Snow and Anderson 1993).

13. For some participant-observers, the distinction between observing and participating is salient, but in my everyday work in Guadalupe and Chávez this was a fairly insubstantial distinction.

14. See Milgram (1983) and Zimbardo (1972).

# Bibliography

Agee, James, and Walker Evans. [1941] 1988. *Let Us Now Praise Famous Men: Three Tenant Families.* Boston: Houghton Mifflin.

Ainsworth-Darnell, James W., and Douglas B. Downey. 1998. "Assessing the Oppositional Culture Explanation for Racial/Ethnic Differences in School Performance." *American Sociological Review* 63:536–53.

Alarcón, Rafael. 1992. "Norteñización: Self-Perpetuating Migration from a Mexican Town." Pp. 302–18 in *U.S.-Mexico Relations: Labor Market Interdependence,* edited by J. A. Bustamante, C. W. Reynolds, and R. A. H. Ojeda. Stanford, CA: Stanford University Press.

Anderson, Elijah. 1978. *A Place on the Corner.* Chicago: University of Chicago Press.

———. 1989. "Sex Codes and Family Life among Poor Inner-City Youths." *Annals of the American Academy of Political and Social Science* 501:59–78.

———. 1990. *Streetwise: Race, Class, and Change in an Urban Community.* Chicago: University of Chicago Press.

———. 1991. "Neighborhood Effects on Teenage Pregnancy." Pp. 375–98 in *The Urban Underclass,* edited by C. Jencks and P. E. Peterson. Washington, DC: Brookings Institution.

———. 1999. *Code of the Street: Decency, Violence, and the Moral Life of the Inner City.* New York: W. W. Norton.

Archer, Margaret. 1990. *Culture and Agency: The Place of Culture in Social Theory.* New York: Cambridge University Press.

Auletta, Ken. 1982. *The Underclass.* New York: Vintage Books.

Basch, Linda G., Nina Glick Schiller, and Cristina Szanton Blanc, eds. 1994. *Nations Unbound: Transnational Projects, Postcolonial Predicaments, and Deterritorialized Nation-States.* New York: Routledge.

Bennett, William J., John J. DiIulio, and John P. Walters. 1996. *Body Count:*

276                                                    Bibliography

*Moral Poverty . . . and How to Win America's War against Crime and Drugs.*
New York: Simon and Schuster.

Blauner, Robert. 1972. *Racial Oppression in America.* New York: Harper and
Row.

Boissevain, Jeremy. 1974. *Friends of Friends: Networks, Manipulators and Coalitions.* Oxford, England: Blackwell.

Bonacich, Edna. 1976. "Advanced Capitalism and Black/White Relations in the
United States: A Split Labor Market Approach." *American Sociological
Review* 41:34–51.

Borjas, George J. 1990. *Friends or Strangers: The Impact of Immigrants on the
U.S. Economy.* New York: Basic Books.

Bourdieu, Pierre. 1977. *Outline of a Theory of Practice.* Edited by R. Nice. New
York: Cambridge University Press.

———. 1990. *The Logic of Practice.* Stanford, CA: Stanford University Press.

Bourdieu, Pierre, and Loïc J. D. Wacquant. 1992. *An Invitation to Reflexive
Sociology.* Chicago: University of Chicago Press.

Bourgois, Philippe. 1995a. "In Search of Horatio Alger: Culture and Ideology in
the Crack Economy." Pp. 77–107 in *Drugs, Crime and Criminal Justice,* vol.
2, *Cultures and Markets, Crime and Criminal Justice,* edited by N. South.
Brookfield, VT: Dartmouth Publishing.

———. 1995b. *In Search of Respect: Selling Crack in El Barrio.* New York:
Cambridge University Press.

Boyd, Monica. 1989. "Family and Personal Networks in International Migration: Recent Developments and New Agendas." *International Migration
Review* 23:638–70.

Burawoy, Michael. 1998. "The Extended Case Method." *Sociological Theory*
16:63–92.

Castells, Manuel, and Alejandro Portes. 1989. "World Underneath: The Origins,
Dynamics, and Effects of the Informal Economy." Pp. 11–40 in *The Informal
Economy: Studies in Advanced and Less Developed Countries,* edited by A.
Portes, M. Castells, and L. A. Benton. Baltimore, MD: Johns Hopkins University Press.

Castles, Stephen, and Mark J. Miller. 1998. *The Age of Migration: International
Population Movements in the Modern World.* New York: Macmillan.

Chávez, Leo R. 1992. *Shadowed Lives: Undocumented Immigrants in American
Society.* New York: Harcourt Brace Jovanovich.

Coleman, James S. 1988. "Social Capital in the Creation of Human Capital."
*American Journal of Sociology* 94:S95–S121.

———. 1990. *Foundations of Social Theory.* Cambridge, MA: Harvard University Press.

Corcoran, Mary. 1995. "Rags to Rags: Poverty and Mobility in the United
States." Pp. 237–67 in *Annual Review of Sociology,* edited by J. Hagan. Palo
Alto, CA: Annual Reviews.

Crane, Jonathan. 1991. "The Epidemic Theory of Ghettos and Neighborhood
Effects on Dropping out and Teenage Childbearing." *American Journal of
Sociology* 96:1226–59.

Cummings, Scott, and Daniel J. Monti. 1993. *Gangs: The Origins and Impact of*

*Contemporary Youth Gangs in the United States.* Albany: State University of New York Press.

Danziger, Sandra, Mary Corcoran, Colleen Heflin, Ariel Kalil, Judith Levine, Daniel Rosen, Kristin Seefeldt, Kristine Siefert, and Richard Tolman. 2000. "Barriers to the Employment of Welfare Recipients." Pp. 245–78 in *Prosperity for All? The Economic Boom and African Americans,* edited by R. D. Cherry and W. M. Rodgers. New York: Russell Sage Foundation.

Danziger, Sheldon. 2000. "Approaching the Limit: Early Lessons from Welfare Reform." Retrieved March 31, 2003, from Joint Center for Poverty Research Web site: www.jcpr.org/wpfiles/ruraldanziger.pdf.

Davis, Mike. 2000. *Magical Urbanism: Latinos Reinvent the US City.* New York: Verso.

Decker, Scott H., and Barrik Van Winkle. 1996. *Life in the Gang: Family, Friends, and Violence.* New York: Cambridge University Press.

Dimaggio, Paul J., and Walter W. Powell. 1983. "The Iron Cage Revisited: Institutional Isomorphism and Collective Rationality in Organizational Fields." *American Sociological Review* 48:147–60.

Duncan, Greg J., and Jeanne Brooks-Gunn. 1997. *Consequences of Growing up Poor.* New York: Russell Sage Foundation.

Duneier, Mitchell. 1999. *Sidewalk.* New York: Farrar, Straus, Giroux.

Durand, Jorge, and Douglas S. Massey. 1992. "Mexican Migration to the United States: A Critical Review." *Latin American Research Review* 27:3–42.

Edin, Kathryn. 1991. "Surviving the Welfare System: How AFDC Recipients Make Ends Meet in Chicago." *Social Problems* 38:462–74.

Edin, Kathryn, and Laura Lein. 1997a. *Making Ends Meet: How Single Mothers Survive Welfare and Low-Wage Work.* New York: Russell Sage Foundation.

———. 1997b. "Work, Welfare, and Single Mothers' Economic Strategies." *American Sociological Review* 62:253–66.

Engbersen, Godfried. 1993. *Cultures of Unemployment: A Comparative Look at Long-Term Unemployment and Urban Poverty.* Boulder, CO: Westview Press.

Fernandez, Roberto M., Emilio J. Castilla, and Paul Moore. 2000. "Social Capital at Work: Networks and Employment at a Phone Center." *American Journal of Sociology* 105:1288–1356.

Fernández-Kelly, M. Patricia. 1995. "Social and Cultural Capital in the Urban Ghetto: Implications for the Economic Sociology of Immigration." Pp. 213–47 in *The Economic Sociology of Immigration: Essays on Networks, Ethnicity, and Entrepreneurship,* edited by Alejandro Portes. New York: Russell Sage Foundation.

Fernández-Kelly, M. Patricia, and Anna M. García. 1989. "Informalization at the Core: Hispanic Women, Homework, and the Advanced Capitalist State." Pp. 247–64 in *The Informal Economy: Studies in Advanced and Less Developed Countries,* edited by A. Portes, M. Castells, and L. A. Benton. Baltimore, MD: Johns Hopkins University Press.

Fischer, Claude S. 1975. "Toward a Subcultural Theory of Urbanism." *American Journal of Sociology* 80:1319–41.

———. 1982. *To Dwell among Friends: Personal Networks in Town and City.* Chicago: University of Chicago Press.

———. 1995. "The Subcultural Theory of Urbanism: A Twentieth-Year Assessment." *American Journal of Sociology* 101:543–77.

Fischer, Claude S., Michael Hout, Martín Sánchez Jankowski, Samuel R. Lucas, Ann Swidler, and Kim Voss. 1996. *Inequality by Design: Cracking the Bell Curve Myth.* Princeton, NJ: Princeton University Press.

Flanders, Stephanie. 2001. "Admired Welfare Plan in Connecticut Meets First Test in Hard Times." *New York Times,* August 13, pp. A15, B1.

Freeman, Richard B., and Harry J. Holzer. 1986. *The Black Youth Employment Crisis.* Chicago: University of Chicago Press.

Furstenberg, Frank F. 1999. *Managing to Make It: Urban Families and Adolescent Success.* Chicago: University of Chicago Press.

Furstenberg, Frank F., Jr. 1993. "How Families Manage Risk and Opportunity in Dangerous Neighborhoods." Pp. 231–58 in *Sociology and the Public Agenda,* edited by W. J. Wilson. Newbury Park, CA: Sage Publications.

Gans, Herbert J. 1962. *The Urban Villagers.* New York: Free Press.

———. 1990. "Deconstructing the Underclass: The Term's Danger as a Planning Concept." *Journal of the American Planning Association* 56:271–77.

———. 1992. "Second-Generation Decline: Scenarios for the Economic and Ethnic Futures of the Post-1965 American Immigrants." *Ethnic and Racial Studies* 15:1734–92.

———. 1995. *The War against the Poor: The Underclass and Antipoverty Policy.* New York: Basic Books.

Geertz, Clifford. 1973. *The Interpretation of Cultures.* New York: Basic Books.

Gibson, Margaret A., and John U. Ogbu. 1991. *Minority Status and Schooling: A Comparative Study of Immigrant and Involuntary Minorities.* New York: Garland.

Gilens, Martin. 1995. "Racial Attitudes and Opposition to Welfare." *Journal of Politics* 57 (November): 994–1014.

———. 1996. "'Race Coding' and White Opposition to Welfare." *American Political Science Review* 90 (September): 593–604.

Glasgow, Douglas G. 1981. *The Black Underclass: Poverty, Unemployment, and Entrapment of Ghetto Youth.* New York: Vintage Books.

Glazer, Nathan. 1986. "Education and Training Programs and Poverty." Pp. 152–72 in *Fighting Poverty: What Works and What Doesn't,* edited by S. H. Danziger and D. H. Weinberg. Cambridge, MA: Harvard University Press.

González de la Rocha, Mercedes. 1994. *The Resources of Poverty: Women and Survival in a Mexican City.* Cambridge, MA: Blackwell.

Gottschalk, Peter, Sara McClanahan, and Gary D. Sandefur. 1994. "The Dynamics and Intergenerational Transmission of Poverty and Welfare Participation." Pp. 85–108 in *Confronting Poverty: Prescriptions for Change,* edited by S. H. Danziger, G. D. Sandefur, and D. H. Weinberg. Cambridge, MA: Harvard University Press.

Granovetter, Mark S. 1973. "The Strength of Weak Ties." *American Journal of Sociology* 78:1360–80.

———. 1974. *Getting a Job: A Study of Contacts and Careers.* Cambridge, MA: Harvard University Press.

———. 1985. "Economic Action and Social Structure: The Problem of Embeddedness." *American Journal of Sociology* 91:481–510.

Gutierrez, David G. 1995. *Walls and Mirrors: Mexican Americans, Mexican Immigrants, and the Politics of Ethnicity.* Berkeley: University of California Press.

Hagan, Jacqueline M. 1994. *Deciding to Be Legal: A Maya Community in Houston.* Philadelphia: Temple University Press.

———. 1998. "Social Networks, Gender, and Immigrant Incorporation: Resources and Constraints." *American Sociological Review* 63:55–67.

Hagedorn, John M. 1988. *People and Folks: Gangs, Crime and the Underclass in a Rustbelt City.* Chicago: Lake View Press.

Haitsma, Martha Van. 1989. "A Contextual Definition of the Underclass." *Focus* 12:27–31.

Hannerz, Ulf. 1969. *Soulside: Inquiries in Ghetto Culture and Community.* New York: Columbia University Press.

Hao, Lingxin, and Mary C. Brinton. 1997. "Productive Activities and Support Systems of Single Mothers." *American Journal of Sociology* 102:1305–44.

Harris, Kathleen Mullan. 1993. "Work and Welfare among Single Mothers in Poverty." *American Journal of Sociology* 99:317–52.

———. 1996. "Life after Welfare: Women, Work, and Repeat Dependency." *American Sociological Review* 61:407–26.

Heisler, Barbara Schmitter. 1991. "A Comparative Perspective on the Underclass: Questions of Urban Poverty, Race, and Citizenship." *Theory and Society* 20:455–83.

Herrnstein, Richard J., and Charles Murray. 1994. *The Bell Curve: Intelligence and Class Structure in American Life.* New York: Free Press.

Hondagneu-Sotelo, Pierrette. 1994a. *Gendered Transitions: Mexican Experiences of Immigration.* Berkeley: University of California Press.

———. 1994b. "Regulating the Unregulated: Domestic Workers Social Networks." *Social Problems* 41:50–64.

Horowitz, Ruth. 1983. *Honor and the American Dream: Culture and Identity in a Chicano Community.* New Brunswick, NJ: Rutgers University Press.

———. 1997. "Barriers and Bridges to Class Mobility and Formation: Ethnographies of Stratification." *Sociological Methods and Research* 25:495–538.

Irelan, Lola M., Oliver C. Moles, and Robert M. O'Shea. 1969. "Ethnicity, Poverty, and Selected Attitudes: A Test of the 'Culture of Poverty' Hypothesis." *Social Forces* 47:405–13.

Jargowsky, Paul A. 1997. *Poverty and Place: Ghettos, Barrios, and the American City.* New York: Russell Sage Foundation.

Jargowsky, Paul A., and Mary Jo Bane. 1990. "Ghetto Poverty: Basic Questions." Pp. 16–67 in *Inner-City Poverty in the United States,* edited by L. E. Lynn, Jr., and Michael G. H. McGeary. Washington, DC: National Academy Press.

Jencks, Christopher. 1991. "Is the American Underclass Growing." Pp. 28–100 in *The Urban Underclass,* edited by C. Jencks and P. E. Peterson. Washington, DC: Brookings Institution.

———. 1992a. "Is the American Underclass Growing?" Pp. 143–203 in

*Rethinking Social Policy: Race, Poverty, and the Underclass.* Cambridge, MA:
Harvard University Press.

———. 1992b. "Making Sense of Urban Ghettos." Pp. 120–42 in *Rethinking
Social Policy: Race, Poverty, and the Underclass.* Cambridge, MA: Harvard
University Press.

———. 1992c. "The Safety Net." Pp. 70–91 in *Rethinking Social Policy: Race,
Poverty, and the Underclass.* Cambridge, MA: Harvard University Press.

Jones, Jacqueline. 1992. *The Dispossessed: America's Underclasses from the Civil
War to the Present.* New York: Basic Books.

Katz, Jack. 1997. "Ethnography's Warrants." *Sociological Methods and Research* 25:391–423.

Katz, Jack. 1983. "A Theory of Qualitative Methodology: The Social System of
Analytic Fieldwork." Pp. 127–48 in *Contemporary Field Research: A Collec-
tion of Readings,* edited by R. M. Emerson. Prospect Heights, IL: Waveland
Press.

Katz, Michael B. 1986. *In the Shadow of the Poorhouse.* New York: Basic
Books.

———. 1989. *The Undeserving Poor: From the War on Poverty to the War on
Welfare.* New York: Pantheon.

———. 1993. "The Urban 'Underclass' as a Metaphor of Social Transformation." Pp. 3–26 in *The "Underclass" Debate: Views from History,* edited by
M. B. Katz. Princeton, NJ: Princeton University Press.

Kelso, William A. 1994. *Poverty and the Underclass: Changing Perceptions of
the Poor in America.* New York: New York University Press.

Kirschenman, Joleen, and Kathryn M. Neckerman. 1991. "'We'd Love to Hire
Them, But . . .': The Meaning of Race for Employers." Pp. 203–32 in *The
Urban Underclass,* edited by C. Jencks and P. E. Peterson. Washington, DC:
Brookings Institution.

Klein, Malcolm. 1995. *The American Street Gang: Its Nature, Prevalence, and
Control.* New York: Oxford University Press.

Kotlowitz, Alex. 1991. *There Are No Children Here: The Story of Two Boys
Growing up in the Other America.* New York: Doubleday.

Lamphere, Louise. 1992. *Structuring Diversity: Ethnographic Perspectives on the
New Immigration.* Chicago: University of Chicago Press.

Lewin, Tamar. 2001. "Surprising Result in Welfare-to-Work Studies." *New York
Times,* July 31, p. A16.

Lewis, Oscar. 1966. *La Vida: A Puerto Rican Family in the Culture of Poverty,
San Juan and New York.* New York: Vintage Books.

———. 1968. "The Culture of Poverty." Pp. 187–200 in *On Understanding
Poverty: Perspectives from the Social Sciences,* edited by D. P. Moynihan.
New York: Basic Books.

Liebow, Eliot. 1967. *Tally's Corner: A Study of Negro Streetcorner Men.* Boston:
Little, Brown.

Light, Ivan, and Parminder Bhachu. 1993. "Introduction: California Immigrants
in World Perspective." Pp. 1–24 in *Immigration and Entrepreneurship: Culture, Capital, and Ethnic Networks,* edited by I. Light and P. Bhachu. New
Brunswick, NJ: Transaction Publishers.

Light, Ivan, and Stavros Karageorgis. 1994. "The Ethnic Economy." Pp. 426–52 in *The Handbook of Economic Sociology*, edited by N. J. Smelser and R. Swedberg. New York: Russell Sage Foundation.

Lofland, John. 1995. "Analytic Ethnography: Features, Failings and Futures." *Journal of Contemporary Ethnography* 24 (April): 30–67.

Lomnitz, Larissa Adler de. 1977. *Networks and Marginality: Life in a Mexican Shantytown*. New York: Academic Press.

MacLeod, Jay. 1995. *Ain't No Makin' It*. Boulder, CO: Westview Press.

Mahler, Sarah J. 1995. *American Dreaming: Immigrant Life on the Margins*. Princeton, NJ: Princeton University Press.

Massey, Douglas S. 1993. "Latinos, Poverty, and the Underclass: A New Agenda for Research." *Hispanic Journal of Behavioral Sciences* 15:449–75.

———. 1997. "When Work Disappears: The World of the New Urban Poor." *Contemporary Sociology* 26 (July): 416–18.

Massey, Douglas S., Rafael Alarcón, Jorge Durand, and Humberto González. 1987. *Return to Aztlan: The Social Process of International Migration from Western Mexico*. Berkeley: University of California Press.

Massey, Douglas S., and Nancy A. Denton. 1993. *American Apartheid: Segregation and the Making of the Underclass*. Cambridge, MA: Harvard University Press.

Massey, Douglas S., and Kristin E. Espinosa. 1997. "What's Driving Mexico-US Migration? A Theoretical, Empirical, and Policy Analysis." *American Journal of Sociology* 102:939–99.

Massey, Douglas S., Luin Goldring, and Jorge Durand. 1994. "Continuities in Transnational Migration: An Analysis of Nineteen Mexican Communities." *American Journal of Sociology* 99:1492–1533.

Massey, Douglas S., A. B. Gross, and M. L. Eggers. 1991. "Segregation, the Concentration of Poverty, and the Life Chances of Individuals." *Social Science Research* 20:397–420.

Maxwell, Andrew H. 1993. "The Underclass, Social Isolation and Concentration Effects: The Culture of Poverty Revisited." *Critique of Anthropology* 13:231–45.

Mead, Lawrence M. 1986. *Beyond Entitlement: The Social Obligations of Citizenship*. New York: Free Press.

———. 1989. "The Logic of Workfare: The Underclass and Work Policy." *Annals of the American Academy of Political and Social Science* 501:156–69.

———. 1992. *The New Politics of Poverty: The Nonworking Poor in America*. New York: Basic Books.

———. 1997. "The Rise of Paternalism." Pp. 1–38 in *The New Paternalism: Supervisory Approaches to Poverty*, edited by L. M. Mead. Washington, DC: Brookings Institution Press.

Merry, Sally Engle. 1981. *Urban Danger: Life in a Neighborhood of Strangers*. Philadelphia: Temple University Press.

Merton, Robert King. 1968. *Social Theory and Social Structure*. New York: Free Press.

Milgram, Stanley. 1983. *Obedience to Authority: An Experimental View*. New York: Harper and Row.

Mines, Richard, and Jeffrey Avina. 1992. "Immigrants and Labor Standards: The Case of California Janitors." Pp. 429–48 in *U.S.-Mexico Relations: Labor Market Interdepedence,* edited by J. A. Bustamante, C. W. Reynolds, and R. A. H. Ojeda. Stanford, CA: Stanford University Press.

Moore, Joan W. 1978. *Homeboys: Gangs, Drugs, and Prison in the Barrios of Los Angeles.* Philadelphia: Temple University Press.

———. 1989. "Is There a Hispanic Underclass?" *Social Science Quarterly* 70:264–85.

———. 1991. *Going Down to the Barrio: Homeboys and Homegirls in Change.* Philadelphia: Temple University Press.

Moore, Joan, and Raquel Pinderhughes, eds. 1993a. *In the Barrios: Latinos and the Underclass Debate.* New York: Russell Sage Foundation.

———. 1993b. "Introduction." Pp. xi-xxxix in *In the Barrios: Latinos and the Underclass Debate,* edited by Joan Moore and Raquel Pinderhughes. New York: Russell Sage Foundation.

Moore, Joan, and James Diego Vigil. 1993. "Barrios in Transition." Pp. 27–49 in *In the Barrios: Latinos and the Underclass Debate,* edited by Joan Moore and Raquel Pinderhughes. New York: Russell Sage Foundation.

Murray, Charles. 1984. *Losing Ground: American Social Policy 1950–1980.* New York: Basic Books.

Nee, Victor, and Paul Ingram. 1998. "Embeddedness and Beyond: Institutions, Exchange and Social Structure." Pp. 19–45 in *The New Institutionalism in Sociology,* edited by M. C. Brinton and V. Nee. New York: Russell Sage Foundation.

Newman, Katherine S. 1992. "Culture and Structure in the Truly Disadvantaged." *City and Society* 6:3–25.

———. 1999. *No Shame in My Game: The Working Poor in the Inner City.* New York: Knopf.

Ogbu, John U. 1974. *The Next Generation: An Ethnography of Education in an Urban Neighborhood.* New York: Academic Press.

———. 1987. "Variability in Minority School Performance: A Problem in Search of an Explanation." *Anthropology and Education Quarterly* 18:312–34.

Ortner, Sherry B. 1984. "Theory in Anthropology since the Sixties." *Comparative Studies in Society and History* 26: 126–66.

———. 1999. "Introduction." Pp. 1–13 in *The Fate of "Culture": Geertz and Beyond,* edited by S. B. Ortner. Berkeley: University of California Press.

Padilla, Felix M. 1992. *The Gang as an American Enterprise.* New Brunswick, NJ: Rutgers University Press.

Park, Robert Ezra, Ernest Watson Burgess, and Roderick Duncan McKenzie. 1967. *The City.* Chicago: University of Chicago Press.

Patterson, James T. 1994. *America's Struggle against Poverty, 1900–1994.* Cambridge, MA: Harvard University Press.

Pattillo-McCoy, Mary. 1998a. *Black Picket Fences.* Chicago: University of Chicago Press.

———. 1998b. "Church Culture as a Strategy of Action in the Black Community." *American Sociological Review* 63:767–84.

Peterson, Jonathan. 2001. "Poverty Study Puts New Wrinkle in Welfare-to-Work

Debate, Services: Families of Single, Employed Women Did Not Fare as Well as Others during Economic Boom, Report Finds." *Los Angeles Times,* August 16, p. 15.

Peterson, Paul E. 1991. "The Urban Underclass and the Poverty Paradox." Pp. 3–27 in *The Urban Underclass,* edited by P. E. Peterson and C. Jencks. Washington, DC: Brookings Institution.

Petterson, Stephen M. 1997. "Are Young Black Men Really Less Willing to Work?" *American Sociological Review* 62:605–13.

Pinderhughes, Howard. 1997. *Race in the Hood: Conflict and Violence among Urban Youth.* Minneapolis: University of Minnesota Press.

Piore, Michael J. 1979. *Birds of Passage: Migrant Labor and Industrial Societies.* New York: Cambridge University Press.

Portes, Alejandro. 1994. "The Informal Economy and Its Paradoxes." Pp. 426–52 in *The Handbook of Economic Sociology,* edited by N. J. Smelser and R. Swedberg. New York: Russell Sage Foundation.

———. 1998. "Social Capital: Origins and Applications." Pp. 1–24 in *Annual Review of Sociology,* edited by J. Hagan. Palo Alto, CA: Annual Reviews.

Portes, Alejandro, and Robert L. Bach. 1985. *Latin Journey: Cuban and Mexican Immigrants in the United States.* Berkeley: University of California Press.

Portes, Alejandro, and Rubén G. Rumbaut. 1990. *Immigrant America: A Portrait.* Berkeley: University of California Press.

Portes, Alejandro, and Julia Sensenbrenner. 1993. "Embeddedness and Immigration: Notes on the Social Determinants of Economic Action." *American Journal of Sociology* 98:1320–50.

Puntenney, Deborah L. 1997. "The Impact of Gang Violence on the Decisions of Everyday Life: Disjunctions between Policy Assumptions and Community Conditions." *Journal of Urban Affairs* 19:143–61.

Quadagno, Jill S. 1994. *The Color of Welfare: How Racism Undermined the War on Poverty.* New York: Oxford University Press.

Rainwater, Lee, and William L. Yancey. 1967. *The Moynihan Report and the Politics of Controversy.* Cambridge, MA: MIT Press.

Riis, Jacob A., and Luc Sante. [1890] 1997. *How the Other Half Lives: Studies among the Tenements of New York.* New York: Penguin Books.

Rivera, Carla. 2001. "Los Angeles; 5 Years Later, Welfare Reform Draws Fire from Recipients and Advocates; Aid: Activists Say the Sharp Decline in Caseloads Stems from an Economic Boom, Not Stringent Guidelines." *Los Angeles Times,* August 23, p. 3.

Rouse, Roger C. 1989. "Mexican Migration to the United States: Family Relations in the Development of a Transnational Migrant Circuit." Ph.D. dissertation, Stanford University.

———. 1995. "Questions of Identity: Personhood and Collectivity in Transnational Migration to the United States." *Critique of Anthropology* 15:351–380.

Rumbaut, Ruben G. 1996. "The Crucible Within: Ethnic Identity, Self-Esteem, and Segmented Assimilation among Children of Immigrants." Pp. 119–70 in *The New Second Generation,* edited by A. Portes. New York: Russell Sage Foundation.

Salzinger, Leslie. 1991. "A Maid by Any Other Name: The Transformation of 'Dirty Work' by Central American Immigrants." Pp. 139–60 in *Ethnography Unbound: Power and Resistance in the Modern Metropolis*, edited by Linda G. Basch, Nina Glick Schiller, and Cristina Szanton Blanc. Berkeley: University of California Press.

Sampson, Robert J., and Walter Groves. 1989. "Community Structure and Crime: Testing Social Disorganization Theory." *American Journal of Sociology* 94:774–802.

Sampson, Robert J., and Jeffrey D. Morenoff. 1997. "Ecological Perspectives on the Neighborhood Context of Urban Poverty: Past and Present." Pp. 1–22 in *Neighborhood Poverty: Policy Implications in Studying Neighborhoods*, edited by J. Brooks-Gunn, G. J. Duncan, and J. L. Aber. New York: Russell Sage Foundation.

Sampson, Robert J., S. W. Raudenbush, and F. Earls. 1997. "Neighborhoods and Violent Crime: A Multilevel Study of Collective Efficacy." *Science* 277:918–24.

Sampson, Robert J., and William Julius Wilson. 1995. "Toward a Theory of Race, Crime, and Urban Inequality." Pp. 37–54 in *Crime and Inequality*, edited by J. Hagan and R. D. Peterson. Stanford, CA: Stanford University Press.

Sánchez, George J. 1993. *Becoming Mexican American: Ethnicity, Culture and Identity in Chicano Los Angeles, 1900–1945*. New York: Oxford University Press.

Sánchez-Jankowski, Martín. 1991. *Islands in the Street: Gangs and American Urban Society*. Berkeley: University of California Press.

Sassen, Saskia. 1988. *The Mobility of Labor and Capital: A Study in International Investment and Labor Flow*. New York: Cambridge University Press.

———. 1990. "Economic Restructuring and the American City." Pp. 465–90 in *Annual Review of Sociology*, edited by W. R. Scott and J. Blake. Palo Alto, CA: Annual Reviews.

———. 1991. *The Global City: New York, London, Tokyo*. Princeton, NJ: Princeton University Press.

———. 1993. "Urban Transformation and Employment." Pp. 184–206 in *Latinos in a Changing U.S. Economy*, edited by R. Morales and F. Bonilla. Newbury Park, CA: Sage Publications.

———. 1995. "Immigration and Local Labor Markets." Pp. 87–121 in *The Economic Sociology of Immigration: Essays on Networks, Ethnicity, and Entrepreneurship*, edited by Alejandro Portes. New York: Russell Sage Foundation.

Sassen-Koob, Saskia. 1989. "New York City's Informal Economy." Pp. 60–77 in *The Informal Economy: Studies in Advanced and Less Developed Countries*, edited by A. Portes, M. Castells, and L. A. Benton. Baltimore, MD: Johns Hopkins University Press.

Scheper-Hughes, Nancy. 1992. *Death without Weeping: The Violence of Everyday Life in Brazil*. Berkeley: University of California Press.

Schiller, Nina Glick, Linda G. Basch, and Cristina Szanton-Blanc. 1992. *Towards a Transnational Perspective on Migration: Race, Class, Ethnicity, and Nationalism Reconsidered.* New York: New York Academy of Sciences.

———. 1995. "From Immigrant to Transmigrant: Theorizing Transnational Migration." *Anthropological Quarterly* 68:48–63.

Scott, W. Richard. 1995. *Institutions and Organizations.* Thousand Oaks, CA: Sage.

Sewell, William H., Jr. 1992. "A Theory of Structure: Duality, Agency, and Transformation." *American Journal of Sociology* 98:1–29.

Sharff, Jagna W. 1987. "The Underground Economy of a Poor Neighborhood." Pp. 19–50 in *Cities of the United States: Studies of Urban Anthropology,* edited by Leith Mullings. New York: Columbia University Press.

———. 1998. *King Kong on 4th Street: Families and the Violence of Poverty on the Lower East Side.* Boulder, CO: Westview Press.

Short, James F., Jr. 1997. *Poverty, Ethnicity, and Violent Crime.* Boulder, CO: Westview Press.

Smith, Robert C. 1998. "Transnational Localities: Community, Technology and the Politics of Membership within the Context of Mexican-US Migration." *Journal of Comparative Urban and Community Research.*

Snow, David A., and Leon Anderson. 1993. *Down on Their Luck: A Study of Homeless Street People.* Berkeley: University of California Press.

Stack, Carol. 1974. *All Our Kin: Strategies for Survival in a Black Community.* New York: Harper and Row.

Sullivan, Mercer. 1989. *Getting Paid: Youth Crime and Work in the Inner City.* Ithaca, NY: Cornell University Press.

———. 1993. "Puerto Ricans in Sunset Park, Brooklyn: Poverty amidst Ethnic and Economic Diversity." Pp. 1–26 in *In the Barrios: Latinos and the Underclass Debate,* edited by Joan Moore and Raquel Pinderhughes. New York: Russell Sage Foundation.

Susser, Ida, and John Kreniske. 1987. "The Welfare Trap: A Public Policy for Deprivation." Pp. 51–68 in *Cities of the United States: Studies in Urban Anthropology,* edited by Leith Mullings. New York: Columbia University Press.

Suttles, Gerald D. 1968. *The Social Order of the Slum: Ethnicity and Territory in the Inner City.* Chicago: University of Chicago Press.

———. 1972. *The Social Construction of Communities.* Chicago: University of Chicago Press.

Swidler, Ann. 1986. "Culture in Action: Symbols and Strategies." *American Sociological Review* 51:273–86.

Uehara, Edwina. 1990. "Dual Exchange Theory, Social Networks, and Informal Social Support." *American Journal of Sociology* 96:521–57.

U.S. Bureau of the Census. 1990. *Census of Population and Housing.* File STF 3A. Washington, DC: U.S. Government Printing Office.

U.S. House, Committee on Ways and Means. 1996. *1996 Green Book: Background Material and Data on Programs within the Jurisdiction of the Committee on Ways and Means.* Washington, DC: Government Printing Office.

Valdez, Avelardo. 1993. "Persistent Poverty, Crime, and Drugs: U.S.-Mexican Border Region." Pp. 173–94 in *In the Barrios: Latinos and the Underclass*

*Debate*, edited by Joan Moore and Raquel Pinderhughes. New York: Russell Sage Foundation.

Valentine, Bettylou. 1978. *Hustling and Other Hard Work: Life Styles in the Ghetto*. New York: Free Press.

Valentine, Charles. 1968. *Culture and Poverty: Critique and Counterproposals*. Chicago: University of Chicago Press.

Valenzuela, Abel, and University of California Los Angeles, Center for the Study of Urban Poverty. 1999. *Day Laborers in Southern California: Preliminary Findings from the Day Labor Survey*. Los Angeles: Center for the Study of Urban Poverty.

Venkatesh, Sudhir Alladi. 1997a. "The Social Organization of Street Gang Activity in an Urban Ghetto." *American Journal of Sociology* 103:82–111.

———. 1997b. "The Three-Tier Model: How Helping Occurs in Urban, Poor Communities." *Social Service Review* 71 (December): 574–606.

———. 2000. *American Project: The Rise and Fall of a Modern Ghetto*. Cambridge, MA: Harvard University Press.

Vigil, James Diego. 1988. *Barrio Gangs: Street Life and Identity in Southern California*. Austin: University of Texas Press.

Wacquant, Loïc. 1996. "The Rise of Advanced Marginality: Notes on Its Nature and Implications." *Acta Sociologica* 39 (July): 121–39.

———. 1997. "Three Pernicious Premises in the Study of the American Ghetto." *International Journal of Urban and Regional Research*, 21 (June): 341–53.

———. 1998. "Inside the Zone: The Social Art of the Hustler in the Black American Ghetto." *Theory, Culture and Society* 15:1–36.

Waldinger, R., C. Erickson, R. Milkman, D. J. B. Mitchell, A. Valenzuela, K. Wong, and M. Zeitlin. 1997. "Justice for Janitors." *Dissent* 44:37–44.

Waldinger, Roger. 1995. "The Other Side of Embeddedness: A Case-Study of the Interplay of Economy and Ethnicity." *Ethnic and Racial Studies* 18:555–80.

———. 1996a. "Ethnicity and Opportunity in the Plural City." Pp. 445–70 in *Ethnic Los Angeles,* edited by R. D. Waldinger and M. Bozorgmehr. New York: Russell Sage Foundation.

———. 1996b. *Still the Promised City? African-Americans and New Immigrants in Postindustrial New York*. Cambridge, MA: Harvard University Press.

Whyte, William Foote. [1943] 1981. *Street Corner Society: The Social Structure of an Italian Slum*. Chicago: University of Chicago Press.

Williams, Terry M. 1989. *The Cocaine Kids: The Inside Story of a Teenage Drug Ring*. Reading, MA: Addison-Wesley.

———. 1992. *Crackhouse*. New York: Addison-Wesley.

Willis, Paul. 1977. *Learning to Labor: How Working Class Kids Get Working Class Jobs*. New York: Columbia University Press.

Wilson, William Julius. 1987. *The Truly Disadvantaged: The Inner City, the Underclass, and Public Policy*. Chicago: University of Chicago Press.

———. 1991. "Studying Inner-City Social Dislocations: The Challenge of Public Agenda Research." *American Sociological Review* 56:1–14.

———. 1996. *When Work Disappears: The World of the New Urban Poor*. New York: Vintage Books.

Wilson, William Julius, and Kathryn M. Neckerman. 1986. "Poverty and Family

Structure: The Widening Gap between Evidence and Public Policy Issues." Pp. 232–59 in *Fighting Poverty: What Works and What Doesn't*, edited by S. H. Danziger and D. H. Weinberg. Cambridge, MA: Harvard University Press.

Zavella, Patricia. 1987. *Women's Work and Chicano Families*. Berkeley: University of California Press.

Zhou, Min. 1997. "Segmented Assimilation: Issues, Controversies, and Recent Research on the New Second Generation." *International Migration Review* 31:975–1008.

Zimbardo, Philip G. 1972. "Pathology of Imprisonment." *Society* 9:4–8.

Zlolniski, Christian. 1994. "The Informal Economy in an Advanced Industrial Society: Mexican Immigrant Labor in Silicon Valley." *Yale Law Journal* 103:2305–35.

Zlolniski, Christian, and Juan-Vicente Palerm. 1996. *Working but Poor: Mexican Immigrant Workers in a Low-Income Enclave in San Jose*. Berkeley, CA: Chicano/Latino Policy Project.

# Index

| | |
|---:|:---|
| Indexer: | Sharon Sweeney |
| Compositor: | BookMatters, Berkeley |
| Text: | 10/13 Sabon |
| Display: | Sabon |
| Printer and Binder: | Malloy Lithographing, Inc |